Chinese Popular Literature and the Child

Chinese Popular Literature
and the Child

Dorothea Hayward Scott

American Library Association

Chicago 1980

Library of Congress Cataloguing in Publication Data
Scott, Dorothea Hayward.
   Chinese popular literature and the child.

   Bibliography
   1.   Children's literature, Chinese—History and criticism.   2.   Chinese literature
   —History and criticism. I.   Title.
PN1009.C5S36   895.1′09′9282   80-10412
ISBN 0-8389-0289-8

Designed by Richard Pace
with modifications by ALA Publishing Services staff
Composed by FM Typesetting Company in Linotype Caledonia
with Garamond and Delphin II display faces
Printed on 50# Warren's 1854, a pH-neutral stock,
and bound by Braun-Brumfield, Inc.
Cover design by Ellen Pettengell

To all my
Chinese friends,
East and West

Contents

Figures

Introduction

Literature written especially for children (apart from school primers) did not exist in China in any appreciable way until the end of the nineteenth century. Instead, from the earliest times, Chinese children were fortunate in being able to listen to master storytellers whose entertainment consisted of every kind of tale drawn from a vast repertoire of literature dating back to the tenth century B.C. Myths; legends; animal fables; stories of gods and ghosts, heroes and villains, of love and war; interspersed with songs, poems, jokes, rhymes, and riddles; all were grist to their mill.

Chinese stories retold for western children always draw on the tales made popular by the storytellers. But what was the origin of these tales? Because a child's first understanding of a people from another country will be gained through stories read or told about them, it is important to know the sources of retold stories so that judgment can be made as to their authenticity. To eradicate from a child's mind a false stereotype implanted through misleading pictures or unauthentic stories introduced to them when very young is extremely difficult. We know from the intensity of the "black is beautiful" campaign in contemporary western children's literature how hard it is to undo the harm of false stereotypes.

For centuries the Bible, an anthology of ancient literature, with the moral precepts it teaches, has dominated the cultural life of the western world, its history and literature, its customs and festivals, and certainly the education of its children. For example, it would only be necessary to mention "Daniel in the lion's den" or the story of Noah's Ark to call forth an immediate imaginative reaction in the minds of most western children, without any further elaboration of the story. Even in this secular age, almost every child knows the story behind the Christmas and Easter festivals. In exactly the same way, the words of ancient Chinese historians, poets, and philosophers, their moral teachings and the stories they told to illustrate their points, written down before the third century B.C. and generally referred to as the Classics, colored the whole cultural life of China and its education system. These were the sources to which the storytellers turned for many of their tales which became elaborated through the ages with

1

countless tellings and retellings. Many of the stories from these ancient sources are as familiar to Chinese children as Cinderella or Little Red Riding Hood are to western children. But the familiar stories collected by Basile, Perrault, and Grimm were not originally told for children. In Europe, as in the rest of the world, the presence of children has always encouraged storytelling from familiar sources nearest to hand.

In China professional storytelling has been a highly developed art from very early times and one whose continuity remains unbroken today. Where did the traditional stories of China come from and how old are they? How is it that China's literature dating from one thousand, two thousand, three thousand years ago is so much alive today? How is it that Mao Tse-tung could refer in two brief sentences to a story from the philosopher-sage Lieh-tzu of the fifth century B.C. and be sure to be understood by the uneducated masses to whom his words were addressed? What really are the sources for stories whose origins are given in the kind of vague reference one sees so often in western translations, "story from the Warring States period, fifth to third century B.C."? These are the kinds of questions this book sets out to answer for the benefit of editors, librarians, teachers, and parents who wish to provide reliable guidance in children's reading about China.

The very word "China" seems to conjure up visions of the exotic and fantastic. From the time of Marco Polo onwards, travelers' tales of the marvels of the East have fascinated the western world. Strange customs still lingering on in overseas Chinese communities provide a living illustration of a different way of life. Why do they have a lion dance procession, why do they set off noisy firecrackers on festive occasions, why do they have dragon boat races, why do they hang up decorated lanterns, and why do they eat moon cakes? All of these customs and many more are rooted in ancient traditions and stories. Their origins are known, but the temptation to invent explanations or embroider the truth has often proved irresistible. The difficulty of learning Chinese, the comparatively few people who have gained sufficient knowledge to translate it, and the even smaller minority of these who have turned their attention to children's literature, the vast amount of existing literature to encompass in order to obtain a perspective view, all this has encouraged both the idea that everything Chinese is different and mysterious and that any out-of-the-way explanation will serve as well as another.

It is impossible to consider children's literature in China without reference to the system of education. Literature and the art of calligraphy were held in such high esteem that from the time of the Han dynasty (206 B.C.–A.D. 220) to the turn of the twentieth century, the educated man deemed fit for government office was the one well versed in the Classics, the literature of the tenth to the third centuries B.C., which included songs and poems of many kinds, official chronicles and histories, and the philosophies and moral sayings of great sages like

Confucius and Mencius. A scholar had to be able to express himself in the accepted form of literary style patterned after these Classics. All education was geared to this ideal. On the one hand this veneration for the Classics has preserved a huge body of work with an unbroken tradition unique in the world. On the other hand, the requirements of classical scholarship led to the establishment of an educated elite writing in a literary style which was divorced from everyday spoken language. A key to the many revolutionary changes which have taken place in contemporary China may be sought in the rejection of the old learning in the earlier part of this century and the call by modern scholars for a new written style more compatible with everyday spoken language.

Parallel in time to the great body of classical literature, there grew up a flourishing colloquial genre, called "small talk," from which the Chinese term for a novel or short story derives. The themes for this popular literature were drawn from many different literary and oral sources and included myths about the creation, the wonders of the natural world and the perils of the infernal regions, tales of gods and supernatural beings, the chivalrous exploits of past heroes, and romantic love stories. Interspersed with the stories there were songs, poems, ballads, and humorous anecdotes. Jokes, rhymes, and riddles were also written down, material which was often culled from marketplace gossip and the talk of the streets. Although this kind of writing was despised by the literati, it is recorded that court chroniclers traveled round the countryside to collect and write down the things they heard as an important reflection of public opinion. The official chronicles of the early periods of Chinese history, therefore, often contained sections with colloquial writing of this kind. In completing their accounts of the past, the early historians drew upon the myths and legends woven around the creation and racial origins thus recorded.

The introduction of Buddhism into China from India in the second century A.D. was a paramount influence on the development of a folk literature based on stories of the supernatural, animal fables, and magic happenings. The early Buddhist monks were often skilled storytellers and ballad singers who used their arts for proselytizing the Buddhist scriptures, and in doing so, laid the foundations for the more sophisticated storytellers of a later age. However, it was not only the Buddhists who used the art of storytelling for religious purposes. Taoists, the intellectual sources of whose faith was derived from the teachings of two philosophers of the sixth and fifth centuries B.C., used storytelling to convert the common people to follow "the Way" (Tao), drawing upon nature myths and primitive beliefs in the supernatural for their tales.

Even though some of this popular oral literature was recorded, many rhymes, riddles, jokes, and tongue twisters repeated by generations of Chinese children had never been written down at all until serious study of oral and folk material was begun in the twentieth century. Then every region was found to have its own repertoire of traditional rhymes for children, the subjects and the types of which are very similar to those we know in English: lullabies; ring-a-roses and hand-clapping rhymes; counting rhymes and those about parts of the body and things to eat; rhymes about animals, birds, fishes, and insects; and rhymes about holidays and festivals. There are also flower-sellers' songs, beggars' chants, birthday songs, riddle rhymes, cumulative rhymes, and rhymes about the weather.

Written and printed Chinese uses characters or symbols that represent whole words. Some, signifying objects like sun, moon, or tree, are derived from ancient and purely pictorial forms; some are simple representations of such basic concepts as above or below, or numbers, such as one, two, or three which are represented by an equivalent number of strokes. But by far the majority are composite characters of either pictorial or ideographic symbols as *moon* and *window* to mean bright, or combinations of an element indicating the meaning and known as a radical, with a purely phonetic element indicating the sound only. For instance, the radical for water is included in a large number of characters signifying liquid of some sort. But because of the comparatively small number of sounds compared to the thousands of characters which can be represented, there are many homophones, that is to say, different characters expressed by the same sound, exactly as in the English *tail* and *tale* which are pronounced in the same way but mean different things. To help avoid confusion with similar-sounding words, the Chinese use a pronunciation system having four different tones for each sound. A child learning to speak a word learns the tone and never afterwards makes a mistake. This tonal quality of the Chinese language readily lends itself to sing-song chanting and recitation, echoed in the techniques of the storytellers. Every visitor to Chinese schools or kindergartens is struck by the universal practice of children learning by reciting aloud in unison. This has always been their method of learning. Primers to the Classics, all were learned in this way.

The literature of China over a long period of time has reflected social and historical events marked by both continuity and change. From the second century B.C. until 1908, China was ruled by an absolute monarchy, then passed through revolution to the establishment of a republic, and after a further period of war and civil strife, became the Marxist People's Republic we know today. In the following pages the writer has traced against this background a profile of Chinese literature and has shown how that literature has influenced the minds of children, literate and illiterate alike. In order to understand the revolution which has taken place since 1950 in Chinese attitudes to children, in their education and the provision of literature written for them, we have first to understand the traditions which shaped them for centuries.

This account does not review the new literature—a separate book is needed for that and can be written only after a comprehensive collection of the first three decades of publications is available for study. It does show how the seeds for a new children's literature were sown in the years of China's first Republic.

Chinese papercut:
a contemporary design

China's long and living tradition of literature, both oral and written, goes back for nearly four thousand years to the period known as the Shang dynasty (1765–1123 B.C.). The story of its preservation and influence is a remarkable one, and any adequate appreciation of the civilization of China must take into account the profound part her literature has played in all aspects of her cultural life. To this earliest recorded period belong a substantial number of written records. Literature proper, the earliest songs, poems, histories, and philosophical and moral writings belong to the next millenium, referred to in Chinese history as the Chou dynasty (1122–221 B.C.), and are known in general terms as the Classics. In the chronicles written in this period historians attempted to trace the origins of their people back to the beginning of time and incorporated in their purely historical accounts of contemporary events stories based on oral sources about how their world began. Once written down, many of these, although known to be mythical, became the authoritative sources for popular stories, told and retold. Comparatively recent archaeological discoveries have thrown new light on this legendary period of Chinese history, a brief description of which gives some background to these early stories.[1]

Oracle Bones

The earliest known written records were inscribed on large animal bones and tortoise shells or on bronze vessels of many kinds. Ancient bronze inscriptions have been known and revered from time immemorial in China, but the many thousands of bone inscriptions now known were only discovered towards the end of the nineteenth century. About that time the attention of two scholars was drawn to pieces of bone with inscriptions on them which were turning up in local medicine shops near the ancient site of An-yang in modern Honan Province (fig. 1). It was ascertained that local farmers were finding the bone fragments when they plowed and were selling them to medicine shops where they were being ground up and sold as "dragon bones," thought to be a good medical remedy by the credulous! The inscribed char-

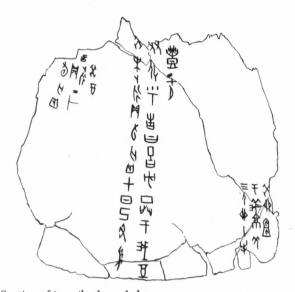

Figure 1. Section of inscribed oracle bone

from Tung Tso-pin, "On the Inscription of Scapulae in Seoul University's Collection" in *Bulletin of the Institute of History and Philology* 28:825–40 (1957). Taipei: Academia Sinica, 1957.

acters were recognized as similar to some found on known ancient seal inscriptions and bronzes. Realizing the importance of these relics, the scholars offered to buy all that were found and also organized careful excavations resulting in thousands of pieces of inscribed bones and tortoise shells being unearthed. A publication by one of the scholars in 1903 was the first systematic account of the discovery.[2] Later two Chinese government institutions, Academia Sinica and the National Academy of Sciences, conducted scientific excavations which are continuing, and which have yielded a number of rich finds. In one of the most important digs made in 1936 a full pit with over seventeen thousand pieces, almost all of tortoise shell, was discovered. Thus far more than one hundred thousand pieces have been found.

Most of the inscriptions have been dated between the early fourteenth and the twelfth centuries B.C., when the capital was situated in the general area where the finds have been made. Many have been deciphered, although a number of personal and geographical names remain obscure. The writing is sophisticated in form and must have been developing for at least a thousand years earlier than this time. All three kinds of characters still in use are found on these bone fragments: the pictorial, characters representing ideas, and characters used for sounds only (*see* fig. 2). The majority of the inscriptions are records of divination by oracles. The practice of divination by placing pieces of bone in fire dates back to earlier neolithic times in China, where bone objects from this period with scorch marks have been discovered. In Shang times records were inscribed with a stylus on the bones and

PRINCIPLES	EXAMPLES								EXPLANATION
Pictograms	man	woman	child	mouth	nose	eye	hand	foot	a. Whole or parts of human body
	horse	tiger	dog	elephant	deer	sheep	silkworm	tortoise	b. Side or front view of animals
	sun	moon	rain	lightning	mountain	river	grain	wood	c. Symbol of natural objects
	vase	tripod	bow	arrow	silk	book	oracle	omen	d. Symbol of artificial objects
Ideograms	two men against each other — fighting	man and a plough — ploughing	weapon and animal — hunting	woman nursing child — suckling	e. Combination of pictograms suggesting action
	sun setting among grasses — sunset	moon-light on window — bright	hand holding brush — writing brush	hand holding object — scribe	f. Assembling ideas
	above	below			g. Indicating position
Phonograms	horse + li — black horse	spirit + ssu — sacrifice	woman + jen — pregnancy	river + huan — Huan River	h. Combination of pictogram and a phonetic element
	lai wheat for lai — to come	feng phoenix for feng — wind			i. Phonetic loan of a word with the same sound to express another idea
	1	2	3	4	5	6	7	8	

Figure 2. Principles and forms of shell and bone inscription

from *Written on Bamboo and Silk* by T. H. Tsien. Reprinted with permission of the University of Chicago Press. Copyright © 1962 by the University of Chicago.

shells themselves and filled in with ink, traces of which have been found.

Divination

The method of divination was as follows. Cavities were drilled in the shells and bones which were then placed in a fire and long vertical or horizontal cracks would occur. The character for oracle, "p'u," among those shown in figure 2, resembles such a crack. The oracular sayings predicted good or bad fortune in hunting and in military expeditions or recorded prayers for rain and sometimes added a statement about when rain had occurred. Events like lunar or solar eclipses and other strange phenomena were recorded as well as accounts of unusual dreams. Writing on bones and shells was used as a means of communication with the spirits of ancestors and with deities during sacrifices and other religious ceremonies. Although popularly known as "oracle bones," some also record purely historical events, unconnected with any oracular pronouncements. It will be seen how stories about the origins of Chinese writing described later were inspired by the practice of attributing symbolic meaning to the lines and cracks on the surface of bones and shells when used in divination ceremonies.

Bronze Inscriptions

Inscriptions on bronze and a few on iron are also known from the Shang dynasty (1765–1123 B.C.), but by far the larger number extant belong to the succeeding Chou dynasty (1122–211 B.C.). Beauty and variety of design and fine craftsmanship are characteristic, whether the objects are sacrificial vessels, musical instruments, weapons, mirrors, coins, seals, or tools. Inscriptions occur on all these artifacts, but the longest, including one of five hundred characters, are found on the larger ritual vessels, tripods, and cauldrons and recount military campaigns, treaties, and ceremonial events. A story is told concerning the legendary Emperor Yü, attributing magical properties to an iron cauldron he had cast with maps of different regions engraved on it.

Inscriptions on Stone

Commemorative inscriptions on stone were also common in China from very early times. Ten stone "drums," as they are popularly called, dome-shaped boulders varying in height between eighteen inches and three feet and dating from about the eighth century B.C., are preserved in Peking today. Each has a rhymed verse of about seventy characters in vertical lines carved on it. Boulders such as these, roughly chiseled into shape from rocks found on or near the site, were used until the Han dynasty (202 B.C. onwards), when rectangular stone tablets or stele were cut and polished ready for engraving. Some of these were only about three feet high but many were as much as seven feet high, about three feet wide, and five inches thick. The larger ones were frequently mounted on sculptured bases in the form of a tortoise (symbolizing longevity) or a mythic animal, and long texts were carved on both sides. Smaller stone tablets were frequently placed in graves of important people, recording the names and dates of the deceased and the honors they had received.

The Classics Written on Bamboo

The Chou dynasty (1122–221 B.C.) saw the beginnings of a real Chinese literature in the poems and songs, the historical chronicles, books of philosophy and moral sayings and of ceremonial and religious ritual written during this period. A large number of these writings have survived and became known as the Classics, for which the Chinese word is *Ching*. The most important are the *Book of Songs*, the *Book of History*, the *Spring and Autumn Annals*, the *Book of Change*, and the *Record of Rites*. Later editing included the sayings of Confucius and Mencius in the canon of classical literature. The ordinary writing material of the time was strips of bamboo, strung together to form a "book." Silk scrolls were also used for more important documents from about the sixth century B.C. The earliest extant bamboo book dates from the Warring States period (480–221 B.C.), but there are many references in the Chou dynasty literature to earlier writing on "tablets," and the early character for book is a pictorial representation of thin strips of material strung together with a cord, shown in figure 2. This character occurs in the earlier bone inscriptions, showing that bamboo tablets were in use in Shang times, but being perishable, none has survived from this period. Bamboo is native to China, as are palm leaves to India and papyrus to Egypt, and its use as a writing material was a natural development. The length of bamboo tablets was dictated by the existence of notches in the wood at growth points but some much longer tablets made of poplar or willow wood have been found. Characters were written with stylus or brush and ink and could be conveniently erased by scraping a thin layer of wood from the surface.

Examples of bamboo tablets have been found in a number of ancient graves where a list of the offerings buried in the tomb was recorded. Archaeological expeditions have also resulted in finds of many thousands of tablets in northwestern China and eastern Turkestan. One of the most dramatic of all finds of ancient Chinese documents was at Tun-huang, beyond the western end of the Great Wall. At the turn of the twentieth century, a Chinese monk, who had taken up residence in a nearby abandoned Buddhist sanctuary known as the Caves of the Thousand Buddhas, discovered a bricked-up cave behind a wall fresco he was restoring. The cave had been closed up in a time of danger during the eleventh century and forgotten until this time.

In it was a huge cache of documents of great historical and biblio-graphic importance, including bamboo tablets, silk scrolls, and later writings on paper. Most interesting to note here are the more than eighty examples of popular literature dating from the eighth and ninth centuries A.D., ballads, stories, Buddhist legends, and storytellers' prompt books, described and in part translated by Arthur Waley.[3]

The "Burning of the Books"

In the third century B.C. occurred the incident, "the burning of the books" ordered by the first emperor of a unified China, Shih Huang-ti, which has been much written about. He feared the teachings of the earlier and now revered philosophers and ordered that all copies of their works be collected and burnt, a fate all too easy for writings on bamboo. Books of a practical nature on medicine, divination, agricul-ture, and the imperial historical archives were to be carefully safe-guarded. The action was part of his general plan of unification of the country which included the standardization of forms of writing in the different feudal states which made up the empire, a unified system of weights and measures, a standard width of road for military purposes, and other reforms. Fortunately there were private libraries owned by scholars who hid or buried their copies of the condemned books. When the succeeding Han dynasty was established, the concealed books were eventually brought out, damaged and mutilated copies compared, edited, and recopied by royal decree.

The Classics Engraved on Stone

Engraving texts on stone had by this time become such a recognized art that the Emperor ordered the re-edited Classics to be carved on stone tablets. This enormous task was begun in A.D. 175 and took eight years to complete. Forty-six giant tablets were erected in a semi-circle, each tablet with a protective roof over it. The tablets were engraved on both sides with about seventy to seventy-three characters in a vertical row and with some forty rows on each stone. All together it has been estimated that they contained over two hundred thousand characters. Several hundred fragments of these original stones have been found and exist today in various museum collections. The enter-prise established the practice and subsequent emperors also com-manded that existing tablets containing the Classics be restored or new ones carved.

Inscriptions in Caves and on Buildings

Walls of caves and grottoes were frequently used for recording religious texts where the inscription would be protected from weather-ing and more easily preserved in troubled times of proscription of the religion. Cave sites such as Tun-huang in modern Kansu province already described, Lung-men in Honan province, Yün-kang in Shansi, and Fang-shan in Hopei are world-famous for the wealth of their inscriptions. In the last mentioned cave, known as the Hall of Stone Sutras, there are more than seven thousand tablets with over one hundred complete Buddhist texts carved on them. Emperors, princes, and other dignitaries or well-known poets visiting a famous mountain beauty spot would record the fact or write a commemorative couplet which would be carved on the face of the rock. City gates; lintels, pillars, and walls of temples; palaces; larger houses; and public buildings were all adorned with decorative inscriptions of quotations from the ancient sages or historical figures which thus became popular sayings. The practice has continued until modern times. The following verse is carved on a peak near Kweilin in South China to commemorate the occasion when Marshal Chu Teh, Commander-in-Chief of the People's Liberation Army and Chairman of the Standing Committee of the National People's Congress under Mao Tse-tung, climbed Bright Moon Crest on 29 January 1963 with an eighty-seven-year-old friend, Hsü T'e-li. He himself was seventy-seven at the time.

Hsü lao lao ying hsiung.
T'ung shang ming yüeh feng,
Teng kao pu yung ch'ang,
T'o mao hsi tung feng.

Old Hsü is a hero.
Together we climbed Bright Moon Crest,
He climbed to the top without a walking stick,
Taking off his cap, he enjoyed the east wind.[4]

Writing on Silk

The cultivation of silk was known as early as the Shang dynasty and characters for silk, silkworm, and silk goods as well as one for the mulberry tree, the leaves of which are necessary to feed cultivated silkworms, have all been found in oracle bone inscriptions. Among the archaeological discoveries at Tun-huang there are a few examples of complete documents written on silk, including two letters complete with silk envelopes. There are a number of stories in ancient literature about silk letters being discovered in the bodies of fishes and birds, and frequent references to records being "written on bamboo and silk," which indeed is the title of Dr. Tsien's authoritative work referred to. There is a famous first century B.C. story in the *History of the Former Han Dynasty* that describes how an emperor secured the release of a general captured by Tartar tribes through a ruse involving a silk letter being sent tied to the foot of a wild goose. The expression "wild goose feet" is now understood to mean a written communication.

Documents on silk written in languages other than Chinese were found at Tun-huang and illustrate the value of silk in trading with other countries. The greater width of the silk scroll, the ease with which silk would take brush writing, and its extreme lightness made it much more convenient for writing on than bamboo tablets. But its cost confined its use to more important documents and to religious writings, or for such purposes as map drawing and illustrations which obviously would be impossible to produce on narrow strips of wood. There are extant examples of silk scroll illustrations added to a text on bamboo.

The Invention of Paper

It is in the *History of the Later Han Dynasty* that the epoch-making invention of paper is recorded with the following laconic words:

> silk being costly and bamboo heavy they were not convenient to use. Ts'ai Lun then initiated the idea of making paper from the bark of trees, hemp, old rags and fishing nets. He submitted the process to the Emperor [in A.D. 105] and received praise for his ability. From this time, paper has been in use everywhere and is universally called the paper of Lord Ts'ai.

Although the invention of paper is so exactly recorded, the character for "paper" containing the radical sign for "silk" was in use before A.D. 105. Scholars think that an experimental quasi-paper made from silk waste pounded to a pulp in water and spread to form a mat when dry was in existence before Ts'ai Lun's method of making satisfactory paper from cheaper materials was perfected. The rapid growth and spread of Chinese civilization in the later Han dynasty was the impetus for improvements in both the quality and quantity of paper produced during the first few centuries. Its use spread throughout the empire and eventually, it was exported to neighboring countries. But it is interesting to note that it took more than a thousand years for the invention and the papermaking process to travel from Asia to the Arab world and with the Moors into Spain and finally into the rest of Europe. Probably the earliest extant fragment of paper is contemporary with Ts'ai Lun's invention; this was found in far northwest China. Other early specimens were found in the Tun-huang caves.

Ink Squeezes or Rubbings

Once the art of papermaking was perfected, an extremely important development was the ability to make multiple copies of writings engraved on stone or other hard materials by a method known as ink squeezes and which anticipated the invention of wood-block printing in the eighth century A.D. The method is somewhat similar to the comparatively modern practice of taking rubbings from engraved brasses on tombs in Europe; in fact, the Chinese method is often called "making a rubbing." A thin sheet of paper, dampened so that it would stretch easily, was laid lightly on the engraved surface and then pressed into every incised line and crevice with a soft brush. After the paper dried, its surface was evenly inked all over with a cotton or silk dabber, so that the parts pressed into the engraved lines remained untouched. When the paper was lifted the result was a white line copy, an exact duplication of the original engraving. There are records in the bibliographies attached to historical chronicles of the sixth century A.D. of copies of stone inscriptions on "rolls" including inscriptions dating from the second and third centuries A.D. Copies of famous inscriptions from these early times were made for the imperial collections and scholars were also encouraged to make copies of the Classics engraved on stone to ensure having accurate texts for commentaries and teaching. The earliest extant ink squeeze copy dates from the seventh century A.D. and was among the documents found at Tun-huang.

Wood-block Printing

It was in the T'ang dynasty (618–906), a period rich in cultural and literary activity, when thousands of new poems, plays, and stories were written, that woodblock printing was invented in China. It was a logical development from another form of woodblock carving popular at the time. From the third century B.C. the custom of using seals for official purposes had been widespread. At first characters were incised into the surface of seals which were carved on jade, stone, ivory, or rhinoceros horn or cast in gold, silver, or copper. Later, in the fifth century A.D., seals began to be carved in relief on wood and when inked and pressed on to the now commonly used paper, a red or black line impression resulted. Large seals carved on blocks of wood were popularly used for religious purposes. Pictures of Buddha with suitable short quotations from sutras were carved and impressed on sheets of paper. These multiple copies were used as "charms" and distributed by monks to believers.

The Traditional Form of a Chinese Book

The same character *yin* is used both for "seal" and for "print" and the connection between large carved wooden seals and the carved woodblock for printing whole books is obvious. The method of printing books from woodblocks has changed little through the centuries, once it was perfected by the tenth century. Even though printing with movable type was developed in the eleventh century, woodblock printing continued to be the most popular method used, right down to the nineteenth century.

To be printed from a woodblock, the text was first handwritten by a skilled calligrapher in vertical columns on thin paper, two pages on one sheet, the center dividing column having a special mark known as a fish tail (*see* in fig. 3). A block of wood, usually pear, the size of

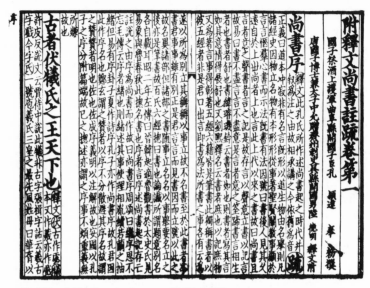

Figure 3. Wood-block printing, ca. 1195–1200
from *Select Chinese Rare Books and Historical Documents in the National Palace Museum, Taiwan*

two pages, was covered with a thin size and while it was still wet the manuscript was laid on it. The Chinese ink would adhere to the size and the characters in reverse would be clearly visible on the block. When dry, the thin paper could be rubbed off and a skilled craftsman would cut away all the surface of the block not inked, leaving the characters in relief. No press was used for printing from this surface, since the paper was too thin. The block was simply inked with one brush, the paper gently pressed on to the inked surface with another, dry brush and then pulled off, resulting in an exact copy of the text the right way round. A skilled workman could easily print two thousand copies in a day. The sheets were folded down the marked center column which formed the outside edge and the loose edges were sewn with silk thread to form the back of the traditional paper-covered Chinese book. A work usually consisted of a number of these paper-covered volumes which in turn were put into a stiff cloth-covered wrapper, a format which did not change, whether the book was hand-written, block-printed, or printed by any other method, until the twentieth century. By the tenth century, woodblock printing had attained a beauty which has never been surpassed, based as it was on the finest calligraphy of the period.

Literature Preserved in Print

The Classics were printed by order of the emperor in 953, using as a model text a new "edition" cut on stone tablets between 836 and 841 at the T'ang capital, Ch'ang-an. Numbers of these stone tablets survive today and are kept in a Confucian temple at Sian, the modern name of that ancient city.[5] In the following two centuries most of the surviving works from previous centuries were edited and printed. This included the great flowering of T'ang dynasty literature, which was the inspiration of popular stories, songs, ballads, and plays for centuries to come. Copies of the books were placed in the Imperial Library and in a considerable number of the private libraries existing at this time. It has been estimated that as late as A.D. 1500, the number of books produced in the whole of the rest of the world did not equal the number which had already been produced in China.

Popular Stories Also Preserved in Print

It was not only highly esteemed literary works which were preserved in this way. Buddhist monks, whose descriptive narrations dealing with the forces of good and evil drew fascinated audiences within the temple courtyards, soon arrived at the need for working scripts as an aid to their technique. With printed outlines of their stories, the Chinese term for them is *hua-pen*, prompt books, much longer stories could be told serially from week to week, keeping ever larger audiences involved in their tales. Copies of these printed prompt books could be widely distributed and some were found among the popular literature discovered at Tun-huang. They were the prototypes for more sophisticated printed aids for the professional storytellers of later dynasties.

Professional Storytellers

Records show that by the Sung dynasty (960–1279) storytellers had become a highly professional body of public entertainers who were organized under guilds, each of which served the exponents of one particular genre or style of presentation. The scripts they used became representative texts for particular styles of storytelling.

Popular Plays

At the end of the Sung dynasty China was conquered by the Mongols who established their own dynasty, the Yüan, from 1260 to 1368, when a Chinese dynasty, the Ming, was restored to power again. The Yüan dynasty has been called the golden age of Chinese drama, for during this period there was a great flowering of dramatic writing. Many innovations were introduced in stage technique and the plays of this period set the pattern for centuries to come. The rise of the drama under Mongol rule was due in great part to the fact that Chinese scholars, who would normally have pursued an official career, were forbidden to enter government service by their conquerors. The result was that many men of considerable literary talent turned their energies to writing for the stage at a time when the theater, under the patronage of an affluent merchant class, was becoming an increasingly popular public entertainment. The great spectacles and performances given for the amusement of the Mongol court provide evidence that the rulers themselves encouraged lavish entertainment.

Novels of the Ming (1368–1644) and Ch'ing (1644–1908) Dynasties

The scholarly elite had always held poetry, philosophy, essay writing, and commentaries on the Classics in the highest esteem and tended to despise colloquial stories. But in the Ming dynasty writers at last turned their attention to the popular story cycles developed by the storytellers and to the highly dramatic incidents from them presented in popular plays. From these sources were woven the first full-length Chinese novels, the enormously popular *Romance of the Three Kingdoms* and the *Tale of the Marshes,* folk epics as alive in the twentieth century as they were when composed in the fourteenth and fifteenth centuries. Collections of short stories taken from existing colloquial sources with new ones written in similar style were also published. Other well-known novels written in the sixteenth, seventeenth, and eighteenth centuries include *The Pilgrimage to the West,* featuring the universally popular character Monkey, and the *Dream of the Red Chamber,* perhaps the most widely known of all Chinese novels. But the conflict between colloquial and literary styles of writing was not over with the publication and success of these popular novels.

The Twentieth Century

It was not until the twentieth century that the language reform movement revolutionized the style of Chinese writing. Following the establishment of the first Republic in 1912 a flood of western literature was translated and freely circulated. It had a dominating influence on all the first generation of writers in the new vernacular style. In the nineteen twenties western films with Chinese subtitles became very popular with audiences of all ages. They were widely shown in the larger cities and influenced the first Chinese films made at this time. Playwrights, too, began writing what were called "speaking" plays in contrast to the traditional dramas which were always accompanied by musicians and partly sung. But the hold of the traditional theater was too strong, and until the majority of the older plays were banned during the Cultural Revolution of the sixties and early seventies, "speaking" plays never gained the universal appeal of the old dramas. Contemporary stories and plays both for children and adults are still experimental in many ways and it is not yet possible to judge them in perspective.

Eventual Use of Modern Mass Production Printing Methods

Several methods of printing from movable types were introduced in China between the eleventh and fifteenth centuries. Technical descriptions of printing with wood, tin, and copper types exist, and examples of books printed in this way are preserved, some of them produced several hundred years before Gutenberg's invention in Europe. The success of moveable type there, in contrast to the slowness of its universal adoption in China, can be explained by the difference in writing systems. With our phonetic alphabet only twenty-six separate letters with numbers, punctuation marks, and the like are needed, compared with the many thousands of different characters needed for a Chinese text. Gutenberg's invention of the adjustable mold for reproducing large numbers of an identical type speeded up the printing process and his adaptation of a press for printing was possible with the thicker type of paper in use. Chinese printers continued to use the wood-block method more widely than any other until the second half of the nineteenth century, when western methods for the mass production of newspapers and cheap, popular books were necessarily introduced.

Summary

In the preceding pages an overview of Chinese literature as it has been produced through the ages and the methods and means of literary communication have been briefly traced in historical sequence over a vast period of time. It has been shown how the invention of sophisticated printing techniques, which have been the prototypes for all later developments, evolved from the earliest primitive forms of engraving on bones and shells. The need to preserve and pass on from generation to generation the wisdom of past ages has always been paramount in the Chinese mind, and even the Draconian "burning of the books" did not succeed, thanks to scholarly concern for guarding ancient texts. It is a story of change within continuity, for not only have the many methods used for the transmission of the written word ensured its preservation, but the chronicles and religious narratives, the songs, poems, ballads, and stories thus preserved have remained an inexhaustible source from which both classical and popular literary forms have been nourished.

Notes

Full bibliographic details of books and other sources cited in the notes of this and succeeding chapters will be found in the bibliography.

1. The writer is indebted to Tsien, *Written on Bamboo and Silk* and Carter, *The Invention of Printing in China and Its Spread Westward* for information in this chapter.
2. For a detailed account see Li, *Anyang*.
3. Waley, *Ballads and Stories from Tun-huang: An Anthology*.
4. This inscription was photographed by Professor Chow Tse-tsung in 1978 and translated by him for the writer.
5. A good illustration of the stone tablets appears in Topping, *Dawn Wakes in the East*, p. 141 (a work to be found in many junior collections).

Chinese papercut: a traditional design

The wonderful flowering of songs and poems and of philosophical, historical, and other prose writings of the Chou dynasty which, when collected and edited with commentaries, became known as the Classics, grew out of an earlier oral literature consisting largely of myths and legends and the written records of divinations and rituals already described. Many of the earliest versions of myths and legends were incorporated in these philosophical writings and historical chronicles and were attributed to ancient sages, records of whom were lost. A brief survey of the more important of these myths and legends will set the stage for a description of the Classics which, for over two thousand years, have had such a profound effect on the intellectual and cultural life of China and, through the education system, on the minds of children.

The Earliest Myths and Their Origins

Myths grew up in ancient times in China as in other early civilizations, through humankind's attempts to explain the world—the changes of seasons; the rain accompanied by the roll of thunder and lightning in the sky; the movements of the sun, the moon, and the stars. As early peoples observed and explored their surroundings, they wove stories to account for the ever-changing world around them: how the mountains were raised, how the lakes were formed, and where the rivers flowed. The origin of many myths dates back to prehistoric times, and because versions were written down very early, they are often quite sophisticated in style. No great traditional collections of myths and legends exist; they have to be culled from the whole corpus of early literature. Most of the earliest versions occur in barest outline, the same stories becoming embroidered in the many retellings. Some of the earliest recorded myths are found in the writings of two philosopher-metaphysicians, Lieh-tzu of the fifth century B.C. and Chuang-tzu of the fourth century B.C. Both used many fantastic stories to illustrate the mystic quality of the ideas they were expounding. Confucius, the most famous of the early philosophers, by contrast, is recorded as saying that he disapproved of stories of the supernatural.

21

Earliest Chinese Chronology

Established Chinese chronology begins with the Shang dynasty (1765–1123 B.C.) but to a period a thousand years earlier than this belong the mythical times of the Three Dynasties and the Five Emperors around whom so many stories have collected. The Hsia dynasty followed the period of the Five Emperors and is traditionally dated from 2205 to 1766 B.C. There is now some archaeological evidence that the legendary Hsia rulers are historical figures.

Fu-hsi, Legendary First Emperor

According to the early chroniclers, Fu-hsi, the first emperor of the Three Dynasties, reigned for more than one hundred years from 2953 B.C. He taught men how to fish, how to domesticate animals, how to cook, and how to breed silkworms. He invented music and the instrument which Yü, the first of the Hsia emperors, used to measure the earth. He introduced a calendar and also invented writing from a system of eight trigrams used for divination which are elaborated in the *Book of Change* (*I Ching*), according to which they symbolize the eight fundamental elements of the universe: heaven, lakes and marshes, fire, thunder, wind, water, mountains, and earth (fig. 4). Fu-hsi is supposed to have received the signs from a tortoise rising out of the water with them written on its back, or from the back of a dragon, according to some versions of the story. Each trigram was associated with a cardinal point, with different abstract qualities such as strength, power, submission, and the like, and with a particular animal—horse, goat, pheasant, dragon, cock, swine, dog and ox. Closely associated with the system of trigrams is the familiar male-female, yang-yin symbol of creation. *Yang* is represented by an unbroken line (——) and *yin* by a broken one (- - -). *Yang* stands for the male principle, heaven, light, vigor, and is symbolized by the dragon and odd numbers. Mountains are said to be *yang*. *Yin* stands for the female principle, for earth and for darkness. *Yin* is symbolized by the tiger and even numbers. Valleys and streams are said to be *yin*.

Chinese Calendars

Early Chinese chronology used several systems but the lunar calendar is the most generally associated with China's festivals.[1] The system of counting the years in cycles of sixty was established in the Han dynasty (206 B.C. to A.D. 220) and continued in use until the first Republic of 1912 when the western calendar was adopted. Based on the lunar year, it was calculated so that New Year' Day would always coincide with the first new moon after the sun enters Aquarius. This means that according to the western calendar the Chinese New Year always falls between 21 January and 20 February. In order that the

Figure 4. The eight trigrams with the symbol of creation in the center
from Williams, *Encyclopedia of Chinese Symbolism and Art Motives*

first day of each month will be the day of the new moon and the fifteenth the day of the full moon, some months have thirty days, some only twenty-nine. Instead of a leap year, an intercalary month is inserted every two or three years between any two of the ordinary months from the second to the eleventh, so that the winter solstice will always fall in the eleventh month, the summer solstice in the fifth, the spring equinox in the second, and the autumn equinox in the eighth.

The sixty-year cycles are denoted by two characters, one of the "Ten Heavenly Stems" and one of the "Twelve Earthly Branches" taken from the list in sequence (fig. 5). Beginning with the first sign in each of the lists, *Chia* of the Heavenly Stems and *Tzu* of the Earthly Branches, the first year of a cycle is *Chia Tzu*. The second year is denoted with signs two and two in each list, the third with three and three, continuing until ten and ten are reached. The next year will be numbered with the first of the Heavenly Stem signs again, *Chia* and the eleventh of the Earthly Branches *Hsü*, then two and twelve, three and one and so on until after sixty combinations, one and one are reached again.[2] This constitutes the sixty-year cycle. The Chinese names of the Heavenly Stems and Earthly Branches are not traditionally translated. The Heavenly Stems are connected in pairs with five planets: Jupiter, Mars, Saturn, Venus, and Mercury. The Twelve Earthly Branches are linked with animals: rat, ox, tiger, hare, dragon, serpent, horse, goat, monkey, cock, dog, and swine, as well as with the signs of the zodiac.

Ten Heavenly Stems	Twelve Earthly Branches
1. *Chia* 甲	1. *Tzŭ* 子
2. *Yi* 乙	2. *Ch'ou* 丑
3. *Ping* 丙	3. *Yin* 寅
4. *Ting* 丁	4. *Mao* 卯
5. *Wu* 戊	5. *Ch'en* 辰
6. *Chi* 己	6. *Ssŭ* 巳
7. *Keng* 庚	7. *Wu* 午
8. *Hsin* 辛	8. *Wei* 未
9. *Jen* 壬	9. *Shen* 申
10. *Kuei* 癸	10. *Yu* 酉
	11. *Hsü* 戌
	12. *Hai* 亥

Figure 5. The Ten Heavenly Stems and Twelve Earthly Branches
from Bodde, *Annual Customs and Festivals in Peking*

The names of the Twelve Earthly Branches were used to denote the points of the compass and twelve two-hour periods of the day long before they were used to name the years of the cycle. Although the use of the traditional calendar was officially discontinued in 1912, the lunar New Year was still widely celebrated in Republican China as the "Old New Year." Overseas Chinese communities, including Chinatowns of the western world, still continue the custom and welcomed 1979, for example, as the year of the goat. In 1949 the government of the People's Republic proclaimed the "Old New Year" a three-day public holiday, but it is now officially called the Spring Festival (*Ch'un Chieh*).

Another traditional system of Chinese chronology was introduced about the same time as the sixty-year cycle calendar. Each emperor was given a reign title and this was combined with the consecutive number of the years of his reign. This system also lasted until the period of the first Republic. Yet another calendar in use from very early times was based on the solar seasons. The year was divided into twenty-four fifteen-day periods which were appropriately named, for example, to mark the spring and autumn equinox, the summer and winter solstices, and such periods as "The Awakening of Insects," "The Little Heat" and "The Great Heat" of summer, and "The Little Cold" and "The Great Cold" of winter. Farmers faithfully followed the seasons noted for planting, reaping, and other agricultural work.

Fu-hsi's method of recording a lunar calendar was most ingenious. He is said to have invented two different calendar plants. One grew a new leaf every day for fifteen days and then lost a leaf day by day for another fifteen. This marked the end of the month of thirty days when the whole process began again. The second tree grew a new leaf every month for six months, then lost one in each of the next six months, and thus a year was recorded. Fu-hsi's magic trees are to be seen carved in stone relief in a Han dynasty tomb (second century B.C. to second century A.D.).

Nü-kua and Creation Myths

As time went on Fu-hsi became connected with many other mythical beings, particularly with Nü-kua, who is sometimes described as his sister and sometimes as his wife. The stories about Nü-kua are connected with the creation of the earth and first appear in written form in the book of *Lieh-tzu* of the fifth century B.C.[3] The author is usually known by this simple form of his name, Master Lieh, and his writings were adopted as part of the canon of the Taoist religion. The *Lieh-tzu* version of the story of the creation goes like this:

> In olden times the four cardinal points were out of place; the nine provinces lay open; the sky did not wholly cover the earth; the earth did not wholly support the sky; fire burnt ceaselessly without dying out; waters flowed on forever; wild beasts devoured peaceful people; birds of prey carried off the aged and children. Then Nü-kua melted colored stones to make good the azure sky; she cut off the feet of a tortoise to fix the cardinal points propping up the extremities of the earth. A monster, Kung Kung, contending for the mastery of the earth, crashed into Mount Pu-chou, breaking the pillars of heaven and earth's foundations. Then heaven tilted down on the northwest and the sun, the moon, and the stars all go that way. The earth has a gap in the southeast where all rivers and streams flow.[4]

A Story from *Lieh-tzu*

An idea of how popular and well known the *Lieh-tzu stories* still are among the ordinary people is shown by Mao Tse-tung's own use of them in his often quoted and frequently published *Three Old Tales* (*Lao San P'ien*). For instance, he used the story "The Foolish Old Man Moves the Mountain" with a moral twist.

> Yü Kung and his family lived on the northern bank of the Yellow River. Two mountains opposite his front door prevented his friends coming to see him, and whenever he wanted to go to the city he had to walk all round the mountains. One day he called all his sons and said "Let us remove the mountains." Thereupon they all started digging together. A clever neighbor who saw them so engaged, laughed at them, saying, "You are such an old man and the mountains are so big, you simply have not enough time left before you die to move them." Yü Kung replied, "Yes, I shall die, but I have sons, and my sons will have sons, and eventually the mountains will be moved." So the whole family kept on digging. The God of the Mountains saw this and was so moved by Yü Kung's spirit that he sent two giant gods and ordered them to carry away the mountains to the sea.[5]

The moral drawn by Chairman Mao was, "The Chinese people have not two mountains to move but three, Imperialism, Feudalism, and Poverty. We don't need the gods to help us move the mountains; if the people work together we can do it."

Tenth-Century A.D. Anthologies of Myths and Legends

The preservation of ancient stories and myths was ensured both by a strong oral tradition and by the work of court historiographers appointed from earliest times to copy and recopy the ancient texts which have thus been preserved through the generations in the imperial libraries. The names and brief descriptions of the most important writings were contained in the bibliographies attached to the official dynastic histories and editors were appointed to copy extracts from the most important works. Many such writings exist, therefore, only in anthologies made by royal decree, in the encyclopedias as they have come to be called in English. Two of the most important collections from the point of view of preserving myths, legends, and tales of fantasy and the supernatural were made in the Sung dynasty. The emperor appointed Li Fang (whose dates were 925–996) to be president of an editorial board and two great collections were compiled.

The first collection, the *T'ai P'ing Imperial Encyclopedia* (*T'ai P'ing Yü Lan*), has one thousand chapters and is a compendium of general knowledge and collections of stories mainly from the fifth to the tenth centuries, but also including selections from older writings. Of nearly seventeen hundred works listed at the beginning, only about one-fifth remain today. This great work was printed from movable types in the sixteenth century and a new edition was also produced in 1812 with many subsequent reprintings.

The second great collection known as the *T'ai P'ing Miscellany* (*T'ai P'ing Kuang Chi*) has five hundred chapters. It is a compendium on the same lines as the *Imperial Encyclopedia* but contains more stories, jokes, poems, and riddles. All that remains of some important sources of myths and legends is preserved in these two collections.

Other Early Story Collections

Stories of the creation similar to that of *Lieh-tzu* come particularly from four of the books preserved by the imperial anthologists. One of them, *The Prince of Huai Nan's Tales* (*Huai Nan Tzu*), was written by Liu An, the great-grandson of the Emperor Wen Ti (179–156 B.C.). Another, *A Sequel to Records of Strange Tales* (*Hsü Ch'i Hsieh Chi*), was written by Wu Chün at the beginning of the sixth century A.D. and was so called because it was modeled on an earlier book of the same title. The other two of these four important source books are *The Travels of King Mu* (*Mu T'ien Tzu Chuan*), recounting the travels of King Mu of the Chou dynasty to the Western Regions in a carriage drawn by eight wonderful horses, and the *Book of Mountains and Seas* (*Shan Hai Ching*), both dating from the third or second centuries B.C. It will be seen how the *Book of Mountains and Seas* continued to fascinate young readers by the references to it in the *Reminiscences of Lu Hsün*, the famous twentieth-century writer.

There is a dramatic story attached to the discovery of contemporary copies of these two last mentioned books. In A.D. 280 a robber, pillaging an ancient tomb, came upon a large cache of bamboo books. The find was reported and carefully documented at the time. The total number of tablets is estimated to have been some two thousand five hundred in seventy-five bundles tied with white silk. There were thirteen different texts in all, among them copies of the *Book of Mountains and Seas* and *Travels of King Mu*. The most important of all the books discovered was a history which became known as the *Bamboo Annals* (*Chu Shu Chi Nien*). Although the find was so carefully documented and the tablets with copies of them preserved in the royal collections, with time, wars, change of dynasty and the site of the royal capital, all of the *Bamboo Annals* were lost by the thirteenth century.

P'an Ku and the Creation Myth

All the creation stories from these aforementioned sources dwell on the emergence of the earth out of chaos. The chief character in the story besides Nü-kua and the monster Kung Kung is P'an Ku:

> Heaven and earth were comingled like an egg in the midst of which P'an Ku was born and he lived for eighteen thousand years. Then heaven and earth split asunder, the pure and the bright element became heaven, the impure and dark element earth, while P'an Ku within underwent nine transformations in one day, turning into a god in heaven and a saint on earth. Heaven grew ten feet higher every day, earth grew ten feet thicker every day, and P'an Ku grew ten feet taller every day. So it went for eighteen thousand years, till heaven was exceedingly high, earth exceedingly thick, and P'an Ku exceedingly tall. Then came the three divine emperors.
>
> When P'an Ku died he is said to have given birth to the various parts of the universe. His head became the mountains, his breath the winds and the clouds, his voice thunder, his left eye the sun, his right eye the moon, his beard the stars, his four limbs the four quarters of the earth, his flesh the soil, his skin and hair the plants and trees, his teeth and bones minerals, his marrow pearls and precious stones and his sweat the rain.

Tradition has it that when P'an Ku is happy the weather is fine and when he is angry the weather changes to fit his mood.

Queen Mother of the West, Hsi Wang Mu

The *Book of Mountains and Seas* is the source of some of the best known stories which concern the Queen Mother of the West, Hsi Wang Mu. She lives in a palace on a mythical jade mountain in the west, said to be part of the great K'un Lun range dividing China from Central Asia. She was originally a monster with a human face, tiger's teeth, and a leopard's tail. But in Taoist legends she became a beautiful goddess embodying the principle of *yin*. On the banks of the Lake of Gems within her palace there grows a miraculous peach tree which blooms only once every three thousand years and those who eat its fruit gain immortality. When the tree blooms it is then the birthday of Hsi Wang Mu, and all the immortals, male and female, attend her feast. It was at this banquet that the legendary character Monkey stole a peach of immortality and was banished from heaven.

Shen-nung, the Divine Husbandman

The second Emperor of the legendary Three Dynasties was Shen-nung. He is supposed to have been miraculously conceived, as was Fu-hsi. Shen-nung is known as the Divine Husbandman. He fashioned wood into plows and taught the people the art of agriculture. Through the cultivation of plants he discovered their curative and poisonous properties, developing the art of medicine on which he is said to have written a learned treatise. To his son, or his minister in some accounts, is credited the invention of war. Many miraculous powers were attributed to the legendary rulers, but among the stories relating to them, traces of actual historical achievements can be found. The early historians, wishing to complete the accounts of the development of Chinese culture from the beginning up to their own day, mixed myth, legend, and fact indiscriminately. Thus it was that the deeds of the ancient heroes, men of outstanding intelligence, strength, and valor, became the themes of stories told and retold. As time went on the heroes were credited with supernatural powers and they became the subjects of legends.

Huang-ti, the Yellow Emperor

To the Yellow Emperor, Huang-ti, the first of the legendary Five Emperors following the Three Dynasties, is attributed the invention of the chariot wheel, the potter's wheel, and the compass. He was also supposed to have invented armor and to have used ships and employed these inventions against a rebellious minister. The Yellow Emperor, wanting to learn the secret of immortality, is said to have discussed Shen-nung's *Treatise on Medicine* with him in order to discover the pill of immortality. This magic pill carried with it the power of making gold, so that many emperors sought for it.

Sun Legends

One of the most widely known myths about the sun is connected with the last but one of the Five Emperors, Yao, who was in danger of losing his throne. According to the story, there were ten suns who lived in the Valley of Light. In the early morning the sun on duty for the day was bathed by his mother; he then mounted an enormous hollow mulberry tree from where he was conveyed in a chariot drawn across the sky by dragons. The other suns lodged in the lower branches of the tree. The Chinese character for "east" is a stylized picture of the sun amidst a tree (*see* fig. 6). In times of disaster all ten suns appeared in the sky at once and everything on earth was in danger of being burnt. Such a period of disaster threatened the Emperor Yao. He gave a magic bow to Yi, the Divine Archer, who shot down nine of the suns, leaving the tenth, the present one, in the sky for posterity. The sun is made of fire and symbolizes, the male principle *yang*.

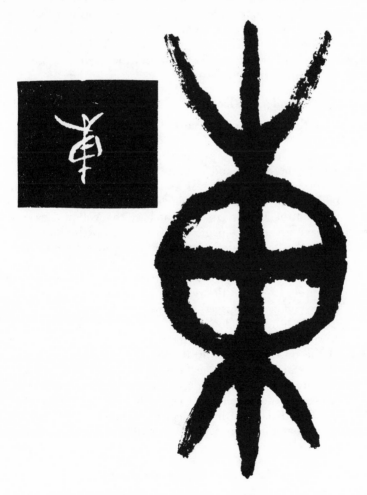

Figure 6. The Chinese character for "east"

Ch'ang-o,   Goddess of the Moon

The Divine Archer had a wife called Ch'ang-o. She stole from him the herb of immortality which he had been given by the Queen Mother of the West. Ch'ang-o fled to the moon with it where she lives on as the Goddess of the Moon, but in the form of a celestial toad with three legs. During an eclipse the toad is said to swallow the moon. Living beside her in the moon is the hare, who stands pounding the elixir of immortality from the leaves of a cassia tree under which he stands. Legends around the world have connected the hare with the moon. The hare is said to conceive by gazing at the moon and to bring forth its young from its mouth. It is supposed to live for a thousand years and this connects it with stories of immortality. As with the sun myths, there is more than one moon. Twelve moons take turns to drive across the sky and bathe in the Western Lake. The moon was worshipped at the mid-Autumn or moon festival on the fifteenth day of the eighth month, when the weather is usually finest and the moon brightest, and is connected with the harvest festival.

Emperor Yü, Controller of Floods

Emperor Yü, the founder of the partly historical Hsia dynasty (traditional dates are 2205–1766 B.C.), is often called Yü the Great. His benefits to mankind were of a practical nature. He mastered the elements of metals and water and became known as the Controller of Floods. By working at his great task for thirteen years, cutting channels and building dikes and embankments, he at last brought the waters under control. In one story about him, the Yellow Emperor is supposed to have given him magic earth to dam up the innumerable springs feeding the flood waters. He is supposed to have built mountains at the four corners of the earth so that there were areas which could not be flooded. A winged dragon used its tail to cut channels to drain the waters back into the river beds. When we remember that ancient Chinese civilization spread along the course of the great Yellow River, whose long history of flooding has lasted up to the present day, it is not surprising that such stories have grown up. Emperor Yü also mapped out the universe, dividing it into nine regions and, with his knowledge of metal, had cast nine huge iron cauldrons on which his maps were engraved. These cauldrons had a magic quality, having been cast when the power of the dynasty was at its height. As the power declined and danger threatened, the weight of the cauldrons became less so that they could be more easily transported to a new capital site.

Ch'ü Yüan, Father of Poetry, and the Dragon Boat Race

Other early written evidence of the popularity of many of these legends is contained in the poems of Ch'ü Yüan, the first great Chinese poet known by name and often called the Father of Chinese Poetry. He lived from about 340 to 278 B.C., a member of the ruling house of the State of Ch'u, situated along the northern and southern banks of the Yang-tze River in central China and south of the Yellow River, the main center of early Chinese civilization. He had a brilliant official career and was sent as an envoy to a northern state. But other officials, jealous of his power, engineered his dismissal from Court and he was sent into exile. Although he was recalled several times, his enemies were always too strong for him. He warned his King of the danger from a powerful neighboring state, but the King, disregarding his advice, went to treat with the enemy and was held prisoner by them, dying in captivity.

The King's son, instead of avenging his father, made a humiliating peace. This did not prevent the enemy from invading and plundering the capital. At the news of this disaster Ch'ü Yüan drowned himself in the River Mi-lo. The people, who loved the poet for his virtue, honesty, and fidelity, sent out boats to search for his body but to no avail. They then prepared a kind of glutinous rice cake wrapped in lotus leaves called *tsung-tzu* and set out in boats decorated with flags, racing to be the first to sacrifice the cakes to the spirit of the dead man. Tradition has it that his death occurred on the fifth day of the fifth month and the event is commemorated still among some overseas Chinese communities in the Dragon Boat Festival, when long, canoe-like boats race each other.

One of Ch'ü Yüan's most famous poems, *The Lament*, or *Encountering Sorrow (Li Sao)*, is largely autobiographical. Another poem, *Heaven Questioned (T'ien Wen)*, refers to many of the myths and legends already described. In this poem Ch'ü Yüan asks Heaven one hundred and seventy-two questions, such as "What virtue has the moon that it dies and is born again? Why is there a toad in the moon? Why did Yi shoot down the suns?"[6] Other poems and elegies are addressed to nature gods and spirits of the rivers and the mountains. A Han dynasty commentator on the poems some two hundred years later says that when Ch'ü Yüan was wandering through the countryside during his exile, he came across temples built to honor ancient kings and sages, on the walls of which were pictured scenes from ancient legends, representations of deities, spirits, and monsters, and that these inspired his poems. Similar pictures have been discovered painted or carved on walls of Han dynasty tombs.

Star Myths

Many Chinese myths are connected with the stars. All the constellations have names and are favorite dwelling places for gods and goddesses. One of the best known of all myths is the story of the Heavenly Weaver Maid and the Celestial Cowherd who live in the constellations of Aquila and Lyra on opposite sides of the Milky Way. This ancient and popular story is referred to in the *Book of Songs* and occurs again in the sources already described. The Heavenly Weaver Maid, the daughter of the Sun God, was a model of industry, weaving from morning to night. When the time came, her father arranged her marriage to the Celestial Cowherd. The couple became so much in love that the Weaver Maid neglected her work. This angered the Sun God so much that he ordered their separation. Only once a year, on the seventh day of the seventh moon, are they allowed to meet. Myriads of magpies form a bridge over the Heavenly Stream, the Chinese name for the Milky Way, which separates them and on this one night the lovers may be together. If it rains, the birds take shelter and the lovers have to wait another long year to meet. The Weaver Maid was honored as the Goddess of Weavers, and the Double Seventh is celebrated as a Festival for Girls.

Myths and Legends of Winds, Waters, and Mountains

Other nature myths and legends from the same sources seek to explain the winds, waters, and mountains. The waters are governed by a whole hierarchy of deities from the Palace of the Waters, where there is a ministry with separate departments for salt and sweet waters. Sometimes the waters are said to be governed instead by dragons who live in a fabulous undersea palace, feeding on pearls and opals. Four dragon kings control the salt waters in the eastern, northern, western, and southern oceans. Four other dragon kings control the sweet waters, one in charge of each of the four great rivers of China, and other lesser dragons control waterfalls, springs, lakes, and pools. The winds are governed by Feng Po, the God of the Winds, often pictured as an old man with a white beard, wearing a yellow cloak and a red and blue cap. Over his shoulder he carries a large sack from which he can release winds in any direction he pleases. Control of the winds is also assigned to a dragon called Fei Lien. Five of the great mountains in China are regarded as sacred. They mark five cardinal points, east, north, west, south, and center. Each mountain is inhabited by a powerful spirit who can control nature and influence the affairs of men. The magic mountain of the west, always associated with the great range K'un Lun, lay beyond known boundaries and there the immortals were said to dwell. Some accounts say that the winds emerge from a cave on this mountain and that the God of Rain also lives there.

Animal Legends

Animals play an important role in Chinese myths and legends. We have seen how the eight trigrams of Fu-hsi, demonstrating the creative forces of the universe, were each linked with an abstract quality and with a particular animal. The animals are the horse, goat, pheasant, dragon, cock, swine, dog, and ox and all existed in China, except, of course, the dragon. We have seen too how the year cycles in the ancient calendar were also linked with animals—the rat, ox, tiger, hare, dragon, serpent, horse, goat, monkey, cock, dog, and swine—again, all but the dragon found in China.

Dragons. The lore which has grown up around the dragon is extraordinarily complicated. Some dragon lore is mentioned in the *Book of Change* (*I Ching*), and the *Record of Rites* (*Li Chi*) lists four kinds of supernatural animals, the dragon, the phoenix, the unicorn, and the tortoise, although the last, the tortoise, was real enough in the south of China. The famous second century A.D. dictionary, the *Shuo Wen,* says that of the three hundred and sixty-nine scaly reptiles the dragon is the chief, with the powers of transformation and of making itself invisible. There are five kinds of dragons and all are beneficent, in contrast to the dragon in western mythology, where it is usually evil. The celestial dragon guards the mansion of the gods in the heavens and prevents their falling down. The spiritual dragon can cause the winds to blow and rain to fall for the benefit of mankind. The earthly dragon marks out the course of rivers and streams and deepens the seas. The dragon of hidden treasures guards wealth concealed from mankind and the imperial dragon, always colored yellow and the only one with five claws instead of four, forms the dragon throne of the emperor in charge of the welfare of mankind.

An early Han emperor adopted the imperial dragon (fig. 7) as his symbol in 206 B.C., and it remained the imperial emblem until the death of the last empress in 1908. It was such a yellow dragon which

Figure 7. The imperial dragon (from a traditional paper cut)

rose from a river to present the legendary emperor Fu-hsi with the elements of writing in one version of the myth, emerging from the waters with the pattern of the eight trigrams on its back. Only the emperor and his sons and princes of the first and second rank could use the emblem of the five-clawed dragon. The imperial dragon is often portrayed holding a flaming pearl in his claw, a symbol of the imperial treasure it guards.

The dragon is said to have nine resemblances, such as the horns of a deer, the neck of a snake, the scales of a carp, and so on. Nine is an odd and a lucky number and the scaly ridge down the dragon's back has nine times nine points. Its breath comes from its mouth like a cloud and can change into fire or into water. Its voice is like the beating of a gong and it is said to be deaf. The written character for "deaf" in Chinese derives from the character for dragon, *lung*, and is pronounced in the same way.

Phoenix. While Chinese emperors have used the dragon as their symbol, empress-consorts have adopted the phoenix, another supernatural creature, shown in figure 8. It was said that the phoenix only

Figure 8. The phoenix (from a traditional paper cut)

appears in times of peace and prosperity, remaining hidden at other times. Its divine origin from the sun or fire connects it with the south, with warmth, and with a bountiful harvest. It symbolizes beauty and in appearance sometimes resembles the pheasant. However, in ancient times the phoenix was portrayed more as a bird of prey with a long swanlike neck and heavy claws.

Monkey. Among the animals the monkey is the most popular, and the Monkey King is the hero of countless exploits in the famous fifteenth-century novel *Pilgrimage to the West,* inspired by the historical account of an actual journey made by a seventh-century Chinese monk to India in search of Buddhist relics and scriptures. Monkey had a supernatural birth from an egg which was formed on a rocky promontory of a mountain in the east. When the wind blew on the egg, a stone monkey was born. The light of the sun animated him and he was given magic powers. He was able to perform seventy-two kinds of transformations, he could turn a somersault which carried him one hundred and eight thousand *li,* and he was armed with an immensely strong, magic iron cudgel which he could reduce in size and keep behind his ear. He proclaimed himself King of the Monkeys.

Foxes. Monkey is a hero, even if mischievous, but the fox, which figures in many stories of the supernatural, is usually regarded as inauspicious or evil. Traditional Chinese tombs were hollowed out of hillsides, and foxes, with their nocturnal life and habit of living in holes, were sometimes seen emerging from the graves at night. For this reason they were thought to be ghosts of the dead. They were also believed to be the steeds on which ghosts could ride. Foxes had the power of transformation either into a man or woman, but most frequently turned into a young and pretty woman whose influence would be evil. Other supernatural powers attributed to the fox were the ability to make fire by striking its tail on the ground nine times and to live for a thousand years.

Snakes. Snakes also had the power of transformation into human beings, usually changing into beautiful young women to enchant unwary men. There is a famous cycle of stories known in varying versions in many parts of China about a white snake which changed itself into a beautiful woman known as White Dawn or Madam White. She had a maid who was originally a green snake or, in some versions, a green fish. A sixteenth-century *Guide to the West Lake,* the famous beauty spot where the city of Hangchow is situated, describes how blind storytellers, accompanying themselves on the *p'i-p'a* (a kind of lute) connected the much older story of the white snake with the building of the Thunder Peak Pagoda on the lake in the ninth century A.D.

Horses. Horses have played an important part in Chinese civilization and magic horses figure in a number of stories. The most famous, perhaps, are the eight wonderful horses of the emperor Mu Wang of the Chou dynasty which drew his chariot on his journey to the west, described in the *Travels of King Mu.* Each horse has a name and they have been depicted by two Chinese artists of the eighth and thirteenth centuries, famous for this type of painting. The horses are shown prancing, tossing their manes, or rolling on the ground, each one in a different attitude, with their famous charioteer herding them together.

Porcelain models of these eight horses are a popular item today in Chinatown tourist shops or those in cities like Hong Kong or Singapore.

Animal Symbolism

Lions are not native to China and so were treated as mythical beasts. Pairs of fabulous-looking seated lions in stone or bronze are popular as door guardians, one of them usually with its paw resting on a ball which is thought to symbolize the sun or a precious stone. The figure of a tiger was also popularly used as a door guardian, carved on a spirit screen guarding the entrance to a courtyard. Sometimes a door handle carved in the form of a fierce tiger's head served the same purpose. The tiger was regarded as the fiercest of all wild beasts and therefore the king of all the animals. The stripes on its head were imagined to form the character *wang*, 王, which means "king." Children's toy tigers always have this character painted or embroidered on their foreheads.

From Han times onward (second century B.C.), animal figures were used to guard the entrances to tombs of members of the royal family and of important dignitaries. The famous avenues of carved stone animals and figures of officials guarding the tombs of the first Ming emperor in Nanking and of the thirteen other emperors of that dynasty (1368–1644) in Peking are still standing and are a great attraction for tourists visiting the cities. There are twenty-four enormous stone beasts arranged in fours on either side of the avenue leading to the tombs, one pair standing, the other kneeling. There are lions, camels, elephants, horses, unicorns, and another kind of fabulous beast for which there is no English equivalent name.

An entire galaxy of animals, birds, and other creatures figure as art motifs in China—some, such as the ox, because of their usefulness and others because of their symbolical significance. For instance, the bat was widely used as a decorative motif because *fu* in Chinese, written with different characters, of course, is the word for bat and also for prosperity or happiness. Many birds are used in this way; for example, the crane signifies longevity and the mandarin duck, beauty and fidelity. This kind of symbolism was so widespread and general that it would be understood by everyone.

Shang-ti, the Heavenly Emperor

Over all the forces of nature, over man, and all other creatures ruled the gods and goddesses. Shang-ti, the Heavenly Emperor, the Supreme Being—his name is translated in various ways—was the ruler from whom the earthly emperor received his mandate to rule. When an earthly emperor's rule was corrupt, when the government was mismanaged, the Heavenly Emperor was said to withdraw his mandate. Beneath this superior deity was a complete bureaucracy of gods and goddesses, similar to government on earth.

The idea of the Heavenly Emperor controlling human affairs is Confucian. With the rise of Taoist philosophy the name given to the Heavenly Emperor was Yü-ti, the Jade Emperor, jade signifying purity. The two concepts of the Heavenly Emperor were combined and sometimes the two names in Chinese are strung together. The Temple of Heaven, sometimes called the Hall of Annual Prayers, with its parasol-like, three-tiered, blue-tiled roof, still standing in Peking, symbolizes the circular sky above with three heavens. There the emperor, the "Son of Heaven," offered sacrifices, interceded for his people for good harvests and prosperity, and received his mandate to rule.

Gods and Goddesses

There are literally thousands of gods and goddesses who were worshipped at different times and places and for different reasons. Their origins are to be found in early shamanistic religions and in the teachings of Taoism and Buddhism. Among them are household and personal gods, gods of cities, towns, and villages, of mountains, rivers, and lakes; intercession with these deities would guard people from the evil influence of demon spirits or save them from danger or bring good fortune. Some gods were purely local, but some, like the God of War, the God of Wealth, the Kitchen God, and Kuan Yin, the Goddess of Mercy, were worshipped everywhere in China and statues of them are to be seen in thousands of temples throughout the land.

The God of War and Literature. Kuan-ti, or Kuan Kung as he is variously known, the God of War, was originally the popular Kuan Yü, one of a band of three sworn brothers who fought together against tyrant rulers in the time of the San Kuo period (A.D. 221–280) and whose exploits are recorded in *The Romance of the Three Kingdoms.* He was later deified and regarded as an upholder of justice and a preventer of strife. Because Kuan Yü studied the ancient classics, he is also regarded as the God of Literature and is often pictured holding a scroll in his right hand.

The God of Wealth. Ts'ai Shen, the God of Wealth, was especially worshipped by poor peasants. He lived on earth as a hermit before he was deified. Among his miraculous powers was the ability to ride on the back of a black tiger. He is sometimes pictured on his tiger, or as a benign dignitary seated beneath a money tree whose branches bear strings of coins instead of leaves. Such pictures were hung up as talismans (*see* fig. 9).

The Kitchen God. By far the most popular god was the Kitchen God, a picture of whom would be pasted up over the cooking stove in every household. He is known as Tsao Chün and many stories exist about his origin. On the twenty-third of the twelfth month, known as "Little New Year," offerings were made to him and paper images of him were burnt to "send him up to heaven" where he made a report on the family. The offerings included honey and other sugary things to sweeten

Figure 9. The money tree
from Williams, *Encyclopedia of Chinese Symbolism and Art Motives.*

his lips so that he would only say good things. On New Year's Eve, after the feast and special dishes had been cooked, other offerings were made and the stove would then be allowed to go cold in readiness for the god's return on New Year's Day, when a new paper image would be pasted up to welcome his return.

Kuan Yin, the Goddess of Mercy. Kuan Yin, the Goddess of Mercy, was known in China before the advent of Buddhism but was also adopted into the Buddhist hierarchy. On entering heaven she is said to have paused to listen to the cry of the world, and her name, when translated, means heeding the cry of the world. A story connected with her is placed in the seventh century B.C. A daughter of the ruler of a northern kingdom, she refused to marry according to the wishes of her parents, but was determined to enter a nunnery and devote her life to the poor and the sick. Kuan Yin suffered many cruelties inflicted on her by order of her father, but she carried on with her work of aiding the poor and healing the sick. At last her father was forced to acknowledge her piety and goodness and ordered a statue of her to be made. When the Emperor Shen-nung of ancient times taught the people how to plow, it was Kuan Yin who, taking pity on the hunger of the people, caused the rice grains they had planted to swell so that they would have plenty to eat.

Door Gods. Door gods were universally popular in China and brightly colored paper pictures of two of the favorites were to be seen pasted on doors everywhere. Their story is as follows. The T'ang dynasty Emperor T'ai Tsung (A.D. 627–650) who lay sick in his palace told the doctors who were attending him that he could rest peacefully by day, but that at night he was disturbed by demon spirits. Two brave noblemen, who had been his sworn brothers when he was fighting for the throne, volunteered to keep watch all night outside the palace gates. Thus guarded, the emperor slept peacefully. As he could not allow the two to be on guard every night, T'ai Tsung ordered their portraits to be painted and pasted up on the gates. This precaution worked perfectly. Eventually the two heroes were deified and the popular custom arose to make prints depicting these door gods, fresh prints being pasted on doors at each New Year (fig. 10).

Figure 10. Door gods
from Williams, *Encyclopedia of Chinese Symbolism and Art Motives*

A much more ancient story says that on the shores of the far eastern ocean there grew a giant peach tree whose branches spread over many acres. Two of the tree's giant branches formed a doorway through which evil spirits, or demons, came and went. Two spirits were stationed there as guards to seize any demons who had harmed mankind and send them to destruction. Gradually the custom grew to paint pictures of these two guards armed with bows and arrows on plaques of peach wood and hang these on doors as guardians. Paper pictures of T'ai Tsung's guards largely replaced the older custom of the painted peach-wood plaques.

The Eight Immortals

The Eight Immortals form one of the most popular decorative motifs in traditional Chinese arts and crafts. They are pictured on scrolls, screens, plates, vases, and fans and carved portraits appear in ivory, jade, wood, and stone. They are not exactly gods and goddesses, but a legendary group of beings who have attained immortality by their knowledge of the secrets of nature. Through their devotion to the Taoist religion the Eight Immortals withdrew from the world and attained the power to become invisible and to change materials they touched into gold. They are honored guests at the Feast of the Immortals presided over by the Queen Mother of the West. Some are historical characters, some legendary. They represent different conditions in life such as wealth, poverty, youth, age, aristocracy and plebeianism, masculinity and femininity (there are two female immortals among the eight). Their life stories are illustrated by emblems which they carry. For instance, the Chief of the Immortals is depicted as a fat man holding the peach of immortality in one hand and in the other a fan with which he was able to revive the souls of the dead.

The myths and legends of China, the stories of their gods and goddesses and other mythical beings and of their heroes and heroines, besides being perpetuated by generations of storytellers and in countless plays and poems, are kept alive for the ordinary people in their customs and traditional festivals. Some of these linger on in present-day China but are probably of greater significance among overseas Chinese communities.[7]

The New Year Festival

The most important festival of the whole year and the one which is still universally celebrated among Chinese is the welcome for the New Year. According to the traditional lunar calendar, New Year's Day comes with the second new moon after the winter solstice. The underlying idea of this festival, as in other cultures, is that of renewal and a fresh start. To ensure this, houses had to be thoroughly cleaned, new clothes had to be worn, and all debts had to be discharged.

Preparations began several weeks beforehand with the "little New Year" ceremony, already described, of sending the Kitchen God back to heaven to make his annual report on the family. On New Year's Day no cooking was done and no knife or other sharp instrument was allowed to be used for fear of cutting the good luck for the coming year. Food for several days in advance had to be prepared that included a number of special dishes always made at this season, and ordinary families who normally ate little meat would have pork as well as duck, chicken, and fish dishes.

On New Year's Eve itself the feast was strictly for members of the extended family and as many relatives as possible would try to be present. On succeeding days of the holiday, courtesy visits would be paid at prescribed times to one's superiors or employers. Friends would call on each other and visitors would be received. There would always be some delicacies—nuts, melon seeds, lotus seeds, and other sweet-meats—to offer guests. Special round lacquer boxes, divided into sections, were made for this purpose, the idea of roundness, completeness, countributing to the idea of good luck.

New Year Prints. Several weeks beforehand shops would display brightly colored New Year prints for sale. These would often depict the door gods, the Kitchen God, the God of Wealth, Kuan Yin or other deities, or illustrate scenes from well-known stories. These and good luck couplets, brush-written in bold characters on red paper, to paste up on each side of doorways, would be so plentiful and cheap that everyone would buy them. In Hong Kong at New Year one can still see literally every apartment and house in the Chinese section of the city decorated in this way. Even the prows of junks and sampans are similarly adorned by the boat people.

Flower Decorations. Flowers too were an important part of the New Year's decorations. Especially popular were branches of peach trees which had been forced into early bloom. There are descriptions of methods for forcing blooms in hothouses written in manuals of horti-culture dating back to the fourteenth century. Most towns of any size would have a regular flower market, but at New Year extra flower markets were set up in temporary mat-sheds. White narcissus also were very popular—the sweet-scented variety with many flowers on one stalk, called in Chinese "water fairy flowers" (*shui hsien hua*). Flowering branches were popular New Year's gifts among friends.

Gifts. Other kinds of gifts were exchanged at New Year, but they had to take a prescribed form according to the person giving and the one receiving. Money, placed in little red paper envelopes decorated with good luck signs printed in gilt characters, had to be left for servants at the houses one visited. Children too were presented with money in these red envelopes.

Firecrackers. With preparations complete and before the New Year's Eve feast, offerings were made to the memorial tablets commemorating the family ancestors. Then all members of the family in order of seniority would in turn kowtow to the grandparents or oldest living family members. A cascade of firecrackers would be set off and the feast could begin. Firecrackers were an essential part of any festivity but especially at New Year there would be a perpetual din as one family after another, to say nothing of the children on the side, set off strings of noisy firecrackers. Some were spectacular as well as noisy. Traditional Chinese firecrackers are a study in themselves, with the makers vying with each other in ingenuity. Many varieties have fancy names, such as flags of fire, falling moons, golden plates, ten explosions flying to heaven, silver flowers, and so on.

Pigeons. In Peking there were often pigeon vendors near the flower markets with dozens of different varieties for sale. The fashion was to fly the pigeons with different shaped bamboo whistles attached to their tails. As the birds wheeled around in the sky the whistles made very sweet music. Being made of bamboo the whistles were very light and did not harm the birds.

Entertainments. From the first to the fifteenth day of the first month all shops would be shut and business would cease. It was and still is the one time when everyone in China takes a holiday. During this season there would be a fair in all the towns and larger villages, culminating in the Lantern Festival at the full moon on the fifteenth day. There would be puppet shows of all kinds (fig. 11), jugglers and acrobats, traveling theater shows, pageants, and a lion dance proces-

Figure 11. A puppeteer
from Constant, *Calls, Sounds and Merchandise of the Peking Street Peddlers*

sion, a traditional folklore relic of an ancient rite of exorcism, but now without any religious significance. Adults and children alike would throng to these entertainments.

Toys and Lanterns. During the festival days, market stalls and itinerant vendors would have displays of all sorts of toys for children. Toys in China had their special seasons as in other countries. There was a kite-flying season, a shuttle cock or diabolo season, and many others. But at New Year all these toys could be bought. There was a New Year or "Peace" drum, which several children would beat together to welcome the New Year, and different kinds of toy trumpets. Red silk lanterns were hung from the eaves of roofs and outside the doors of houses at New Year, but particularly on the fifteenth day, the Feast of Lanterns, there would be many different, gaily decorated kinds available for sale and hung up everywhere. Sometimes at night there were lantern processions. Some of the lanterns were ingeniously made—the "pacing horse lantern" (*tsou ma teng*) would have painted mounted horses on a moving shade which would revolve with the movement of hot air from a lighted candle inside. Many varieties of these revolving lanterns are still made today to use with electric lights. In Hong Kong one may find very elaborate and expensive kinds.

Crickets. Caged fighting crickets were very popular with boys and with men as well, who would bet on their "champion" cricket. Two combating insects were placed in a wide bowl and irritated with a straw until they fought each other, often to the death. Crickets symbolized summer and courage when used as decorative motifs. The summer was, of course, their natural season and they were popular then. However, ways were found to rear them so that they hatched out in the winter, when their cheerful chirring notes were welcome reminders of warmer days to come. The many varieties of crickets were greatly prized by connoisseurs and wealthy owners would keep them in elaborately decorated porcelain cricket cages.

New Year Foods and Fruits. Also at the fairs there were stalls selling the special New Year candies and cakes, baked sweet potatoes, and hot roasted chestnuts. Also very popular were the colorful candied fruits: red crabapples; purple, yellow, and green plums; and other fruits—threaded on skewerlike sticks often with decorative streamers hanging at the ends.

Ch'ing-Ming Festival

The next important festival was Ch'ing Ming, the Festival of Pure Brightness, in the second month soon after the Spring Equinox, when families went to "sweep the graves" of the ancestors. Each extended family traditionally had its own burial ground, and hillsides outside the towns and villages were the chosen sites. This festival was not a solemn one; besides tidying up the graves it was usually the occasion for a family picnic in the country.

The Dragon Boat Festival

On the fifth day of the fifth month the Dragon Boat festival would be held to commemorate the death of Ch'ü Yüan, the Father of Poetry, referred to earlier. Some authorities think it possible that the origins of the festival go back earlier than the time of Ch'ü Yüan, that it may have been part of a ceremonial sacrifice to the dragon of the waters to bring rain in the early summer and only later was associated with Ch'ü Yüan. The typical dragon boat was one hundred and twenty-five feet long, a narrow canoe-like structure with a high, curving prow ornamented with a dragon's tail. A single oar was held in two hands by the men who paddled at a furious pace, urged on by their leader standing at the prow and loudly beating a gong or clanging cymbals. Steamed, spiced, triangular-shaped glutinous rice cakes wrapped in lotus leaves, commemorating the offerings made to the spirit of the drowned poet, were on sale everywhere at the time of the festival. Dragon boat races were still being held when the writer lived in Nanking in the late nineteen forties and are still held in Hong Kong and Singapore.

The Double Seventh and the Festival of the Spirits

The Double Seventh, the Lucky Seventh, or *Ch'i Ch'iao* (Begging for Skillful [Fingers]) was a special festival for girls. It had no particular ceremony attached to it but was linked with the story of the Heavenly Weaver Maid and the Celestial Cowherd. Inspired by the skill and industry of the Weaver Maid, girls prayed for skill in their sewing and embroidery. *Ch'iao*, besides meaning "clever" or "skillfull" can also mean "lucky," and *ch'i*, besides meaning "begging," can also mean "seven," the different meanings written with different characters, of course. So *Ch'i Ch'iao* is a punning name for the festival. On the fifteenth day of the same month comes Chung Yüan, the Festival of the Spirits, when prayers are said and offerings made for the dead. An old custom was for children to carry lanterns made of freshly cut lotus leaves with a lighted candle buried in the deep hollow of the leaf so that a soft green light shone through and to sing this song:

Sage-brush lantern,
Lotus leaf lantern,
Alight today
Tomorrow thrown away.

Hou-tzu teng,
Ho yeh teng,
Chin-erh tien,
Ming-erh ko jeng.[8]

Paper lanterns made in the shape of lotus flowers could also be bought from peddlers. Sometimes groups of people with lighted lotus flower lanterns would gather by a stream or lake and float the lighted lanterns on the water to placate the spirits of those who had been drowned.

The Moon Festival

The Moon Festival, or Mid-Autumn (Chung Ch'iu), was celebrated on the fifteenth day of the eighth month, toward the end of the western calendar September, when, with the clear skies usual in China at that season, the moon seemed to be at its brightest. Big round moon cakes made of pastry stuffed with meat and spices or with sweet bean paste were offered at temples. People presented each other with smaller moon cakes or with round fruits to symbolize the full moon. The cakes often had small squares of paper stuck on the top with pictures of the three-legged toad or the hare, the animals who lived on the moon (fig. 12). Popular prints of the hare and the toad were sold for decoration at the time of the festival. Moon Festival parties were often held and, if there was a lake nearby, parties would row out on the lake for moon viewing.

Figure 12. Moon cake peddler
from Constant, *Calls, Sounds and Merchandise of the Peking Street Peddlers*

The Double Ninth

Very soon after the Moon Festival came the Double Ninth, the ninth day of the ninth month, when it was customary for families to take wine and food and climb to the top of a high hill for a picnic. The origin of this practice dates back to a legend from the third century A.D. A man well known for his knowledge of the art of magic, warned his friend that a great disaster would befall him and his family on this particular day, but if he and his family climbed to the top of a high hill, they would escape the worst disaster. The family followed his advice and were unharmed, but found on returning home that all their livestock had been killed. "That is the fate which would have befallen you if you had not followed my advice," said the magician.

Other Ceremonies

The eight festivals under discussion were universally observed in China with local variations at least until the founding of the Republic in 1912 and some of them linger on in varying degrees today, more especially among overseas communities. There were, besides, many local temple fairs, festivals, and observances which varied from place to place. Weddings and funerals were occasions when all families indulged in as much elaborate ceremonial as they could possibly afford. Families have frequently been known almost to bankrupt themselves with expenditure on lavish feasting and entertainments provided on the occasion of a marriage[9] or on elaborate processions and ceremonies for a funeral.

With this background description of the traditional myths, legends, and customs of China, a description of her classical literature, its importance and dominating influence on the life and culture of her people may now be more readily understood.

Notes

1. For a more detailed explanation of the Chinese calendar written for the layman, see Appendix A, The Chinese Calendar, in Tun, *Annual Customs and Festivals in Peking*, translated and annotated by Derk Bodde, pp. 106–10.

2. Readers wishing to test the sixty-year cycle numbering system for themselves (it is a little confusing) are advised to try it by numbering the Heavenly Stems one through zero and the Earthly Branches with the letters "a" through "m" (omitting the letter "i") and making the combinations one-a, two-b, etc., through zero-k, then one-l, two-m, three-a, and so on. It should work out!

3. Graham, *The Book of Lieh-tzu*.

4. Versions of the creation myths in this chapter are a synthesis of those quoted in Christie, *Chinese Mythology*, and Lu, *Brief History of Chinese Fiction*.

5. See also Gebhardt, *The Foolish Old Man Who Moved Mountains*.

6. Quoted by Lu, *Brief History of Chinese Fiction*, p. 18. The work of Ch'ü Yüan has been translated in *Chu Tzu: The Songs of the South*, and *Li Sao and Other Poems of Chu Yüan*.

7. Reliable and more detailed descriptions of Chinese festivals can be found in Tun, *Annual Customs and Festivals in Peking*, and Eberhard, *Chinese Festivals*.

8. Vitale, *Chinese Folklore: Pekinese Rhymes*, no. 95, pp. 133, 134.

9. A detailed description of traditional marriage ceremonies may be found in Williams, *Encyclopedia of Chinese Symbolism and Art Motives* under "Marriage."

Any study of children's literature in China must take into consideration the dominating role which that country's system of education has played in shaping the culture. Education in China until the late nineteenth century, when political events forced a gradual change, meant a knowledge of Chinese classical literature. Some understanding of the system and the curriculum is essential if we are to appreciate the deep impact of classical literary sources on the minds of children in every stratum of society and how the stories enshrined in this literature were ingrained in their imagination.

Importance of the Classics

As early as the Han dynasty in the first century B.C. an imperial civil service examination system was established, success in which led to coveted employment in the extensive government bureaucracy. A thorough knowledge of classical literature formed the basis of all traditional education and was the sole criterion on which fitness for positions of authority was based. This system lasted with modifications and changes for close on two thousand years. Examinations were held at the local and the provincial level and finally at the capital every third year. The majority of the candidates never got further than the first level, many failed at the second level, and very few reached the highest degree. The system, therefore, provided a number of scholars of varying degrees of ability and accomplishment who could not hope to advance in public life. These "failed" scholars traditionally became schoolteachers.

Primary or Village Schools

Two levels of schools for poorer children grew up from early times onward. First there were village or primary schools (*ts'un shu* or *hsiao hsüeh*) which would be opened by one of these teachers, very often in his own house. Not every village had such a school, but every five or six villages would have one. Parents would pay what they could to the schoolmaster, but it was often very little. If a boy from a poor family

47

seemed gifted, it was not unusual for the whole village to help support his education. In this way it was hoped that benefits from any influential position he later attained would redound to the whole village.

Some primary schools could prepare a student for the first provincial examination, but others stopped at a lower level. As soon as a boy from an ordinary family was old enough to help in the fields or become apprenticed in a trade or a shop he would most probably have to leave school. This type of school continued until well into the twentieth century and such well-known modern Chinese scholars as Lu Hsün, who died in Shanghai in 1936, and Hu Shih, who died in Taiwan in 1962, had part of their early education in such a primary school.

Two descriptions, one from a poem by a well-known eighteenth-century poet, Yüan Mei, about peasant children at school, and one by Lu Hsün, in some reminiscences of his own childhood included in his *Dawn Blossoms Plucked at Dusk*, paint graphic pictures of such schools. Yüan Mei's poem was written on a journey to Kueilin and describes a village school in what was then a remote part of the country:

> I saw in the distance peach-orchards in leaf,
> But did not know what village it was,
> I stopped the boat, tucked up my coat-tails and walked
> Attracted by hearing the sound of a book being read,
> At a wicker gate schoolchildren were gathered,
> Sitting in rows, decent and orderly.
> When they heard that I came from Hangchow
> A look of delight stirred in every face.
> They all came to me bringing their lesson books,
> Wanting to hear something they had never heard.
> Seeing they wished it I explained a few passages
> While they sat in a circle, constantly nodding their heads.
> When I turned to leave, they brought me chicken and millet
> And lifted for me the earthern jar of wine.
> Shouldering their hoes, fathers and elder brothers
> Back from the fields also came to peep. . . .
> I was touched by their simple, unspoiled kindness;
> It was like meeting peasants of a pristine reign.[1]

Reprinted from *Yuan Mei, Eighteenth Century Chinese Poet*, by Arthur Waley, by permission of George Allen and Unwin Ltd. and Stanford University Press. © George Allen and Unwin Ltd., 1956.

Lu Hsün says in his reminiscence, "From Hundred Plant Garden to Three Flavour Study"[2]:

Behind our house was a great garden commonly known as Hundred Plant Garden. It has long been sold and the last time I saw it, seven or eight years ago, there were only weeds there. But it was my paradise when I was a child.

I don't know why my family decided to send me to school, or why they chose the school reputed to be the strictest in town. At all events I would no longer be able to go so often to Hundred Plant Garden.

Less than ten minutes' walk east of our house, across a stone bridge was my teacher's home. You went in through a black-lacquered bamboo gate, and the third room was the study. In the center hung a placard on which was written "Three Flavour Study." Under this was a picture of a very fat spotted deer lying beneath an old tree. Since there was no shrine to Confucius, we kowtowed to the placard and the deer. The first kowtow was for Confucius, the second for our teacher. When we kowtowed the second time, our teacher bowed in return.

At midday I practised calligraphy, in the evening I made couplets. For the first few days the teacher was very stern, though later he treated me better; but by degrees he increased the amount of reading to be done and the number of characters in each line of the couplets, from three to five, and finally to seven.

There was a garden behind Three Flavour Study. Although it was small, you could climb the terrace there to pick winter plum or look for cicadas' skins on the cassia trees. But it was no use too many of us slipping out into the garden at the same time or staying out too long, for the teacher would shout from the study, "Where has everyone gone?" Then everyone would slip back, one after the other. He had methods of punishment which were seldom used. Generally he simply glared round and shouted "Read your books!" Then all of us would read at the tops of our voices and the noise was like a seething cauldron.

The teacher read aloud too. Later our voices grew lower, but he would read as loudly as ever. I used to draw, using thin paper to trace the illustrations in various novels, just as you trace calligraphy. By the time I had studied a good many books, I had also traced a good many illustrations. I never became a good student, but I made not a little progress as an artist, for I had a big volume each of illustrations from *Suppressing the Bandits*[3] and the *Pilgrimage to the West*.[4]

College-type Schools

Then there were college-type schools known as *shu yüan*. Students preparing for the examinations would attend these schools from the age of about seventeen onward. Well-known scholars would come from districts nearby to lecture on their special subjects. Confucius himself (551–479 B.C.) could be said to have instituted such a school, for he taught a group of young scholars who gathered around him, but of course there was no examination system at that time.

As part of the nationwide organization there were prefectural and provincial hostels where students could live among people from their own province while taking the examinations. College-type schools were often attached to these hostels where students could practice their essay writing and have their work criticized before eventually taking the examination. Local guilds supported the hostels and often contributed to the support of the schools. An eleventh-century reform recorded in the official dynastic histories called for the establishment of schools in every prefecture and subprefecture.[5]

Family Schools

In wealthier families private tutors would be employed. The extended family, living in a large courtyard complex, would set up a schoolroom for brothers and cousins alike. They were known as *chia hsüeh*, family schools, and sons of more distant relatives, if living within traveling distance would often attend the school as well. Some of these family schools would allow other local children to attend free of charge, they were then known as *i hsüeh*, public schools.

Education for Girls

Girls too would attend the family school until they reached the age of puberty, when they would be separated from the boys and have to concentrate on embroidery and household arts in preparation for marriage. But in any case, mothers, aunts, or grandmothers would see that girls in this type of family could at least read and write. And once they could read they would go on studying by themselves, and many became exceedingly well read. Calligraphy, painting, and writing poetry are among the traditional arts of China which women have always shared. Examples of cultured women from ancient times are to be found in *Biographies of Chinese Women (Lieh Nü Chuan)*,[6] an extant first-century collection of accounts of one hundred and twenty-five women. Girls were encouraged to read this book and also to study *The Teaching of Girls (Nü Chieh)*, a book of moral precepts for women by the famous historian, Pan Chao. Arthur Waley's life of the eighteenth-century poet Yüan Mei says:

> At this time too [1790 in Nanking], his practice of accepting lady pupils was at its height. . . . He had at this period thirteen principal lady pupils, of whom a picture was once made. But in an anthology of *Poems by My Lady Pupils* he included work by no less than twenty-eight ladies. I will not burden you with a long list of names, but I think we may take as typical Chin I, called Hsien-Hsien (Slender). Frail, ailing, plaintive, doomed to an early death, she reminds one at once of Lin Tai-yü, the heroine of the novel *The Dream of the Red Chamber*, which was first printed in 1792.[7] . . . Her poem says, "On a cold night, waiting in vain for my husband to come home and reading *The Dream of the Red Chamber*. . . .[8]

Reprinted from *Yuan Mei, Eighteenth Century Chinese Poet*, by Arthur Waley, by permission of George Allen and Unwin Ltd. and Stanford University Press. © George Allen and Unwin Ltd., 1956.

Tai-yü, the heroine of this novel, comes from a poorer branch of the Chia family, around which the story centers, but she can brush write a poem on an old handerchief which the young hero, Pao-yü, sends her to dry the tears she sheds when he is sick.

In spite of the immense traditional respect for learning and the written word, the fact remains that the opportunity for education was denied in the past to a majority of the population. These were the poor in the cities and the peasants who lived in the smaller, scattered village communities. They remained illiterate until universal primary education was made mandatory by the People's Republic.

Primary School Textbooks

Children began reading and writing with several traditional primers such as the *Thousand Character Classic* (*Ch'ien Tzu Wen*), written in the early sixth century and used in schools until twentieth-century reforms were introduced. As its title denotes, it is made up of two hundred and fifty lines, each containing four characters, none of which is repeated. It deals with the names of the early emperors and other famous names in history, and with facts about nature and farming and so on. A later but no less popular schoolbook, again reprinted until modern times, was the *Three Character Classic* (*San Tzu Ching*), written in the thirteenth century by Wang Ying-lin. The author compiled it as an elementary guide to knowledge in alternately rhyming lines of three characters each. There are about five hundred different characters in the book. Another popular rhyming book was the *Hundred Family Names* (*Pai Chia Hsing*) in which traditional family names are arranged in rhymes. Chinese, when they want to refer to "the man in the street," say "old hundred names," a saying inspired by this book.

Again quoting from Lu Hsün's reminiscences, he says his primer was the *Rhymed History* (*Chien Lüeh*) by Wang Shih-yün. This book gives a rhymed account of Chinese history to the end of the Ming dynasty (1644), and Lu Hsün says that he remembers people saying it was more useful than learning the *Three Character Classic* or the *Hundred Family Names*. He makes fun of another textbook he remembers, *The Treasure House of Primary Learning* (*Yu Hsüeh Ch'ung Lin*). This was printed as four small books, each having four sections with such titles as astronomy, geography, anatomy, and so forth. But he says that the text, written in rhyming couplets, was mostly sheer nonsense.

Primers varied from period to period and also from province to province. A few early textbooks have been preserved, more as curiosities than as standard school texts. One, translated by Goodrich as *Fifteenth Century Illustrated Chinese Primer* (*Hsin Pien Tui Hsiang Szu Yen*), is attributed to the Ming dynasty, the earliest known extant copy being dated 1436, although some scholars think it is actually a reprint of a book written several hundred years earlier (fig. 13).[9] The book consists of only sixteen pages with three hundred and six small woodcuts of everyday things with the accompanying characters. In the traditional way the pictures begin with heavenly things, clouds for the sky and for rain; then there are pictures of the sun, the moon, and the stars; then come pictures of animals, birds, trees, flowers, insects, buildings, musical instruments, and the like, ending with pictures of

Figure 13. A page from an early, illustrated Chinese primer
from Goodrich, *Fifteenth Century Illustrated Chinese Primer*

such household items as a broom and a saw. It is interesting to compare it with the *Orbis Sensualium Pictus* of 1658 by Comenius, so often referred to as the first picture book for children.[10] A Buddhist tract exhorting people not to eat beef in deference to vegetarian principles, the *Do Not Eat Beef Chant* (*Chieh Shih Niu Jou Ko*), exists in several versions.[11] Not a very suitable subject for children, one would think, but the whole tract consists of characters arranged in the shape of a water buffalo (fig. 14), which because of its pictorial quality has intrigued generations of children. The writer has met one elderly Chinese who does remember chanting from such a text at school just before the turn of the present century.

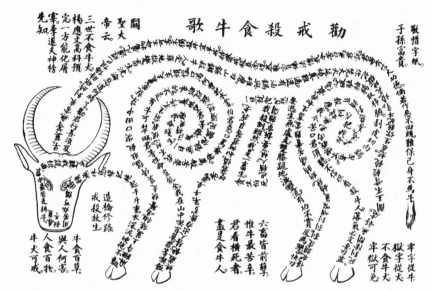

Figure 14. The *Do Not Eat Beef Chant*
from Doré, *Recherches sur les Superstitions en Chine*, vol. 4, p.308

There were also a number of anthologies of poetry used, and children learned many poems by heart before they could fully understand their meaning. *Poetry from a Thousand Poets (Ch'ien Chia Shih)* was popular, as were other similar anthologies. The tradition of learning classical poetry by heart was so strong that even today many Chinese who are old enough to have received some of the lingering traditional as well as a modern education can recite by heart many of the poems in the *Book of Songs (Shih Ching)*, an ancient compilation, and in other collections, such as the famous anthology of T'ang poetry *Three Hundred Poems of the T'ang Dynasty (T'ang Shih San Pai Shou)*,[12] compiled between the seventh and tenth centuries A.D.

Reading for Pleasure

Once children could read freely there were a number of favorite collections of old stories they would read by themselves, especially if there were illustrated editions. In another of his reminiscences Lu Hsün describes how as a young boy he coveted an illustrated copy of the *Book of Mountains and Seas,* already described as an important source of myths and legends:

I was also longing for an illustrated copy of the *Book of Mountains and Seas*. This longing had been aroused by a distant great-uncle of ours. A fat and kindly old man, he liked to grow plants such as chloranthus or jasmine, or the rare silk tree which is said to have come from the north. This old man was a lonely soul with no one to talk to, so he liked children's company and often even called us his "young friends." In the compound where several branches of our clan lived, he was the only one with many books and unusual ones at that. He had volumes of the essays and poems written for the examinations, of course; but his was the only study where I could find *Commentaries on the Flora and Fauna in the Book of Songs* by Lu Ch'i of the third century A.D. and many other strange titles. My favorite in those days was *The Mirror of Flowers* with all its illustrations. He told me there was an illustrated edition of the *Book of Mountains and Seas* with pictures of man-faced beasts, nine-headed snakes, three-footed birds, men with wings, and headless monsters who used their teats as eyes. . . . Unfortunately, he happened to have mislaid it.

Eager as I was to look at pictures like these, I did not like to press him to find them for me. He was very indolent. And none of the other people I asked would give me a truthful answer. I had several hundred coppers of New Year money, but no opportunity to buy that book. The main street where books were sold was a long way from our house and the New Year holiday was the only time in the year when I was able to go there to look around; but during that period the doors of both bookshops were firmly closed.

As long as I was playing it was not so bad, but the moment I sat down I remembered the illustrated *Book of Mountains and Seas*.

Probably because I harped on the subject so much even Ah Chang [his old nurse] started asking what this *Book of Mountains and Seas* was. I had never mentioned it to her, for I knew she was no scholar, so telling her would serve no purpose. Since she asked me, however, I told her.

About a fortnight or a month later, as I remember, four or five days after she had gone home on leave, she came back wearing a new blue cloth jacket. The moment she saw me she handed me a package.

"Here, son!" she said cheerfully. "I've bought you that *Book of Holy Seas* with pictures!"

This was like a thunderbolt. I was struck all of a heap. I hastened to take the package and unwrap the paper. There were four small volumes and, sure enough, when I flipped through the pages, the man-faced beast, the nine-headed snake . . . all of them were there.[13]

The Traditional Curriculum

As soon as children could read and write, the curriculum was based on the classical texts known as the Five Classics and the Four Books.[14] The Five Classics are the *Book of Change,* the *Book of History,* the *Book of Songs,* the *Record of Rites,* and the *Spring and Autumn Annals* with the *Commentary of Tso.* The Four Books are the *Analects of Confucius, The Great Learning, Mencius,* and the *Doctrine of the Mean.*

The Five Classics

The Five Classics (*Wu Ching*) consist of the greater part of existing ancient Chinese literature dating from the tenth to the third centuries

B.C. The *Book of Change* (*I Ching*) is a manual of divination and a metaphysical treatise. In it are to be found the eight trigrams of Fu-hsi, one of the most popular Chinese decorative motifs, symbolizing the eight fundamental elements of the universe, and containing a description of the qualities associated with them. It also contains a description of the *yin* and *yang* principles and other metaphysical doctrines. The *Book of History* (*Shu Ching*) is an anthology of documents such as speeches and exhortations by ancient rulers, proclamations, and other records. The *Record of Rites* (*Li Chi*), a restoration of an earlier classic lost in the third century B.C., is a book of ancient rituals and ceremonies. In it children would read:

> In ancient times, a boy would move to lodgings outside his home at the age of eight to learn the lesser arts and practice the lesser etiquette. When he bound his hair and undertook more advanced studies, he would learn the greater arts and practice the greater etiquette. At home he would study ceremony and literature, abroad his jade pendants would tinkle and when riding in his carriage he would hear harmonious bells. Thus no improper ideas could enter his heart.[15]

The *Book of Songs* (*Shih Ching*), also commonly known in translation as the *Classic of Poetry* or the *Book of Odes*, is the only truly literary work among these ancient classics. It is an anthology of three hundred and five poems, traditionally supposed to have been collected and edited by Confucius himself in the sixth century B.C. for teaching purposes from a much larger number, but the collection was probably made before his time. He is recorded as saying "I transmit but I do not create: I have faith in and love for ancient studies." The poems are arranged in four sections. The first consists of ballads sung by people of the various states, followed by a section with songs for festal occasions, then compositions for occasions of worship and ceremony at court, and finally hymns sung during religious ceremonies and sacrifices. Arthur Waley, in his well-known translation, *The Book of Songs*, arranges the poems under such headings as courtship, marriage, poems of welcome and of feasting, warriors and battles, sacrifice, music and dancing, building, hunting, lamentations, and dynastic songs and legends.

The *Spring and Autumn Annals* (*Ch'un Ch'iu*) cover the period 722 to 468 B.C. and chronicle the events in the State of Lu, the birthplace of Confucius. It is one of the most important source books for the history of the feudal kingdoms of the period. The spare outline of events recorded in the *Annals* is expanded in the *Commentary of Tso* (*Tso Chuan*).

The Four Books

The Four Books (*Ssu Shu*) were edited in their standard form in the seventh century A.D. from the then existing canon and are regarded as the embodiment of Confucian teaching. They are the *Analects of Confucius (Lun Yü)* which is an anthology of the sayings of the Master, the *Great Learning (Ta Hsüeh)*, and the *Doctrine of the Mean (Chung Yung)* which also consist of sayings by Confucius and his followers, and finally there is the book of the philosopher *Mencius (Meng Tzu)*. Study of these books and their classic commentaries was largely through memory learning, with essay writing on interpretation.

Confucius

Not much is known personally of any of the writers of the classic texts, except for Confucius and Mencius. Confucius, whose actual name was K'ung Ch'iu, was known as K'ung the Master (K'ung Fu Tzu), Confucius being a Latinized form of this title. He was born about 551 B.C. Well known in his lifetime as a teacher and philosopher, the little exact information we have about him comes from his own sayings in the *Analects,* which were collected soon after his death, about 479 B.C.[16] His was a respectable but impoverished family in the ancient State of Lu in eastern China, modern Shantung Province.

During the lifetime of Confucius, China was divided into a number of semiautonomous feudal states which were often warring among themselves. His lifelong ambition was to bring about a return to a more unified and peaceful society which he believed had existed in an earlier time. He spent many years traveling far and wide, teaching groups of young men by a system of debate and question and answer. Good government could only be achieved by men of virtue and integrity; men should therefore regulate their lives in the family and in all positions of authority according to the five principles of benevolence, justice, propriety, wisdom, and sincerity. He respected people of all classes and welcomed them as students as long as they were intelligent. Confucius believed the state existed for the people, not the people for the state. He never achieved any very important official position himself, but his pupils formulated and preached his doctrines, becoming very influential in public life. In the second century B.C., Confucianism became the official state doctrine.

Mencius

Mencius (Meng-tzu) was born about 372 B.C, also in eastern China. He became an ardent follower of the doctrine of Confucius and was important as a teacher. Because his father died when he was only three years old, he was brought up with great care by his mother who saw to it that her son, who was very clever, was surrounded with only good influences. Many stories are told of her devoted care for her son. He became famous as a debater and he used many colorful anecdotes to illustrate his points. Like the writings of Confucius himself, those of Mencius emphasize the fundamental goodness of man.

Other Arrangements of the Classics

A standard textbook for the study of the Classics was *Chu-tzu Chuan Shu* (*Collected Works of Chu Hsi*), a commentary by the eleventh-century philosopher Chu Hsi. Another arrangement of the Classics exists, known as the *Thirteen Classics* (*Shih-san Ching*); this collection, in addition to other ancient histories and a dictionary, contains the *Book of Filial Piety* (*Hsiao Ching*), quotations from which often appear in translation, as well as the *Ritual of Chou* (*Chou Li*). In the latter it is written, "The sons of nobles entered primary schools (hsiao hsüeh) at eight, and the imperial tutors taught them the six classes of characters to begin with." The literature itself indicates that from late Han times (second century A.D.), study of the Chinese language was part of the traditional curriculum.

The Histories

Besides the standard Classics, excerpts from other philosophers' writings and from later historical chronicles were studied. The early *Book of History* and the *Spring and Autumn Annals* with the *Commentary of Tso*, already described, established a tradition of writing a chronological account of the events of each dynasty. All of these are preserved in the collection known as the *Twenty-Four Histories*.

Among the histories, those of the Han dynasty (206 B.C.–A.D. 220) contain some of the most valuable as well as memorable records. The *Record of History* (*Shih Chi*), also translated as *Historical Memoirs,* compiled by the famous historian Ssu-ma Ch'ien (145–86 B.C.), whose family name is one of the few with two characters, not only chronicles the events of the Han dynasty so far, but gives a general outline of Chinese history from mythical times.[17] Ssu-ma's work includes treatises on the calendar and astrology, on sacrifices and rites, and on music, as well as seventy biographies of members of the royal and other noble families and of statesmen. These are to be expected in an official history, but there are also accounts of poets, court favorites, and even actors. Stories woven from these bare chronicles form an important part of popular literature. One of the celebrated twentieth-century actor Mei Lan-fang's most popular plays, *The Emperor's Farewell to His Favorite* (*Pa Wang Pieh Chi*), was based on a *Shih Chi* story. It is in this history that it is recorded that officials of the earlier Chou dynasty (1122–221 B.C.) were sent into the streets and marketplaces to gather the stories and sayings circulating among the people.

A continuing contemporary history of the Han times known as the *History of the Former Han Dynasty* (*Ch'ien Han Shu*) was written by Pan Ku (A.D. 32–92) and continued after his death by his sister, Pan Chao, one of the most remarkable woman scholars in Chinese history.[18] Pan's *History* included a bibliographic section based on a system devised for the Imperial Library that contained seven classes of literature.

This system of classification of literature continued until modern times. The list of books recorded amounted to some six hundred titles in over thirteen thousand volumes. About one-quarter of these works are extant today.

The Literature of Buddhism and Taoism

From the third century A.D. onward, Buddhism played an important part in Chinese cultural life, and the growing number of translations of sacred and secular texts from India influenced Chinese literature. Parallel with the spread of Buddhist literature was that of Taoism, a religion which had become formalized in the second century A.D., adopting some of the classic texts as its doctrine. Most widely known were the philosophies of Lao-tzu and Chuang-tzu and the *Book of Change* already described.

Lao-tzu, whose writings and sayings became the basis of Taoism, was an elder contemporary of Confucius. The name by which he has been known through the ages simply means "Old Master" and is a sign of the respect in which he was held. The few facts known about Lao-tzu come from the *Record of History* of Ssu-ma Ch'ien. He held an official appointment at the Imperial Capital which seems to have been that of Keeper of the Imperial Records. A meeting between him and Confucius is documented. His sayings and philosophy are recorded in *The Way and Its Power* (*Tao Te Ching*), at one time attributed to Lao-tzu himself, but now thought to be a later, third century B.C. compilation from his teachings and sayings.[19]

Chuang-tzu (Master Chuang), whose name was Chuang Chou, is well known as a follower of Lao-tzu. He was born about 369 B.C. in a small state in east central China and lived until about 286 B.C. After some experience as a minor government official, he refused higher appointments and retired into private life. The story goes that while Chuang-tzu was fishing one day, a royal emissary arrived to offer him a high appointment. He pointed to a tortoise on the mudbank and said that he would rather be a live tortoise waving its tail in the mud than a dead one in a golden casket decorating the King's ancestral shrine. His teachings and sayings are recorded in the book which bears his name, most of which is thought to have been put together by a later commentator.[20] Many, many stories are based on or quoted from his book, perhaps the most universally known being the story of his dream about the butterfly:

> Once upon a time, Chuang Chou dreamt that he was a butterfly, a butterfly flying about, enjoying itself. It did not know that it was Chuang Chou. Suddenly he awoke, and there he was, veritably Chuang Chou himself. Now he does not know whether the butterfly is a dream of Chuang Chou or whether Chuang Chou is a dream of the butterfly.

The Tradition of the Couplet

The foregoing brief discussion of the Classics and other early literature and their important role in the traditional educational and cultural
life of the people explains why so many of the characters and stories
have become familiar to everyone, child and adult, who received any
schooling at all. From the Classics and other early books and inter-
woven into the very fabric of the language spoken and written today
are innumerable quotations, references to events, and sayings composed
of four- and five-, and seven-character-line couplets. The structure of the
language and its conciseness make the couplet a natural form of expression; their rhythm and tonal quality make them easy to memorize
and easy to chant. Their influence on the Chinese language is even
stronger than that of the Bible and Shakespeare on English in its for-
mative stage.

As has been noted earlier, the practice of writing quotations in public
places and their use as decorative motifs are universal in China. The
pictorial quality and beauty of the calligraphy make such quotations
appropriate for decoration as well as exhortation. Couplets, known as
tui-lien, were carved in stone or painted on parallel plaques or scrolls
and hung on either side of doorways or on the columns of an archway.
They also were painted on screens, on pottery, on fans, and on pictures.
When written on paper scrolls in bold calligraphy, even the poorest
household could buy them for a few copper cash, particularly for decorating their houses at New Year and other festivals. Written characters
wishing good luck and good fortune would appear on all wedding
decorations, and suitable inscriptions would be used to embellish the
customarily lavish funeral decorations. Here are examples of New Year
couplets:

Firecrackers signal the end of the year,
Fruit trees announce a new spring,

P'ao chu ch'u chiu sui,
T'ao li pao hsin ch'un.

Distance may separate true friends,
Minds and hearts remain united.

Hai nei tsun chih chi
T'ien ya jo pi lin.

So ingrained in Chinese tradition is this form of couplet that Mao
Tse-tung framed his well-known pronouncement to the people in this
way:

Let one hundred flowers bloom
Let one hundred schools (of thought) contend.

Pai hua ch'i fang
Pai chia cheng ming.

The illiterate peasant, the man in the street, the educated and the uneducated alike would grow up familiar with a rich legacy of sayings from the poets and the sages. And it is to this age-old tradition, both visual and oral, that we must turn to understand how the best stories came to be so well known through the centuries. It is through the story-tellers and through plays based on the old stories that a strong collo-quial literature has been preserved and made a part of everyday life in China.

Notes

1. Waley, *Yüan Mei: Eighteenth Century Chinese Poet*, p. 17.
2. Quoted and condensed from Lu, *Dawn Blossoms Plucked at Dusk* included in *The Selected Works*, vol. 1, pp. 387–93.
3. *Suppressing the Bandits (Tang K'ou Chih)*, a novel by Yu Chung-Hua (1794–1849), written as a sequel to *The Tale of the Marshes (Shui Hu Chuan)*.
4. *Pilgrimage to the West* (Hsi Yu Chi) by Wu Cheng-en.
5. Goodrich, *A Short History of the Chinese People*, p. 155.
6. O'Hara, *The Position of Woman in Early China According to the Lieh Nü Chuan, "The Biographies of Chinese Women."*
7. Tsao, *The Dream of the Red Chamber (Hung Lou Meng)*.
8. Waley, *Yüan Mei: Eighteenth Century Poet*, pp. 179–80.
9. Goodrich, *Fifteenth Century Illustrated Chinese Primer (Hsin Pien Tui Hsiang Szu Yen)*.
10. Originally written in Latin and printed at Munich in 1658, this primer by Jan Amos Comenius, a Moravian bishop, was translated into several European languages, including English, by 1659. Facsimile editions of the English translation available in many libraries are often known by the abbreviated title of *Orbis Pictus*.
11. See Doré, *Recherches sur les superstitions en Chine*, vol. 2, p. 308.
12. Selections from *Three Hundred Poems of the T'ang Dynasty (T'ang Shi San Pai Shou)* translated into English appear in Jenyns, *Selections from the Three Hundred Poems of the T'ang Dynasty;* Obata, *The Works of Li Po;* Waley, *One Hundred and Seventy Chinese Poems* and *Chinese Poems*.
13. Lu, *Selected Works*, vol. 1, pp. 367–69.
14. Legge, *The Chinese Classics*. "One of the earliest and in some respects still the best translation of the Confucian Classics," Liu, *An Introduction to Chinese Literature*, selected bibliography of books in English, p. 295. The brief descriptions of the Five Classics and the Four Books are based on those in chaps. 1 and 3 of Liu's *Introduction*.
15. From the *Record of Rites*, quoted by Lu in *A Brief History of Chinese Fiction*, p. 28.
16. Waley, *The Analects of Confucius*.
17. Watson, *Ssu-ma Ch'ien: Records of the Grand Historian of China*.
18. Dubs, *The History of the Former Han Dynasty (Ch'ien Han Shu)*.
19. Waley, *The Way and Its Power: A Study of the Tao Te Ching and Its Place in Chinese Thought*.
20. Fung, *Chuang Tzu*, p. 64.

Children on the streets would sit down to listen to old stories, including ones about *The Three Kingdoms*. When they heard of Liu Pei's defeat they would fret and even shed tears. When they heard of Ts'ao's defeat they would brighten up and applaud.[1]

Early Popularity of Storytellers

The foregoing is a quotation from an eleventh-century scholar-poet who was appointed an official in Hangchow, a large, flourishing city in south central China, famous as a center for the performing arts. There is evidence of the popularity of storytellers from the second and third centuries A.D. onward, and in the succeeding centuries their role as popular entertainers became increasingly more important. The storyteller was at once a public entertainer and a teacher who, with his cunning skills, stirred the imaginations of young and old alike, while instilling the precepts of Chinese society deep within their minds. In the T'ang dynasty (618–906), which has often been called a golden age of Chinese culture, music, literature, and poetry flourished. Storytellers, together with actors, musicians, dancers, puppeteers, acrobats, and jugglers, contributed to a flowering of the performing arts. They popularized favorite stories from preceding dynasties, which they changed, adapted, and expanded to suit their own dramatic needs, at the same time enriching their repertoire with many contemporary stories and ballads.

T'ang Dynasty (618–906)

It was at this time that the country became united once more after three centuries of civil wars. The capital at Ch'ang-an (present day Sian) became a center for all the arts and the fame of its lavishly cultured court spread far beyond the frontiers of the country. Transportation was greatly improved, especially through a magnificent system of canals built in the century before T'ang which linked the capital and the Yellow River cities of the north with the Yangtze River cities in central China, a distance of some six hundred miles, and with important ports at the estuary of that river. Luxury goods were imported by   61

Chinese, Indian, and Arab merchants and Chinese silks, porcelains, and other artistic manufactures were exported by ship not only throughout Southeast Asia, but as far away as Egypt. The overland route through central Asia to India and beyond to Arab lands, the famous "Silk Road" and caravan route of Roman times, continued to be extensively traveled.

The Effect of Foreign Influences

This lively commerce naturally enriched Chinese life. Schools and colleges throughout the land were encouraged and the famous Hanlin Academy of Letters was founded in 754. The most eminent scholars and literary figures of the day were appointed to membership and the Academy was responsible for all the literary activities of the Court, the continued editing and copying of texts for the Imperial Library, and the writing of state papers of all kinds. The Academy and its official functions continued until the end of the imperial era in 1908.

China's music repertoire was enriched by the introduction of new kinds of musical instruments from India and central Asia. More translations were made from Sanskrit following the epic journey of the monk Hsüan-chuang to India in search of Buddhist texts and relics, a journey which lasted from 629 to 645. The account of Hsüan-chuang's journey itself, the famous *Pilgrimage to the West* (*Hsi Yu Chi*), inspired countless stories and dramatic pieces, culminating in the great sixteenth-century novel of the same title, translated in part by Arthur Waley in his book, *Monkey*.

Poetry and Prose Writing

Poetry blossomed. Some fifty thousand poems by more than two thousand poets have come down to us from this time. The beauty and appeal of many of these short lyrics for young readers can be appreciated from an anthology of translations designed for readers of all ages, *The Moment of Wonder: A Collection of Chinese and Japanese Poetry*.[2] Every educated man was supposed to be able to compose poems. Candidates for the imperial examinations were in the habit of giving samples of their writing to influential figures at court who would perhaps be among their examiners. Most young scholars offered samples of their poetry, but some writers at this time began writing stories in a consciously literary style, sometimes using the themes of the old, colloquial anecdotes, the type of story previously regarded as being simply "the talk of the market place." Several collections of stories of this period have been translated, among them *The Dragon King's Daughter: Ten T'ang Dynasty Stories*.[3]

Professional Academies for the Performing Arts

Royal patronage of the arts led to the establishment of professional schools and academies for training actors and other performers.[4] The most famous was known as the Academy of the Pear Orchard, at which the best actors trained for appearance at Court. In later times the title "Leader of the Pear Orchard" was an honor bestowed on outstanding actors. Young girls too were chosen from ordinary families for their grace and beauty to be trained in a school supported by the Court. They learned to sing and dance and play musical instruments, such as the flute and a type of lute. Besides performances at Court, there were many other companies or groups of actors who traveled from city to city and through the countryside, performing for the ordinary people during festivals and fairs. Small companies of from five to seven people often belonged to one family but gave themselves professional nicknames like "Big Head," "Orange Peel," or "Silver Fish." Some of these itinerant companies became well known and would be commanded to perform at the big courtyard residence of a local official for a wedding or similar festive occasion.

Script Writers and Writing Guilds

There was a special class of writers, members of writing guilds, who provided play scripts, songs, and poems for the various dramatic forms. As is the case with so much early popular writing, it is known from references that there were masked dramas and plays with domestic themes in T'ang times. The titles of two hundred and eighty plays from this period are known from references, but all the texts are lost. The only copies made would have been for the actors and these naturally would easily become worn out. Many of the themes of these early plays were copied and adapted in later times in the "variety" plays of the eleventh and twelfth centuries that combined dialog, song, dance, and acrobatics.

Stick, Glove, String, and "Human" Puppets

Of all the dramas perhaps the puppet plays were the most loved, especially by children. Puppet plays were popular in China from the third century onward. During the T'ang dynasty and in the following centuries there were several highly developed kinds of puppet shows. Carved and articulated wooden puppets were made with great artistry and ingenuity, the limbs of which were moved with sticks. These puppets had painted faces and were elaborately dressed to represent different roles, with silk gowns and appropriate wigs and headdresses, the female characters wearing flowers and imitation jewels. In addition to the wooden stick puppets there were glove and string puppets, the strings being made of white silk, and there were even puppets "in the flesh." Children were held up to mime the actions of the story in the same way as would an actual puppet. This "full circle" of influence when a child would imitate a puppet imitating a human being is found also in Japanese drama where kabuki actors are strongly influenced by their own highly sophisticated puppet drama, the *bunraku*.

Shadow Puppets

The origin of shadow puppets is lost in the mists of antiquity. Chinese legend has it that the famous Han emperor Wu-ti (140–87 B.C.), heartbroken at the death of his favorite concubine, commanded the necromancers to recall her spirit from the dead. At last one of them achieved this by projecting the shadow of a puppet representation of the dead concubine on a curtain. The story is immortalized in the poem which Wu-ti then wrote:

Is it or isn't it?
I stand and look
The swish, swish of a silk skirt.
How slow she comes![5]

Reprinted from One Hundred Seventy Chinese Poems, translated by Arthur Waley, by permission of Constable & Co. Ltd. and of Alfred A. Knopf, Inc. Copyright 1918 by Constable & Co. Ltd. Copyright 1919 by Alfred A. Knopf, Inc.

It is also said that shadow puppets were introduced as a dramatic form through their use by Buddhist monks who, when preaching to the populace, used reflections of the image of Buddha on a screen and combined storytelling with teaching and chanting the sutras. In any case, by the eleventh century shadow puppets had become a very popular form of entertainment.

Donkey skin, which is very durable, was used to make shadow puppets. When treated and stretched it became translucent. After the puppet figures were cut out, they were painted in bright colors and supported by thin sticks, separate ones for the arms for independent movement. The puppets, with a lamp behind them, were held up to the screen to cast their shadows in color on it, creating a most decorative effect. The puppeteers were highly skilled and served a long apprenticeship before becoming master puppeteers. In their hands the puppets seemed to take on a life of their own. Because the equipment was easily portable, shadow shows were set up at street corners and in marketplaces, as well as in the regular places of entertainment. Music, song, and dance accompanied all puppet shows. Cymbals and drums were used, as were flutes and stringed instruments. All the different kinds of drama were adapted for the puppet stage, but among the most popular were the historical plays when well-known figures of the past were shown in their hero and villain roles. Shadow puppets have enjoyed a recent popular revival in the People's Republic.

Sung Dynasty (960–1279)

The flourishing T'ang dynasty ended in internal strife in 906 with a number of rival claimants to the throne. It was followed by a period known as the Five Dynasties, which, in turn, came to an end in 960.

The Sung dynasty was established in the same year and lasted until 1279, but toward the end of the period, from 1138 onward, the northern part of China was invaded and gradually conquered by the Mongols. Kubla Khan proclaimed himself Universal Ruler in 1260. One of the Chinese princes escaped and set up his temporary capital in Lin-an, present-day Hangchow, the picturesque city with its famous West Lake surrounded by mountains whose slopes are dotted with monasteries and temples, well known to tourists today, one hundred and twenty miles south of Shanghai. Contemporary descriptions tell of the parks surrounding the lake, of its entertainment centers and its pleasure grounds, enriched during the royal residence in the city. Here permanent theaters were built and variety plays were performed. Puppeteers also had special theaters and storytellers had their own booths and wooden sheds, so that their art could continue all the year round. In the city itself there was a well-known "Street of Puppeteers" where the puppetmakers lived and had their workshops.

The Capital at Hangchow

Hangchow was the scene of the children listening to the storyteller described by the scholar-official and poet Su Tung-p'o, quoted at the beginning of the chapter. Appointed governor of the city in 1089, Su Tung-p'o did much to enhance its natural beauty. He had the lake dredged and the earth removed in the dredging built into a beautiful causeway about five miles long, thus forming an inner lake on the western shore opposite the main city. He had the causeway planted with peach trees and willows. It has been known ever since as the Su Tung-p'o Causeway and is restored today according to his plan.

There is yet another, earlier, causeway still standing; named after an eighth-century poet, Po Chü-I, this one ends or is "interrupted" by a bridge which is known, therefore, as Interrupting or Broken Bridge. This bridge is the traditional setting for the well-known story of the White Snake Fairy's meeting with her mortal husband who later had her imprisoned beneath the Thunder Peak Pagoda. The pagoda stood until 1924 when it collapsed and hidden in hollow bricks eighty-four thousand Buddhist miniature scrolls were found.

Poets and philosophers like Po and Su have through the ages endowed Hangchow with a variety of romantic names: Lonely Hill, Three Pools that Mirror the Moon, Pavilion of the Calm Lake, Autumn Moon, and many more. One of the most appealing of its appelations is The Peak that Flew Over. When a fourth-century Indian Buddhist monk visited one of the mountain-top monasteries overlooking the lake, he mused that it reminded him of a famous peak in India and said, "I wonder when it flew over?" From then on that became its name. A well-known book, *Guide to the West Lake (Hsi Hu Yu Lan Chih)*, which was published in 1547, recounts the history of many of the monasteries, pavilions, and beauty spots surrounding it and the stories connected with them.

Marco Polo's Description of Hangchow. Marco Polo, who paid several extended visits to the city some two centuries after the poet's time there, between 1276 and 1292, said ". . . without doubt the finest and most splendid city in the world."[6] He describes the city's wide and spacious streets and canals with the hundreds of bridges, the great marketplaces, the variety of foods on sale there, and the number of bathhouses with hot and cold water. There were drum towers for watchmen who kept order and who marked the hours of the day and night with drum beats. He mentions the guilds organized for the many different artisans and skilled craftsmen working in the city and the beauty of the manufactures. He talks of the throngs of people of peaceful temperament, courteous in speech and manner, all of whom were bent on pleasure as soon as their work was done. Chinese records corroborate most of the descriptions of Marco Polo.[7] An often quoted saying runs, "Above lies heaven, below Soochow and Hangchow."

Mongol (Yüan) Dynasty (1260–1368)

Strong Mongol forces continued the invasion of northern China in 1234 and gradually the Mongols established their own dynasty, with its capital in Peking, the Sung dynasty coming to an end. The Mongol or Yüan dynasty lasted from 1260 until 1368 when a Chinese dynasty, the Ming, was restored. After the Chinese surrender, the Mongols, rather than attempting to destroy the high level of Chinese civilization which they found, adopted many of the customs and manners as well as the culture of the Chinese, and in a way contributed to a new flowering of playwriting and drama. The conquerors suspended the civil service examinations as a means of obtaining government employment and the system remained in suspension for about fifty years. The lack of demand for writing in the traditional literary styles made writers turn to other forms of literature, among them to the writing of plays which previously had been the responsibility of the writing guilds.

Yüan Plays

Theater was immensely popular at this time, especially in the northern and southern capitals and the larger prosperous cities, where a sophisticated urban population flourished. Its importance in the social and cultural life of the people cannot be exaggerated. The new plays were written to appeal to all classes of society and dealt with the lives of corrupt officials and courtesans, ambitious young scholars and virtuous maidens, outlaws and murderers, as well as the glories of the historical past as evidenced in plays about the Three Kingdoms period. Although the plays were written by men of literary talent with classical backgrounds, they were essentially aimed at an ordinary public who demanded that virtue should triumph in the end, but expected their dramatic entertainment to provide them with a full quota of sensationalism in the process. The Yüan dramatists were unique of their kind as they utilized their literary skills to create new kinds of plays, all combining dialog and song with dance and acrobatics. One hundred and seventy of the more than six hundred Yüan plays recorded survive today and hold an honored place in the history of China's folk literature.

A few Yüan plays have become well known in the West through translations. For instance, a tragedy, the *Orphan of Chao (Chao Shih Ku Erh)*, inspired Voltaire's *L'Orphelin de la Chine*. One of the best known Yüan dramatists was Kuan Han-ching, who was born about 1210 and died about 1298. He was a prolific playwright and a true man of the theater, sometimes acting himself. His seven hundredth anniversary was celebrated in 1958 in the People's Republic, the themes of his plays, often featuring the wrongs of poor people, still being acceptable. His plays were frequently rewritten and adapted for later forms of drama and remained popular as long as the traditional theater lasted.[8]

Another famous Yüan play, *The Romance of the Western Chamber (Hsi Hsiang Chi)* by Wang Shih-fu (1279–1368), translated by S. I. Hsiung in 1935,[9] tells the love story of the beauty Ying-ying and the young scholar Chang Chun-jui, which had already been made famous by a T'ang dynasty poet. A finely illustrated serial picture book of the story for young people was published in Peking in 1958 and an English-language edition was published at the same time.[10] S. I. Hsiung also translated the play *Lady Precious Stream (Wang Pao Ch'uan)*, which was staged with extraordinary success in London in 1934, although the translator himself admits in his preface that it is a play with little literary merit. These plays may not seem suitable for children, but in China they habitually accompanied their relatives or amahs to the theater. It is enough to know that the plays were popular to know that they were seen by countless generations of children.

Storytellers' Techniques and Repertoire

It was plays like these described which helped to keep alive the many exciting tales from popular literature and which formed the plots of the first full-length novels which were written in the fifteenth, sixteenth, and seventeenth centuries. They also formed the stock-in-trade of the storytellers who were in a way one-man theaters.

Four main styles of storytelling with considerable local variations had evolved: a simple narrative style; narration with rhyme, punctuated by bamboo clappers; half-narration, half-singing accompanied by one or two instruments; and sung narrative with occasional breaks into speech and patter and with this fourth style there would be two or three accompanying instruments. The different kinds of storytellers each had their own guilds. From the wide and varied repertoire the public could choose among romantic stories, including many accounts of animal spirits transforming into beautiful maidens, ghost stories and other tales of the supernatural; murder and law-court stories; religious stories, mostly Buddhist; hero tales or tales of knights-errant and tales from the historical chronicles, these last often being told in serial form and going on from week to week. Stories from the books of Confucius and Mencius were also told. Some names of outstanding storytellers of this period have been recorded, and among them there were some women, but little else is known about them.

Comparison with Twentieth-Century Storytellers

Down the centuries the technique of the storyteller has changed very little. During the writer's own residence in Nanking from 1947 until 1950 she frequently listened to the storytellers who gathered in the open space around the ancient Drum Tower. This area was used as a sort of fairground at festival times, with flower stalls and others selling candies, soft drinks, cheap toys, and balloons. The storyteller, usually a middle-aged man dressed in typical black cotton trousers and jacket, was often accompanied by a teen-age girl, also dressed in black cotton trousers, but with a bright colored shirt and with her hair in two plaits tied with red ribbon. She carried a small shoulder drum and a tambourine. Besides punctuating the chanting of the storyteller with drumbeats, she would also shake the tambourine, and after about half an hour, she would use the tambourine to go round the audience collecting coins.

When the drumbeats announced the storyteller, throngs of children would appear as if by magic. Amahs, the maidservants who looked after the small children even in quite humble families, would bring their small charges and sit down beside them. On the outside of the crowd there were always a number of adults listening. Not many sat down; it was as though they were reluctant to admit their interest, but all the same they could not tear themselves away.

Storytellers' Prompt Books

Although the storytellers were well known for their inventiveness and ingenuity in adding new episodes to traditional stories, they also had a growing number of prompt books to rely on. A story from one of these, found among the popular literature texts at Tun-huang, has been translated by Arthur Waley. It is a version of the crane maiden story, so popular in a variety of versions in both China and Japan and with a motif found in many other folk literatures. The story first occurs in the collection known as *Records of Spirits* (*Sou Shen Chi*) which is associated with a well-known fourth-century writer, Kan Pao, but the collection as it exists today has many later interpolations.

The Crane Maiden Story. The story is in simple narrative form and a good example of the kind which would naturally appeal to children when told by a skillful storyteller.[11]

Once upon a time there was a man called T'ien K'un-lun. He was very poor, and was not able to marry a wife. In the land he owned there was a pond which was deep, clear and beautiful. Once when the crops were ripe he went to his field and saw that there were three beautiful girls washing themselves and bathing in the pond. Wanting to have a look at them he watched them from a hundred paces away. They at once changed into three white cranes, two of which flew to a tree that stood by the pond and perched on top of it. But the third stayed in the pond, washing herself.

T'ien K'un-lun pressed low down between the cornstalks and crept forward to look at her. These beautiful girls were Heavenly Maidens. The older ones clasped their heavenly robes and rode off into the sky. But the youngest, who was in the pond, did not dare come out. She made no secret of this, saying to K'un-lun: "We three sisters, who are Heavenly Maidens, came out to amuse ourselves for a while in this pond. But you, the owner of the pond, saw us. My two elder sisters were able to rescue their heavenly robes in time and escape. But I, the youngest, lingered all alone in the pond and you, the owner of the pond, took away my heavenly robe and I cannot come naked out of the pond. Please do me the kindness to give it back to me, that I may cover my nakedness and come out of the pond. If you do so, I will marry you." But K'un-lun debated the matter in his mind and decided that if he gave her the heavenly robe, there was a danger she might fly away. So he answered: "Madam, it is no use your asking for your heavenly robe, for you will never get it. But how would it be if I were to take off my shirt, so that for the time being you could cover yourself with that?"

At first the Heavenly Maiden refused to come out on these terms, and K'un-lun at last declared that it was getting dark and he must go. She tried to detain him, still asking for her robe; but when she found she could not get it, her tone changed and she said to K'un-lun, "Very well then! Give me your shirt to cover me while I come out of the pond, and I will marry you." K'un-lun was delighted. He rolled up the heavenly robe and hid it away. Then he took off his shirt and gave it to the Heavenly Maiden, to cover her when she came out of the pond. She said to K'un-lun, "Do not be afraid I shall go away. Let me put on my heavenly robe again, and I will go along with you." But K'un-lun would rather have died than give it to her, and without more ado he took her home with him to show her to his mother. The mother was delighted and ordered mats to be set out. All the friends and relatives of the family were invited and on the appointed day the girl was hailed as New Bride. Although she was a Heavenly Maiden, they had intercourse after the manner of people in this world and lived together. Days went and months came, and presently she bore him a son, a fine child, whom they named T'ien Chang.

Soon afterwards K'un-lun was marked down for service in the west, and was away a long time. The Heavenly Maiden said to herself, "Since my husband went away I have been bringing up this child for three years." Then she said to her mother-in-law, 'I am a Heavenly Maiden. At the time I came, when I was small and young, my father made for me a heavenly robe, and with it I rode through the sky and came here. If I were to see that robe now, I wonder what size it would be. Let me have a look at it; I would dearly love to see it!"

Now on the day that K'un-lun went away, he had given strict orders to his mother, saying, 'This is the Heavenly Maiden's robe. Keep it hidden away and do not let her see it. For if she sees it, she will certainly ride away with it through the sky, and will never be seen again." Whereupon the mother had said to K'un-lun, "Where would be the safest place to hide it?" So K'un-lun made a plan with his mother, deciding that nowhere would it be more secure than in the mother's bedroom. The thing to do was to make a hole under one of the bed-legs, stuff the robe into it and herself always lie on top. Then the Heavenly Maiden would certainly not get at it. So they hid it away like this, and K'un-lun went off to the west.

After he went away, she thought constantly about the heavenly robe, fretting about it all the time and never knowing a moment's happiness. She said to her mother-in-law, "Do let me just have a look at the heavenly robe!" She kept on worrying her about this, and at last her mother-in-law decided to fall in with her wish. So she told her daughter-in-law to go outside the gate for a little while and then quietly come back. She went out at once and the mother-in-law took out the heavenly robe from under the bed-leg, and when the Heavenly Maiden came back, showed it to her. When she saw it, her heart was cut to the quick, her tears fell like floods of rain, and she longed to ride off through the air. But having thought out no plan to do this, she had to give it back to her mother-in-law, who again hid it away.

Less than ten days later she said once more to her mother-in-law, "Let me have another look at my heavenly robe." The mother-in-law said, "I was afraid you might put it on, and fly away from us." The daughter-in-law said, "I was once a Heavenly Maiden. But now I am married to your son and we have had a child. How can you think I would leave you? Such a thing is impossible." The mother-in-law gave in, but was still afraid that she might fly away, and set someone to keep strict watch at the main gate.

But the Heavenly Maiden, as soon as she had put on the robe, flew straight up into the sky through the roof-vent. The old woman beat her breast and in great distress hurried out of the door to see what happened to her. She arrived in time to see her soaring away into the sky. The mother-in-law, when she knew that she had lost her daughter-in-law, let out such a cry as pierced the bright sky; her tears fell like rain, she became utterly desperate and in the bitter sorrow of her heart all day she would not eat.

The Heavenly Maiden had passed more than five years in the world of men, and now she had spent her first two days in heaven above. When she escaped and reached her home both her sisters cursed her for a shameless baggage. "By marrying that common creature of the world of men," they said, "you have made your father and mother so sad that they do nothing but weep." "However," the two elder sisters said to the younger sister, "it is no good your continually lamenting as you are doing now. Tomorrow we three sisters will go together and play at the pool. Then you will certainly see your child."

The child T'ien Chang had just reached his fifth year. At home he was constantly sobbing and calling out for his parents, and out in the fields he continually wailed in sadness. At that time there was a certain Master Tung Chung who was always seeking for persons of superior conduct. He knew that this was the child of a Heavenly Maiden and knew that the Heavenly Maiden was about to come down to the lower world. So he said to the child, "Just at midday go to the side of the pond and look. Three women will come all dressed in white silk robes. Two of them will raise their heads and look at you; but one will lower her head and pretend not to see you, and that one will be your mother."

T'ien Chang did as Tung Chung told him, and just at midday he saw beside the pond three Heavenly Maidens, all dressed in white silk robes, cutting salad-herbs at the edge of the pond. T'ien Chang went nearer and looked at them. Seeing him from afar they knew that it was the child who had come, and the two elder sisters said to the younger, "Your child has come." Then he wailed and called out to his mother. But she, although she hung her head in shame and did not look at him, could not stop her sorrow from coming out of her heart, and she wept bitterly. Then the three sisters took their heavenly robes and carried the child away with them into the sky. (A continuation of the story is thought to have been added later.)

Reprinted from *Ballads and Stories from Tun-huang*, translated by Arthur Waley, by permission of George Allen and Unwin Ltd. © George Allen and Unwin Ltd., 1960.

Story Collections

Systematic official and unofficial collections of colloquial stories like this were made and recorded in the bibliographies which were a regular feature of the dynastic histories from the third century onward. By the fourth century many stories began to show the strong influence of Buddhism and their style can be traced directly to Indian origins. Two collections of the Jataka tales were translated by the fourth century and inspired other animal fables. Tales of the marvelous were used to illustrate the life of Buddha and had great popular appeal. Collections of stories of the supernatural were given such titles as *The Book of Deities and Marvels (Shen I Ching)*, an anthology of the late third century, *Records of Strange Things (Po Wu Chi)*, and *Garden of Marvels (I Yüan)*, both of the fourth century. Besides the stories with Buddhist origins, others contain stories of favorite mythical characters like the Queen Mother of the West.

Stories and anecdotes abounded too about ordinary men and women, and many collections were made, such as *A New Account of Tales of the World (Shih Shuo Hsin Yu)*, *Forest of Sayings (Yu Lin)*, and *Forest of Jokes (Hsiao Lin)*, all of the fourth to the sixth centuries. The tales were simple and short. These books exist now only in a fragmentary way, but parts are preserved in the many quotations from them found in later works and in the "encyclopedia" collections like the *T'ai P'ing Miscellany*, the important tenth-century anthology made at the Emperor's command. *Popular Stories of the Capital (Ching Pen T'ung Su Hsiao Shuo)* dates from the eleventh century. Originally there were sixteen books but now only ten remain. One of the stories in this collection forms the plot of a later seventeenth-century play, *Fifteen Strings of Cash (Shih-wu Kuan)*[12] which enjoyed a popular revival in 1956 in the People's Republic before the Cultural Revolution transformed the popular theater. It is a typical crime play in which a young couple are wrongly accused of murder and sentenced to death by a corrupt local magistrate. A righteous judge reverses the judgment, the real culprit is revealed, and the young couple go free. As was often the case, the villain is a traditional "clown" role, and the enormous popularity of the play depends on the miming and by-play in the unmasking of the murderer, "Lou, the Rat."

Stories from History. The almost legendary accounts of the brave exploits of historical figures in the official records gave rise to historical romance stories. Early examples were written in classical style which in turn became favorites with storytellers who retold the stories in ballad form and colloquial language. An extant prompt book of the eleventh century, known as *Popular Tales of the Five Dynasties (Wu Tai Shih P'ing Shuo)*, is a collection of historical stories. It begins with a chronological outline of the main events in Chinese history, from the legendary Emperor Fu-hsi receiving the eight trigrams on the back of a tortoise, continuing to the tenth century. Each tale ends with "If you want to know what happened afterwards you will find the answer in the next chapter." This was undoubtedly originally an invitation from the storyteller to come to his next session.

Knight-errant Stories. Equally popular were tales of imaginary heroes, based on adventures of knights-errant, perhaps the nearest translation of *yu-hsia*, the Chinese term for these wandering brave men who traveled the country defending the weak against the strong and the poor against the rich. Such heroes had been the subjects of popular stories from earliest times. Particularly during periods of war and social unrest, men of outstanding talent and courage, excelling in the arts of fighting and horsemanship, would travel from state to state and offer their services to those in need. Renowned for their strong ideals of justice, altruism, and individual freedom, these wandering heroes had a contempt for money. Though they would not accept payment for their deeds, the rich were expected to make gifts to them so that they could help the poor.[13]

The prompt book versions of the most well known of these popular historical and knight-errant stories were finally woven into full-length novels in the fourteenth century. *The Romance of the Three Kingdoms (San Kuo Chih Yen I)* and *The Tale of the Marshes (Shui Hu Chuan)* are classic folk epics, universally known and appreciated in China. They have provided a rich repertoire for countless generations of storytellers and have inspired so many well-known plays that the characters have passed into popular legend forever, just as Robin Hood and Paul Bunyan have done in the West.

Notes

1. From the words of the poet Su Tung-p'o, quoted in Lu, *A Brief History of Chinese Fiction*, pp. 419, 420.
2. Lewis, *The Moment of Wonder: A Collection of Chinese and Japanese Poetry.*
3. Yang, *The Dragon King's Daughter: Ten T'ang Dynasty Stories.*
4. Liu, *An Introduction to Chinese Literature*, chaps. 11, 12; Lu, *A Brief History of Chinese Fiction*, pp. 139–51; and Scott, *The Classical Theatre of China*, the chapter, "A Short Historical Survey."
5. "Li Fu-jen," in Waley, *One Hundred and Seventy Chinese Poems*, p. 49.
6. Polo, *The Travels of Marco Polo.* pp. 184–201 describe Hangchow (Kinsai).
7. Ibid. Introduction, p. xvi.
8. Kuan, *Selected Plays.*
9. Hsiung, *The Romance of the Western Chamber (Hsi Hsiang Chi): A Chinese Play Written in the Thirteenth Century.*
10. Hung, *The Western Chamber.*
11. Waley, *Ballads and Stories from Tun-huang: An Anthology*, pp. 149–53 and "Afterword."
12. A description of the play and a translation appear in Scott, *Traditional Chinese Plays*, vol. 2.
13. Liu, *The Chinese Knight-errant*, pp. 1–12.

Papercut of scene depicting the Monkey King from *Pilgrimage to the West*   (*see* Chapter 6)

The Romance of the Three Kingdoms and Its Historical Setting

The drama of the wars of the Three Kingdoms period provided story-tellers and playwrights with countless tales of glowing military exploits, of cunning strategy, and of magnificent bravery. The brief historical background to the stories is as follows. The last of the Han Emperors was assassinated by rebels in A.D. 192. A loyal minister summoned a district governor, Ts'ao Ts'ao, known for his military prowess, to the capital to exterminate the rebels. He was successful and helped to establish a new young emperor on the throne who claimed to be loyal to the Han dynasty. Ts'ao Ts'ao himself became prime minister in whose hands the new young emperor was nothing but a puppet. There also were other claimants to the Han throne, further rebellions broke out, and China once more was divided into three feudal kingdoms which gave the period its name.

Ts'ao Ts'ao seized power over the northern kingdom of Wei with the original Han capital of Loyang. The south and southeast formed the kingdom of Wu with the capital in Nanking, and the west and southwest became the kingdom of Shu-Han with the capital at Chengtu. Controlling this last kingdom was Liu Pei, who had formerly been a commander under Ts'ao Ts'ao. He claimed to be the uncle of the murdered emperor and therefore to have a stronger right to the throne than the newly installed young emperor. A third rival for the throne was Sun Chuan, who asserted that he had in his possession the imperial seal, which gave him the right to rule the country. These three contestants for the throne fought for a long time until finally Ts'ao Ts'ao's son was established on the throne, founding the Chin dynasty which lasted from A.D. 265 to 420.

The History of the Novel

Prompt book versions of Three Kingdoms stories were finally woven into a full-length novel by a writer and playwright, Lo Kuan-chung.[1] He was born in north central China about 1330 and led a wandering life until he finally settled in Hangchow, the city which had become a center of the performing arts as described in the preceding chapter.

Lo died about 1400 and, although his novel was not published until 1522, more than one hundred years after his death, references show that handwritten copies were circulating freely before this time.

In the next hundred years a number of editions appeared (their bibliographical history is very complicated), until in the mid-seventeenth century, a new version was edited by Mao Tsung-kang. It is this version of the novel which remains the most popular today. His editing of the novel was quite extensive; he polished its style, making events follow the historical record more closely and generally tidying it up. But traces of its storytellers' prompt-book origin remain. Each chapter in the original has a linking ending with the beginning of the next, such as, "Chang-fei's fate will be told in the next chapter"; or "Who offered this plan? Succeeding chapters will tell."

The Leading Characters

The novel follows the popular storytellers' versions which favor Liu Pei as the legitimate heir, regarding Ts'ao Ts'ao's influence as corrupt, and Ts'ao Ts'ao himself as the most wicked of villains, treacherous and hypocritical, ruthlessly pursuing his own ends without regard for either friend or foe. In the many plays in which he appears, Ts'ao Ts'ao is easily recognizable, the personification of the stage villain with a matte white, painted face and thin, black lines showing the wrinkles of cunning. The historical Ts'ao Ts'ao was not so bad a character as the fictional one and, in fact, has recently been "devillainized" in the People's Republic.

In the first chapter of the book when Ts'ao Ts'ao asked for an assessment of his character from a sage renowned for his insight into human nature he received the reluctant reply, "You could be a statesman capable of bringing order to the age, or a traitor in an age of sedition." This appraisal elated Ts'ao Ts'ao.[2] One can imagine how children would easily recognize this white-faced archvillain when personified on the stage or when his cunning countenance was mimicked by a storyteller. As the quotation at the beginning of the preceding chapter shows, ". . . when they [the children] heard of Ts'ao Ts'ao's defeat they would brighten up and applaud."

Liu Pei, on the other hand, appears as a kind-hearted and generous man who sincerely loves his country and the people. He was one of a band of three sworn brothers who dedicated their lives to saving their country from the rebels. For this cause they pledged themselves to fight to the death. The first chapter of the book introduces Liu Pei and the other two heroes with the following graphic description of both their appearances and their first meeting:

THE OATH OF FRATERNITY IN THE PEACH GARDEN

Liu Pei's father, a government official, was cited by the court for integrity and filial devotion. He died early, however, and Liu Pei remained with his mother, serving her with unstinting filial piety. He supported their poor household by selling sandals and weaving mats.

The family lived in a village of Cho county called Double Mulberry because of the giant mulberry tree near their home. It was over fifty feet high. Tall and proud, the tree seemed from afar like the canopy of a chariot. A fortune-teller had seen in it a sign that the family would produce a man of destiny. As a youth Liu Pei had played under the mulberry, saying, "I'll be the Emperor and take my seat on this chariot." An uncle, struck by the figure of speech, had remarked, "This is no ordinary child."

Liu Pei was already twenty-eight when the provincial authorities issued the call for volunteers to fight the rebellions. The rebels were known as the Yellow Scarves. . . .

Reading the order posted in Cho county, Liu Pei sighed with indignation that traitors would attack the throne. Someone spoke roughly behind him: "What are the long sighs for? A hardy fellow like you should be giving his all for home and country."

Liu Pei turned to see a man even taller than he, with a blunt head like a panther's, huge round eyes, a swallow's cheek, a tiger's whiskers, a thunderous voice, and a stance like a horse in stride. To Liu Pei, who asked his name, he said, "My surname is Chang, my given name Fei ['flying']. . . . We've been in this county for generations and farm a bit of land, sell wine, and slaughter pigs. I was looking for men of adventure and, coming upon you reading the recruitment call, took the liberty of addressing you."

"Actually," Liu Pei replied, "I am an imperial relation, and I want to raise troops to destroy the Yellow Scarves and defend the people. I was reflecting on my limitations when you heard me sigh."

Chang Fei said, "I have resources that could be used to outfit some local youths. What if you were to join with me in serving this great cause?" Liu Pei was elated, and together they went to a nearby inn. As they drank, they noticed a striking fellow stop at the inn's entrance to rest.

"Some wine, and quickly," the stranger said. "I'm off to the town to volunteer." Liu Pei observed him: gleaming skin, glistening lips, eyes like the crimson phoenix, brows like nestling silkworms. His appearance was stately, his bearing awesome. Liu Pei invited him to share their table and asked who he was.

"My surname is Kuan," the man replied, "my given name Yü ['plume']. . . . One of the notables in our district was using his position to exploit people. I killed him and had to flee. I have been on the move these past five or six years. When I heard of the mobilization I came to answer the call."

Liu Pei then told of his own ambitions, to Kuan Yü's great excitement. Together the three men went to Chang Fei's farm to talk further. Chang Fei proposed: "Behind the farm is a peach garden. The flowers are at their fullest. Tomorrow we must make offerings there to Heaven and Earth, declaring that we three join together as brothers, combining strength and purpose." To this Liu Pei and Kuan Yü agreed.

The next day they prepared their offerings, which included a black bull and a white horse. Amid burning incense the three men performed obeisance and spoke their vow:

"We three, Liu Pei, Kuan Yü, and Chang Fei, though of separate birth, now bind ourselves in brotherhood, combining our strength and purpose to relieve the present crisis. Thus we may fulfill our duty to home and country and defend the common folk of the land. We could not help our separate births, but on the selfsame day we mean to die! Shining imperial Heaven, fruitful Queen Earth, witness our determination, and may god and man jointly scourge whichever of us fails his duty or forgets his obligation."

The oath sworn, Liu Pei became the eldest brother, Kuan Yü the second, and Chang Fei the youngest. When the sacrificial ceremony was concluded, they butchered the bull and spread forth the wine, gathering three hundred youths in the peach garden, where they drank themselves to sleep.[3]

From *Three Kingdoms: China's Epic Drama* by Lo Kuan-chung, translated and edited by Moss Roberts. Copyright © 1976 by Moss Roberts. Reprinted by permission of Pantheon Books, a division of Random House, Inc.

This scene of the three men swearing brotherhood in the peach orchard is a very famous one in the *Three Kingdoms* cycle of plays.

After their meeting, the three heroes, with a local army now five hundred strong, almost immediately got into an encounter with the rebels who "wore their hair flying about their shoulders and their foreheads . . . bound with yellow turbans." If the reader has seen contemporary troops of Chinese acrobats visiting the West, he will have some idea of how such an encounter was shown on the stage. The three leaders would wear elaborate stage armor and, posturing in front of the audience, would twirl their ceremonial spears with great dexterity. Stage bandits and rebels always appeared with loose hair and turbans tied roughly round their foreheads, exactly as the book describes. Hair worn loose was always a sign that the person was distraught or mad. The leaders would then withdraw and the battle begin. A dozen or more soldiers and bandits would appear, making mock battle with swords and spears, leaping over each other, turning somersaults in the air, turning handsprings across the stage, twirling their spears, and making feint attacks to the accompaniment of a crescendo of clashing cymbals. The whole stage would seem to be alive with bodies leaping in midair in every direction.

Acrobatic tours de force like these always gave immense delight to the children in the audience. Such episodes chosen for plays were the ones which were most frequently retold by the storytellers and which have been most often translated. Because of the quick-moving action and exciting incidents, several of the *Three Kingdoms* stories have been adapted for young western readers. To savor the style of the original novel, following are several examples of differing scenes and in the well-known stories of "The Hundred Thousand Arrows" and "The Strategy of the Unguarded City," the reader will be able to compare an adaptation in English for children with a translation of the original.

A Story of Kuan Yü

Kuan Yü is the best loved of the three sworn brothers; in fact he became so deeply revered that he was deified as the God of War, usually known as Kuan Kung. He was a loyal and righteous man, remarkable for his bravery and stoicism. There is a dramatic description of how he played chess and drank wine while a surgeon was operating on a wound in his arm caused by a poisonous arrow. Although the wound had to be opened to the bone, he betrayed no emotion. When the surgeon had finished the operation he thanked him saying that now his arm was as good as new. He gave a great feast to honor the doctor and offered him a large sum of money, but the surgeon refused it saying "he had come to treat his patient from admiration of his great virtue and not for money."[4]

Chu-ko Liang

Another outstanding character in the book besides the three sworn brothers is Chu-ko Liang (he also has one of the few double-syllable Chinese family names). He is introduced to Liu Pei as a man who "has the talent to measure the heavens and mete the earth; . . . a man who overshadows every other in the world." At this time Chu-ko Liang was living as a recluse in the mountains at Sleeping Dragon Ridge where, because of his wisdom, he was known locally as Master Sleeping Dragon. Twice Liu Pei and his two sworn brothers make an expedition to see Chu-ko to beg for his help. Twice they found him away from home and when Liu Pei insisted on going a third time to find him, his two companions impatiently protested. But Liu Pei still insisted that they should go and this time they found Chu-ko who eventually received them courteously.

In a masterly summary of the situation, remarkable in a recluse from the world, Chu-ko had a map brought and outlined the strategy of a whole campaign which Liu Pei should follow if he were to regain the Han empire. After many protestations of modesty, Chu-ko agreed to accompany Liu Pei.[5]

The Story of the Hundred Thousand Arrows

This episode is an excellent example of Chu-ko's handling of a crisis, showing how he was able to foresee results with almost supernatural powers, remaining calm as befits a superior man of letters, and outwitting his opponent with the least display of strength or energy. At this time Chu-ko was fighting with an allied state against Ts'ao Ts'ao, and the general in command had become jealous of his superior intelligence and strategies. The general, Chou Yü, devised a plan to trick Chu-ko into failure so that his life would be forfeited. The scene is a prelude to the famous Battle of the Red Cliff against Ts'ao Ts'ao.

Chou Yü: "When we engage Ts'ao Ts'ao in battle, crossing arms on the river routes, what weapon should be our first choice?"

Chu-ko: "On the Yangtze, the bow and arrow."

Chou Yü "Precisely. But we happen to be short of arrows. Dare I trouble you, master, to take responsibility for the production of one hundred thousand shafts? This is a public service which you would favor me by not declining."

Chu-ko: "Whatever you assign I will strive to achieve. Dare I ask by what time you will require them?"

Chou Yü: "Can you finish in ten days?"

Chu-ko: "Ts'ao's army will arrive any moment. If we wait ten days, it will spoil everything."

Chou Yü: "How many days do you estimate you need, master?"

Chu-ko: "It will take only three before I can respectfully deliver the arrows."

Chou Yü: "There is no room for levity in the army."

Chu-ko: "Dare I trifle with the chief commander? I beg to submit my oath in writing. Then if I fail to finish in three days, I deserve the maximum punishment."

This elated Chou Yü, who accepted the document.

Chu-ko: "On the third day from tomorrow, send five hundred small craft to the river to transport the arrows."

. . . Chu-ko said to Lu Su: "I need you to lend me twenty vessels, with a crew of thirty for each. On the boats I want curtains of black cloth to conceal at least a thousand bales of straw that should be lined up on both sides. But you must not let Chou Yü know about it this time, or my plan will fail." And Lu Su obliged him, and . . . held his tongue.

The boats were ready, but neither on the first day nor on the second did Chu-ko make any move. On the third day he secretly sent for Lu Su: "I called you especially to go with me to get the arrows." And linking the vessels with long ropes, they set out for the north shore and Ts'ao Ts'ao's fleet.

That night tremendous fogs rolled over the heavens, and the river mists were impenetrable. People could not see their companions who were directly in front of them. Chu-ko urged his boats on.

At the fifth watch the boats were already nearing Ts'ao Ts'ao's river stations. Chu-ko had the vessels lined up in single file, their prows pointed west. Then the crews began to volley with their drums and roar with their voices.

Lu Su was alarmed: "What do you propose if Ts'ao's men make a coordinated sally?"

Chu-ko smiled: "I would be very surprised if Ts'ao Ts'ao dared plunge into this heavy fog. Let us attend to the wine and take our pleasure. When the fog breaks we will return."

In his encampment, Ts'ao Ts'ao listened to the drumming and shouting. His new naval advisers rushed back and forth with bulletins. Ts'ao sent down an order: "The fog is so heavy it obscures the river. Enemy forces have arrived from nowhere. There must be an ambush. Our men must make absolutely no reckless movements. But let the archers fire upon the enemy at random." The naval advisers, fearing that the forces of the Southland were about to breach the camp, ordered the firing to commence. Soon over ten thousand men were concentrating their fire toward the center of the river, and the arrows came down like rain. Chu-ko ordered the boats to reverse direction and press closer to the shore to take the arrows, while the crews continued their drumming and shouting.

When the sun rose high, dispersing the fog, Chu-ko ordered the boats to rush homeward. The straw bales in gunnysacks bristled with arrow shafts. And Chu-ko had each crew shout its thanks to the Chancellor for the arrows as it passed. By the time the reports reached Ts'ao Ts'ao, the light craft borne on swift currents were beyond overtaking, and Ts'ao Ts'ao was left with the agony of having played the fool.

Chu-ko said to Lu Su: "Each boat has some five or six thousand arrows. So without costing the Southland the slightest effort, we have gained over one hundred thousand arrows, which tomorrow we can return to Ts'ao's troops—to their decided discomfort."

Lu Su: "You are supernatural! How did you know there would be such a fog today?"

Chu-ko: "A military commander must be versed in the patterns of the Heavens, must recognize the advantages of the terrain, must appreciate the odd chance, must understand the changes of the weather, must examine the maps of the formations, must be clear about the disposition of the troops—otherwise he is a mediocrity! Three days ago I calculated today's fog. That's why I took a chance on the three-day limit. Chou Yü gave me ten days, but neither materials nor workmen, and plainly meant for my flagrant offense to kill me. But my fate is linked to Heaven. How could Chou Yü succeed?" When Chou Yü received Lu Su's report, he was amazed and resigned. "I cannot begin to approach his uncanny machinations and subtle calculations!"

When Chu-ko came to Chou Yü, he was received with cordial admiration. "Master, we must defer to your superhuman powers of calculation."

Chu-ko: "A petty subterfuge of common cunning, not worth your compliments."[6]

From *Three Kingdoms: China's Epic Drama* by Lo Kuan-chung, translated and edited by Moss Roberts. Copyright © 1976 by Moss Roberts. Reprinted by permission of Pantheon Books, a division of Random House, Inc.

This is the original of one of the stories most frequently chosen for retelling by western authors[7] and is naturally loved by Chinese children who are thoroughly familiar with the story from plays, from storytellers, and from their serial picture books.

The Strategy of the Unguarded City

Another famous story about Chu-ko Liang and one of the most popular and frequently performed *Three Kingdoms* plays in the traditional theater is "Chu-ko's Lute Repulses the Enemy," or "The Strategy of the Unguarded City" as the play is often called, or "The Loss of Chieh-t'ing," as it may appear in children's books.[8] After one of his generals has suffered heavy losses of men through disobeying his orders, Chu-ko is left with only a small force in a beleaguered city to face a huge army from Ts'ao Ts'ao's state of Wei.

Chu-ko soon learned of the catastrophe at Chieh T'ing. He ordered a retreat into Han Chung . . . (and) was directing the complex retreat when, well before the expected time, emergency reports arrived telling of a massive force of fifteen legions, led by Ssu-ma Yi, swarming toward the city. Chu-ko had not even a ranking general with him, only a cadre of officials and officers and twenty-five hundred troops.

There was panic among the cadre as Chu-ko climbed the wall to scout the horizon. Dust was billowing up to the skies. Two columns of northmen were bearing murderously down on them. Chu-ko ordered all flags and banners put away. The commanders of the watchtowers were cautioned, on their lives, against any unauthorized movements or audible conversation. Then Chu-ko had the main gates thrown open and twenty men stationed at each to sweep and damp down the roadway. They were to appear oblivious when the northerners arrived. Chu-ko decked himself in crane feathers, wound a white wrap on his head and, followed by two lads and carrying a zither, braced himself upon the city wall. Incense burned as he struck up the instrument.

When Ssu-ma Yi's forward units came within sight of the scene that Chu-ko had contrived, they were afraid to advance. Incredulous, Ssu-ma Yi ordered a halt and raced to the front. There indeed was Chu-ko, seated on the upper wall, appearing palpably amused as he strummed his zither amid the incense. The lad to the left held his sword; the lad to the right the yak-tail. In and around the gates, twenty-odd villagers concentrated on their sweeping as if no one were near.

Ssu-ma Yi viewed the scene with skepticism, but he immediately ordered a general about-face and retreated north to the mountain roads. His second son, Ssu-ma Chao, said: "You can be sure we have caught Chu-ko without his forces, and that explains this exhibition. Why are we retreating, Father?"

"Chu-ko is a man of meticulous caution," replaid Ssu-ma Yi," "He never takes reckless chances. These gates are an invitation to an ambush. If we advance, we spring the trap. You young men do not know of such things. We should pull back without delay."

When he saw the northmen moving back, Chu-ko rubbed his hands slowly and smiled. The cadre in the city were dumbfounded to see how the sight of Chu-ko put to flight a mighty general and his fifteen legions.

Chu-ko explained: "He paid heed to my lifelong reputation for caution. When he saw how things were, he suspected an ambush. But I was not taking a risk, actually; there was simply no alternative. Now he will be heading out to mountain roads in the north, where I have already placed forces to greet him."

The cadre said: "Prime Minister, neither gods nor demons could fathom your machinations. We would have abandoned the city."

Chu-ko: "With twenty-five hundred men we would hardly have been able to get far enough to avoid capture." Then he clapped and grinned: "But if I were Ssu-ma Yi, I'd never have pulled away." Then he continued the retreat into Han Chung.[9]

From *Three Kingdoms: China's Epic Drama* by Lo Kuan-chung, translated and edited by Moss Roberts. Copyright © 1976 by Moss Roberts. Reprinted by permission of Pantheon Books, a division of Random House, Inc.

The lasting appeal which the *Three Kingdoms* stories made to the popular imagination is shown by the number of plays which were based on episode after episode in them, and which continued to be presented as long as the traditional theater lasted. And as long as the plays were current, so they were echoed by the storytellers, the "one-man" theaters so much beloved by ordinary men and women and children. The book ends, "The tale is told. The three States have been rewelded into one empire." And as at the end of many chapters, there is a fifty-line poem, written to be chanted, with the final lines:

> The Kingdoms Three have vanished as a dream,
> The useless misery is ours to grieve.

The Historical Setting for *The Tale of the Marshes*

The Tale of the Marshes (Shui Hu Chuan),[10] the second great full-length novel to be composed from storytellers' prompt books and plays some time in the fourteenth century, centers round a later period of Chinese history than the Three Kingdoms stories. The events on which it is based took place during the Northern Sung dynasty, which came to an end in 1126. China was suffering from a number of invasions from the north, it was a time of great unrest, and tribute had to be paid to the conquerors. Bands of disaffected people of all classes, from minor officials to peasants and fishermen, protesting against the high taxes and in conflict with the authorities, became outlaws and went to live in hideouts among the inaccessible marshes surrounding Mount Liang in modern Shantung Province. Their leader was Sung Chiang, a brief account of whom appears in the official historical chronicles of the time. Always loyal to the emperor, though opposed to local officials, it is stated that in the end he helped government forces against another bandit leader.

The History of the Novel

The title is difficult to render satisfactorily in English. *The Tale of the Marshes,* is the title used by Liu Wu-chi in his published excerpts which are quoted here. The novel is well known in English in the abridged version by Pearl Buck, who, abandoning any attempt at translating the title, called it *All Men Are Brothers.* It is also translated as *The Water Margin* by J. H. Jackson. Its bibliographical history is even more complicated than that of *The Romance of the Three Kingdoms.* An account of the genesis of the novel with a synopsis of the complete version can be found in Richard Irwin's *The Evolution of a Chinese Novel.*[11]

The authorship of the novel *The Tale of the Marshes* is uncertain. It is attributed both to Shih Nai-an, about whom nothing is known except the attribution of this book to him, and to Lo Kuan-chung, the well-known writer and collector of historical tales, to whom is attributed also *The Romance of the Three Kingdoms*. Both names appear on some early editions. The first known printed edition is the hundred-chapter version of 1540, but again references indicate that the book must have circulated in manuscript long before this. In all versions, it retains its vigorous use of colloquial language, showing clearly the influence of existing prompt books and the force of the storytellers' art. The longest and most complete version of one hundred and twenty chapters was published in 1614; between these two dates there were a number of printed editions with variations in the text. In 1641 a much abbreviated seventy-chapter version was edited by Chin Shih-t'an; this became so popular that it completely eclipsed the earlier versions, until the twentieth century when interest in folklore traditions led to a new evaluation of the complete book.

Chin Shih-t'an's version, it was realized, had radically altered the role of the famous band of outlaws. The longer version of the novel is in two parts; the first dealing with the adventures of the outlaws in the mountains, and the second, as history records, with the aid they gave to government forces in suppressing other rebel bands. The second part is completely omitted from Chin's version. Instead, he supplied a substitute ending in which the second-in-command of the outlaws has a dream in which he sees them all put to death, thus destroying the heroic quality of their past. This contradicts the spirit both of the longer version of the novel and the many stories and plays in the dominating folk tradition, which regarded the outlaws as heroes, defenders of the oppressed against their oppressors. Even so, the two English versions are based on the shortened version.

The Main Characters

The novel is an outstanding example of knight-errant stories based on a group of historical characters whose exploits soon became legendary in the hands of the storytellers. Sung Chiang is presented as the leader of one hundred and eight bandit outlaws living a Robin Hood kind of life, often helping the poor and oppressed by robbing the rich. All the outlaws are drawn as picturesque characters. Sung Chiang himself, in the longer version, although he meets an untimely death by drinking poisoned wine given to him by jealous court officials, was honored by the Emperor. Learning of Sung's death, the Emperor issued a decree posthumously creating him a Marquis, Loyal and Upright, and ordered a temple with a statue of him and of his thirty-six most loyal followers to be erected to his memory. The decree also provided his son and family with gifts of money and land.

The most popular of the outlaws were known by nicknames which described either their character or temperament, their appearance, or their fighting characteristics. Sung Chiang himself was known as Opportune Rain for his generosity. The four other most popular outlaws were Li K'uei, known as the Black Whirlwind for his impulsiveness; Lu Chih-shen, known as the Tattooed Monk and Lin Ch'ung as the Leopard Head, both from their appearance; and Wu Sung, known as the Itinerant, from his initiation into a Buddhist order. Others, also because of their appearance, were known by such names as the Blue-faced Beast, the Red-headed Devil, and Nine Blue Dragons. This last bandit had nine blue dragons tattooed on his chest. Big Knife, Double Whip, and Featherless Arrow were so named because of the weapons they used. The last name, "Featherless Arrow," stemmed from the extraordinary accuracy of this bandit's aim with a stone with which he could kill an enemy from a great distance.

Two Fights with Tigers

It is easy to imagine how these bandit heroes, with their outlandish names, would become favorites with the storytellers' audiences and in the many plays which featured them. Both Wu Sung and Li K'uei have dramatic fights with tigers and the bloodthirsty scenes in the novel are almost universally known in China. The stories provided a great opportunity for dramatic gesture for the storytellers, which the children loved, and on the stage, the terrific fight between the bandit and the tiger, both played by acrobatic actors would bring shouts of approval. In the first story Wu Sung sets out alone at night on a journey over a mountain, regardless of warnings that it is haunted by a fierce tiger. No sooner had Wu Sung sat down to rest on a green rock than he sees the beast:

Seeing it thus, Wu Sung cried "Ah-ya!" then rolled down from the green rock. Cudgel in hand, he slipped away alongside the rock. The big beast was both hungry and thirsty. Barely touching the ground with its paws, it sprang upward with its whole body and then swooped down from midair. . . . In a moment Wu Sung saw the tiger was about to pounce on him and he quickly dodged behind the beast's back. It was most difficult for the beast to find anyone from that position, so planting its front paws on the ground and raising its legs at the waist, it lifted itself up. Wu Sung again dodged and slid to one side. When the tiger saw that it had failed this time, it gave out a big roar like a thunderbolt from the mid-sky, shaking the mountain ridge. Then it made a scissors-cut, its iron cudgel-like tail standing upside down, but Wu Sung again slipped aside. . . . After a second failure with a scissors-cut, it roared once more and moved around in another circle. When Wu Sung saw the beast turn back, he lifted his cudgel with both hands and brought it down from midair with one swift and mighty blow. There was a loud sound and a tree fell, its twigs and leaves streaming down all over his face. Opening his eyes, he gazed fixedly. In his excitement, he had missed the big beast but struck instead an old withered tree. The cudgel had broken in two, and one half of it he now held in his hand.

Its temper now thoroughly aroused, the big beast bellowed and again turned round with a forward thrust. Wu Sung made another leap, retreating ten steps. The creature had barely managed to place its forepaws in front of Wu Sung when, throwing away his broken cudgel, he clutched the tiger's mottled neck with a cracking sound and pushing it down, held it tightly. The animal attempted to struggle, but Wu Sung grabbed it with all his might and never relaxed his grip for a moment. With his foot he kicked the beast over its face and eyes. The tiger started roaring again and dug up with its paws two heaps of yellow mud beneath its body, forming an earthern pit. Wu Sung pressed the beast's mouth straight down the yellow mud pit. It became helpless and impotent. With his left hand grasping tightly the beast's mottled neck, Wu Sung freed his right hand and lifting up his fist—the size of an iron hammer—kept pommeling it with all his strength. After it had been struck fifty to seventy times, fresh blood began to gush out from its eyes, mouth, nose, and ears. We Sung, using all his superhuman strength and inborn prowess, in a short while pounded the tiger into a heap as it lay there like an embroidered cloth bag.[12]

From *An Introduction to Chinese Literature* by Liu Wu-chi. Copyright © 1966 by Liu Wu-chi. Reprinted with permission of Indiana University Press.

Li K'uei's encounter is even more gruesome. He is returning to the bandit's hideout, after going back to his home to fetch his blind old mother whom he has to carry on his back. He leaves her seated on a rock while he goes off to find her some water and returns to find nothing but a pool of blood.

Following the traces of blood in his search, he soon reached the mouth of a big cave and saw there two tiger cubs. . . .
Fire erupted from his bosom and his red-yellow whiskers stood erect. Lifting up the big knife in his hand, he rushed forward to thrust at the two cubs. Terrified by the blows, one of the young beasts crawled forward, flashing its teeth and flourishing its paws. Li K'uei raised his hand and at once stabbed it to death. The other crawled straightway into the cave but Li K'uei pursued it and killed it also.
Having crept into the tiger's cave, Li K'uei hid himself inside. As he looked out, he saw a mother tiger come charging to the den with flashing teeth and menacing paws. Li K'uei cried: "So you are that accursed beast that ate my mother!" . . . Then Li K'uei took his knife and pursued it out of the cave. The tigress, in great pain, rushed straightway down the mountain precipice.
Li K'uei was about to hasten after her when he saw a gust of wind roll up from the trees beside him, and all the withered leaves and twigs fall down like rain. It has been said since ancient times that "clouds come with the dragon and winds with the tiger." From where the gust of wind rose beneath the bright light of the stars and moon, suddenly a slant-eyed, white-browed tiger leaped out with a great roar. The big beast pounced fiercely at Li K'uei. Li K'uei, however, was neither flustered nor excited. Taking advantage of the force of the tiger's attack, he lifted his knife and struck straight below the tiger's chin. The tiger no longer charged or

pounced. First, it had to nurse the wound and moreover its windpipe was broken. It had not retreated five or seven steps before uttering a sound as loud as though one half of the mountain had crumbled. In the next moment, the big beast lay dead below the cliff.[13]

From *An Introduction to Chinese Literature* by Liu Wu-chi. Copyright © 1966 by Liu Wu-chi. Reprinted with permission of Indiana University Press.

Plays and Pageants from *The Tale of the Marshes*

In one scene after another robberies, kidnappings, and murders lead to dramatic fights with fists or with weapons. In between there is humorous relief with drinking scenes and ludicrous incidents. Expeditions are made to rescue or avenge the wronged or oppressed. There are large-scale battle scenes in which whole armies sent out by the Emperor against the outlaws are routed. Spectacular hand-to-hand fights are always part of these scenes. It is true to say that there is scarcely a Chinese who does not know at least some of the stories from the *Three Kingdoms* cycle and from *The Tale of the Marshes*. They have been kept vigorously alive both in the oral tradition and in popular plays, in innumerable printed editions of the novels, and in serial picture books for children[14] since the stories were first collected. Biographies of Mao Tse-tung say that he, like countless other schoolboys, "devoured" *The Romance of the Three Kingdoms* and *The Tale of the Marshes* when young.

A vivid description of the acting of scenes from *The Tale of the Marshes* in a street pageant as described by a seventeenth-century writer is quoted by Lu Hsün, who remembers as a boy how much he wanted to be chosen to take part in a similar pageant when the annual Spring Fair was held in his town.

In the old days they acted plays, and it was most spectacular. Here is Chang Tai's description of a pageant from *The Tale of the Marshes*.

". . . They went out in all directions to find one fellow who was short and swarthy, another who was tall and hefty, a mendicant friar, a fat monk, a stout woman, and a slender one. They looked for a pale face too and a head set askew, a red moustache and a handsome beard, a strong, dark man and one with ruddy cheeks and a beard that covered his chest. They searched high and low in the town, and if they failed to find any character they went outside the city walls, to the villages and hamlets in the hills, even to neighbouring prefectures and counties. A high price was paid to the thirty-six men who played the heroes of Liangshan; but each looked his part to the life, and they went out in force on horseback and on foot. . . .

Who could resist watching such a lifelike pageant of the men and the women of days gone by?[15]

Other Hero-bandit or Knight-errant Stories

The hero-bandit, knight-errant type of story continued to be popular right down to the present day, many inspired by the popularity of *The Tale of the Marshes*. But when the later stories came to be written, social conditions were different and the heroes often fought on the side of the law instead of against authority. This kind of story was often combined with the ever-popular crime or detective story.

Many such stories were based on the life of Pao Cheng, a famous judge of the Sung dynasty, whose life is recorded in the official history of the period. He was stern but very honest and upright and his judgments in famous cases became legendary. In the two centuries following his death in 1062, in addition to the versions of the storytellers, at least twelve plays were written about him, including the well-known *Circle of Chalk* (*Huai Lan Chi*), later translations of which have inspired western dramatists, including Brecht. A collection of stories about him was published in 1594, the *Cases of Prefect Pao* (*Pao Kung An*). Inspired by this, many other popular detective or law-suit novels were published in the nineteenth century but have little claim to be called literature. *The Cases of Lord Shih* (*Shih Kung An*), published in 1838, and *The Cases of Lord Peng* (*Peng Kung An*), published in 1891, are widely known and they continued to be read into the twentieth century. But the most familiar story of this kind and the best written is *The Three Knights-errant and the Five Altruists* (*San Hsia Wu Yi*), also known as *The Three Heroes and Five Gallants* (or *Five Champions*). This book returned to the stories of the famous Judge Pao Cheng, but to appreciate the combination of the exploits of knights-errant or bandit-hero characters with detective stories, a little understanding of the Chinese traditional legal and administrative system is necessary.

The District Magistrate, a universal figure in tales of this kind, was commonly spoken of as the "father-mother official." Under an empire-wide system he was the supreme local authority. His "seat" was in a town, the market center of a district usually about sixty or seventy miles in extent, and his jurisdiction would cover all the large or small villages in that area. He would be in charge of land administration; the collector of taxes; the registrar of births, deaths, and marriages; the census-taker; and, in the court of law held at his office-residence, he would be prosecutor, judge, and jury. Under him would be court scribes, guards, wardens and their assistants, but the detective work necessary for unraveling a crime would usually be done by the magistrate himself.

To help him in this important and difficult work the magistrate would have a small band of staunch supporters on whose unswerving loyalty he could count. He would often recruit them from a local outlaw band, men who, as in *The Tale of the Marshes*, had to escape the law and live by their wits because they had been falsely accused of a crime, or because they had killed a cruel official who was oppressing the poor, or for some similar reason. These men would be renowned for their prowess in wrestling, boxing, archery, swordsmanship, or in fighting with cudgels. In describing their feats of strength, the storyteller often allowed elements of the supernatural to creep into the tales. The power of a blow of the fist could emanate by itself and fell an enemy to the ground although not actually struck. An arrow or a sword could fly an impossible distance through the air and strike an invisible target with unerring aim. The descriptions of fights by wrestling were in most picturesque language. The hero would "carry the tiger and push the mountain" (*pao hu t'ui shan*) or "creep like a snake" (*she shen hsia shih*) or be "like a wild horse tossing its mane" (*yeh ma fen tsung*) and thus vanquish the most powerful enemy. The audience would recognize immediately that these were terms used to describe specific movements in the ancient system of Chinese physical culture *t'ai chi ch'üan*, which was regularly practised by large numbers of people and still is today.

Loyal followers of a powerful official would serve their master during his whole lifetime, following him if he were transferred from one district to another. In return for their reform from outlaw life and for the dedicated service they would give without thought of personal gain, the official would bestow on them rank and position in his entourage above his other assistants. It was these trusted supporters who often undertook the difficult and dangerous missions connected with the investigation of a crime.[16]

The Three Knights-errant and the Five Altruists was published in 1870 and was based on the recitals of a professional Peking storyteller named Shih Yü-k'un, whose performances were popular between the years 1851 and 1875. Shih's recitals included songs but these were omitted when the stories were published. And when Shih came to use the tales, his plots were based on the exploits of the judge's brave companions rather than on the law cases themselves.

Ten years later, in 1889, a revised version of the book was published by a more scholarly writer, Yü Yüeh, who changed the title to *The Seven Knights-errant and the Five Altruists (Ch'i Hsia Wu Yi)* because there were in fact seven heroes who figure in the story. Two other continuations were published in the same year about the sons of the seven heroes. It was claimed that these were based on Shih's own drafts of further stories, but they are not considered so good as the original two books. All together, twenty-four sequels or imitations of *The Seven Knights-errant* were published. Featuring eight, thirteen, or eighteen altruists or gallants, they were repetitious and, according to Lu Hsün, written in abominable Chinese.[17]

Not only full-length novels but serial stories about "flying swordsmen" and other heroes capable of fantastic feats of fighting prowess, were popular newspaper features until 1949 and even into the fifties and sixties in Hong Kong and Taiwan. Known as *wu hsia* stories (chivalrous tales of fighting), they were avidly read not only by children but by many adults as well. Similar stories also appeared in daily strip-cartoons from the nineteen twenties onwards. Gradually they became influenced by the James Bond, space-men type of stories of the West, their distinctive style has been lost, and their popularity has declined.

Notes

1. Lo, *Three Kingdoms: China's Epic Drama.* [*San Kuo Chih Yen I.*] Characters are referred to by their best-known names.

2. Ibid., p. 11.

3. Ibid., pp. 5–9.

4. Ibid., pp. 231, 232

5. Ibid., pp. 111–19.

6. Ibid., pp. 173–78.

7. Compare Lu Mar, *Chinese Tales of Folklore,* and Wyndham, *Tales the People Tell in China.*

8. Compare "Chu-ki Liang" and "The Loss of Chieh-t'ing" ("Shih Chieh-t'ing") in Bonnet's *Chinese Fairy Tales.*

9. Lo, *Three Kingdoms,* pp. 285–90.

10. *The Tale of the Marshes (Shui Hu Chuan).* Quotations are from the translated excerpts by Liu in *An Introduction to Chinese Literature.* References to other translations are given in the bibliography.

11. Irwin, *The Evolution of a Chinese Novel: Shui Hu Chuan,* sec. 5, Conclusion, pp. 114–16.

12. Liu, *An Introduction to Chinese Literature,* pp. 207, 208 (chapter 23 of the novel).

13. Ibid., pp. 208, 209 (chapter 43 of the novel).

14. *The Lion Tavern (Shih-tzu Lou),* a story from *The Tale of the Marshes (Shui Hu Chuan),* is such a serial picture book.

15. Lu, *Selected Works,* vol. 1, "The Fair of the Fierce Gods."

16. Liu, *The Chinese Knight-errant,* pp. 116–37, and Van Gulik, *Celebrated Cases of Judge Dee (Dee Goong An): An Authentic Eighteenth Century Chinese Detective Novel.* Preface, pp. ix–xxiii.

17. Lu, *A Brief History of Chinese Fiction,* p. 369.

The Pilgrimage to the West

Monkey, a character famous in legend, and hero of the epic novel *The Pilgrimage to the West*,[1] is as well known throughout China as the characters in the *Three Kingdoms* cycle. The origins of the novel date back to the historic account of the journey made by the monk, Hsüan Chuang (known also as Tripitaka), to India early in the seventh century in search of Buddhist sutras. The journey is recorded in the official chronicles of the period. Storytellers, in spreading the word of Buddhism, used incidents from the famous journey, combining them with fantastic tales of the supernatural which were part of their stock-in-trade, until the story of Monkey reached epic proportions. An incomplete tenth-century storyteller's version was found among the manuscripts in the Tun-huang Caves. There was a well-known version written in verse and chanted by storytellers in the twelfth and thirteenth centuries. At the same time popular plays were written around incidents from the story. Finally these earlier versions were combined and expanded into a hundred-chapter novel written by a well-known scholar, writer, and poet named Wu Cheng-en who retained much of the semicolloquial style of his source materials.

Wu was born about 1510 and lived until about 1582. He served as a district magistrate in central China. He died relatively poor and, having no son, his name was for a time forgotten, although his book lived on in numerous editions. It was first published ten years after his death without his authorship being acknowledged. Later eighteenth-century editors rediscovered the real author from records in local archives and his name was included in subsequent editions.

The story begins with an account of how Monkey, always referred to in China by his name, Sun Wu-k'ung, was born, how he attained his magic powers, became Monkey King, and achieved sainthood. His exuberance created havoc in Heaven; and because he stole a peach of immortality, the Jade Emperor had to send a god to subdue him. In a great fight between them, Monkey went through a number of transformations but the god always outwitted him. For instance, when

Monkey changed into a sparrow to fly away, the god changed into a kite to pursue him; when Monkey changed into a fish and plunged into a river to escape, the god changed into a cormorant to catch him, and so on until Monkey was finally captured and imprisoned in the Mountain of Five Elements. The monk, Tripitaka, setting out on his journey to the West, rescued Monkey who became his faithful disciple on the journey. Pigsy, a pig spirit, and Sandy, the spirit of a black-grass carp, also became Tripitaka's disciples, and the four set out on the long journey with Monkey in the lead (fig. 15). On the way they encountered eighty-one perils—nine times nine, the magic number. In

Figure 15. The monk Tripitaka, with Monkey leading the way
Characters in theatrical costume from *Monkey Subdues the White Bone Demon*

spite of fierce, man-eating monsters, terrifying demons, and goblins, they finally obtained the sacred sutras and arrived safely back in China.

The book has been interpreted in different ways and, according to critics, elements of all three of the great religions of China have been found reflected in it, Confucianism and Taoism, as well as the obvious Buddhist background. In spite of the demons and monsters and hair-raising adventures the pilgrims encounter, the tone of the book is humorous and witty, accounting for its enormous popularity. The exciting adventures have provided storytellers with boundless opportunities for dramatic effect in their retelling, and the author's own funny asides and sly allusions were an inspiration to them to outdo the original. Here is an example:

> (When Monkey is defeated by the Rhinoceros Monster and loses his gold-tipped wand, he asks the Jade Emperor for reinforcements.)
>
> The Four Heavenly Masters reported this to the court and Monkey was led to the steps where he bowed and said: "Excuse me for troubling you, old man, but I am helping a monk to find sutras in the West and I've had more than my share of trouble on the way. I won't go into that now. But since we came to Gold-Helmet Mountain, a Rhinoceros Monster has dragged my monk into its cave—I don't know whether it means to eat him steamed, boiled or baked. When I went to fight it, the monster proved so powerful that it took away my wand and I couldn't beat it. Since it said it knew me, I suspect it is some fallen angel. So I have come to report this, and I hope you will be kind enough to order an investigation and send troops to conquer it. I await your answer in hope and trepidation." Then with a deep bow he added: "I beg to submit my humble report."
>
> Saint Ko who was standing beside him burst out laughing. "What has humbled the proud Monkey all of a sudden?"
>
> "Nothing has humbled me all of a sudden," retorted Monkey. "But I have lost my job. . . ."[2]

A summing up of the most well known of the many Chinese commentaries on the novel would say that it could best be described as an allegory of the human condition, written to suit popular taste. Lu Hsün said, "To my mind the book was written solely to give pleasure." An excellent idea of the spirit of the novel can be obtained from the English translation, *Monkey* by Arthur Waley, even though it represents only about one-third of the whole book.

Monkey symbolizes man's intelligence and ambitions. At first he oversteps the mark but then calms down, and when he uses his magic powers for a just cause, he succeeds. Sandy typifies the loyal, honest, dogged character of the peasant. Pigsy provides comic relief. He represents man's physical desires and Monkey jeers at him for his greed, his lustful actions, and his stupidity. The monk represents man as he really is; in spite of his learning he is afraid of demons and monsters, yet his invincible faith carries him through to the end. In the book the monk says, "It is the mind that gives birth to monsters of every kind, and when the mind is at rest, they disappear.[3] In present-day China a different interpretation is put upon the still universally popular story of Monkey, which, it is now suggested, represents the people's ability to subdue the forces of nature and the triumph of their struggle against the old ruling class.

Monkey in Plays, Puppet Shows, and Picture Books

Numerous plays with Monkey as the central character were included in the traditional repertoire until the recent cultural revolution. Monkey's stage costume was yellow and black and on his head he wore a tam-o'-shanter-type hat with a pom-pom in the middle or a yellow and black skullcap. He wore realistic painted-face makeup and his elaborate facial contortions and grimaces were most monkeylike. His was the supreme athletic role and a performance especially loved by children. He would leap about the stage, jumping high over the heads of his opponents, turn dozens of cartwheels with such rapidity that he could scarcely be seen, turn backwards and forwards somersaults in the air, and perform miracles of dexterity with his magic wand, symbolized by a slender silver-colored metal stave, some four feet long. This he would twist and turn over his head and behind his back, with such lightning speed that it would become almost invisible; then it would be thrown in the air and finally caught with a magnificent flourish. The dance tour de force of Monkey is frequently performed as a variety act in contemporary Chinese acrobatic and dance shows.

Numbers of serial picture books for young people that show episodes of Monkey's adventures have been published and are still being published in the People's Republic. Some, with excellent illustrations of the characters depicted very much as they might be in their traditional stage costumes, such as in *Monkey Subdues the White Bone Demon*,[4] are available in English as well as Chinese. Mao Tse-tung himself wrote a poem on this episode, and there are contemporary puppet shows, shadow plays, even cartoon films, all featuring Monkey (fig. 16).[5]

Book Trade

The popularity of the different kinds of stories in the storytellers' repertoire created a demand for printed collections of the best-known tales. This led to the growth of a flourishing book trade in the great cities of central China like Nanking, which became the capital when the Chinese Ming dynasty (1368–1644) replaced Mongol rule. Although after the death of the first Ming emperor, Peking again became the capital, Nanking, like Hangchow, already described in detail in chapter 4, and other cities of the Yangtze valley, among them Soochow and Yangchow, remained important centers of cultural life housing large, prosperous urban populations with sophisticated tastes. Although moral

THE MONKEY KING SUN WU-KUNG

Figure 16. Title picture from the cartoon film *Uproar in Heaven*

or didactic elements were still present, stories had above all to be entertaining for this class of reader. The prompt-book versions of many other popular stories from earlier dynasties were collected, improved upon, or sometimes entirely rewritten, and new, original stories, often imitating the style of the older ones, were added.

Stories Old and New

Most famous of the author/editors of short stories during the late Ming dynasty was Feng Meng-lung, who lived from 1574 to 1646. He was a scholar, but having failed the advanced imperial examinations, served only as a minor official for a short period. He became well known as a writer of plays and stories and as an editor of older tales. Through his literary work he became intimately connected with the book trade in Soochow as author, editor, and publisher.

Feng was responsible for one of the best known of all Chinese anthologies, *Stories Old and New (Ku Chin Hsiao Shuo)*,[6] which he published in three volumes between 1620 and 1627. The stories were, as the title describes them, retellings of old tales from previous centuries and new stories written in colloquial style similar to the old story-tellers' prompt-book versions. Each volume contained forty stories and had its own title as follows: *Instructive Words to Enlighten the World (Yü Shih Ming Yen)*, *Popular Words to Admonish the World (Ching*

Shih T'ung Yen), and *Lasting Words to Awaken the World* (*Hsing Shih Heng Yen*). As the subtitles of each volume all end with "*yen,*" meaning "words," the collection became known as *San Yen, Three Words*, and descriptive titles were given to the stories. Each begins with a four-line verse which is followed by a brief prologue, often unconnected with the main theme. This is a relic of the original, story-telling technique when the prologue would give the audience time to settle down before the beginning of the story proper. A couplet then announces the main story.

Many types of stories are represented in the collection: historical romances, anecdotes about famous people, domestic dramas, and love stories. The love stories were written in a more realistic manner than they were in older collections and even supernatural tales were told with greater realism, so that the reader is almost unaware of the transition from human to supernatural characters. In fact, the stories of the late Ming period, with their detailed descriptions of the manners and customs of the day, form a fascinating mirror of society at that time.

> Just ask the story-teller to describe a scene on the spot and it will gladden and startle, sadden and cause you to lament; it will prompt you to draw the sword; at other times to bow deeply in reverence, to break someone's neck, or to contribute money. The timid will be made brave; the lewd, chaste; the niggardly, liberal; and the stupid and dull perspiring with shame. Even though you recite every day the *Classic of Filial Piety* and the *Analects* you would never be moved as swiftly as by these story-tellers.[7]

This quotation from Feng's preface to his collection gives a good idea of his approach. He kept the original style of the tales by his use of colloquial language for which he apologizes, saying, "In this world literary minds are few but rustic ears are many." As was usual at that time, his editing and his preface were anonymous and he signed himself "Master of the Green Sky Lodge" ("Lü-t'ien-kuan-chu-jen").

Marvelous Tales, New and Old

Feng's books were extremely popular, so much so that the anthology was almost immediately imitated by Ling Meng-ch'u (1580–1644) with two collections, the first published in 1628 under the title, *Striking the Table in Amazement at the Wonders* (*Ch'u K'e P'o An Ching Ch'i*), with thirty-six stories. The second volume was published in 1632 with a similar title, second series, but with thirty-nine stories. The two volumes became known as *The Two Strikes* (*Erh P'o*). Ling too wrote a preface for his collection. In it he acknowledges his debt to Feng and explains how he picked up plots for his stories when wandering around Nanking.

So popular were both collections that the best stories from each were made into yet another anthology, *Marvelous Tales, New and Old* (*Chin Ku Ch'i Kuan*). This contains twenty-nine stories from Feng's collection and eleven from Ling's. The name of this compiler has not yet been discovered. He signed himself "Old Man Hugging a Jar" (Pao-Weng-Lao-Jen), and his collection in turn became so popular that for many years it overshadowed the originals. Thus the best of the short stories of the thirteenth to the seventeenth centuries, some five hundred years, were collected, re-edited, or rewritten in these three anthologies and preserved.

The Story of the White Snake

One of the most popular of all Chinese legends, that of the White Snake, is to be found retold in the second volume of the *San Yen* collection, *Popular Words to Admonish the World*. It is one of many versions of a story common to different parts of China, and in this version became connected with the Thunder Peak Pagoda, one of the ten famous beauty spots on the West Lake at Hangchow, described in chapter 4. The Supplement to the sixteenth-century *Guide to the West Lake,* already mentioned, lists four tales about unusual happenings occurring around the West Lake, stories recited by blind storytellers accompanying themselves on the lute (*p'i-p'a*), of which one is a version of the White Snake. Thunder Peak Pagoda was built in the tenth century A.D., but the White Snake legend was in existence long before this time. Following is the story in summary:

A young man named Hsü Hsüan worked in his uncle's medicine shop. As he was unwed, he lived with a married sister. One Spring, during the Ch'ing Ming festival, he went to honor his ancestors' graves and to burn incense at a monastery on the far side of the lake. As he crossed Broken Bridge on the Po Chü-i Causeway seeking a ferry boat to return home, it began to rain. A beautiful young girl, dressed in white, and attended by her maid, dressed in green, accosted him and asked for shelter under his umbrella. They crossed the lake together in a boat. The young man fell madly in love with the girl and with the ready connivance of her maid, who acted as a go-between, they declared their marriage vows on the spot. Madam White, as she was called, helped her husband set up an independent herbalist's shop. They became prosperous and were happy together, but the husband gradually became suspicious of his wife's seemingly magical powers with herbs and medicines.

A year went by and Hsü Hsüan went again to burn incense at the monastery. He told the Abbot how he had become a married man and at the same time revealed his suspicions about his wife. The Abbot warned him that he was under the enchantment of a white snake spirit who would certainly eventually devour him. The young man was horrified and the Abbot offered him sanctuary. When the young man failed to return home, Madam White went to the monastery and demanded her husband's release. This the Abbot refused. In revenge Madam White caused a great flood, the waters of the lake rising to a terrifying height, but the Abbot was able to quell them with his own magic powers.

The Abbot then gave the young husband a magic begging bowl and told him he must go back home, catch his wife unawares, put the bowl over her head, and press down as hard as he could until the bowl touched the floor. He did this and Madam White was revealed in her true shape as a white snake and the maid as a green one. The Abbot, who had followed Hsü Hsüan to his house, then picked up the two snakes, placed them in the bowl, and sealed it with a piece of cloth from his magic robe. He ordered the bowl to be bricked over so that the spirits could not escape. The young man then took another begging bowl and wandered round until he had collected enough money to build a pagoda over the bricked-up bowl which would forever prevent the influence of the imprisoned spirits from doing harm. This was how the Thunder Peak Pagoda came to be built.[8]

> Condensed from the version by H. C. Chang in his *Chinese Literature: Popular Fiction and Drama* with permission of Edinburgh University Press and Columbia University Press. Copyright © 1973 by H. C. Chang.

The White Snake story provided the theme for several plays which became some of the most frequently presented in the traditional repertoire. A modern version of the play that was published by T'ien Han in 1957 has been translated into English.[9] In the various theatrical versions based on the story, White Snake gradually becomes more human, her great love for her husband is the dominating theme, and the evil inherent in her is largely suppressed. In one variation the Abbot discovers that the White Snake is pregnant, so he tells her husband not to imprison her until after the child is born. Twenty years later she is rescued by her son, now grown to man's estate. New plays, written since 1950 for shadow puppet performance with propaganda undertones, include both the story of Monkey and the White Snake.

Curiously enough, the flood theme in the White Snake story is based on historical fact. In A.D. 726, two centuries or so before Thunder Peak Pagoda was built, and again in 1539, a few years before *The Guide to the West Lake* was published, a flood occurred when the River Yangtze changed course at Golden Island, two hundred miles northwest of Hangchow. This caused a great surge of water to sweep down the Grand Canal which connected the river with the city, resulting in severe flooding in the West Lake.

Strange Stories from a Chinese Studio

One other popular anthology of short stories universally known in China was published more than a hundred years after the *San Yen*. This collection, with the loosely translated title, *Strange Stories from a Chinese Studio (Lao Chai Chih I)*, has become quite well known in the English version of H. A. Giles. In it, one hundred and sixty-four tales, "the best and most characteristic," as the translator says in his preface, have been chosen from the original four hundred and thirty-one.

The author, P'u Sung-ling, like the other anthologists already described, was a scholar who passed the first but not the higher imperial examinations, and so devoted his whole life to writing. He was the son of a poor country scholar and was born about 1640, a few years before the end of the Ming dynasty, but all his adult life was spent during the Ch'ing, or Manchu, dynasty which succeeded the Ming. This was once more an alien dynasty that lasted from 1644 until 1908, after which the first Republic was established. P'u died in 1715. During his lifetime there was no longer the complete freedom to publish anything in popular demand; instead the Manchus imposed a strict imperial censorship. P'u, therefore, did not dare to publish contemporary stories of everyday life, but instead followed the time-honored custom of collecting folktales, popular stories, and anecdotes from previous centuries and rewriting them. In many of his stories there are sly criticisms of corrupt government officials and bureaucrats whom he despised, perhaps because of his own failure to reach their ranks. In addition to this collection, he also wrote four volumes of essays and six books of poems. None of his writing was published during his lifetime, but manuscript copies circulated freely. His grandson finally published the *Strange Stories* (*Liao Chai*) in 1740, explaining in a note that his grandfather had been too poor to undertake the considerable cost of printing such a large work. The book immediately became very popular and numerous editions were published in the succeeeding two centuries.

In his own preface P'u says that he collected many tales from his friends, then rewrote them. He says of himself that he is like the poet Su T'ung-po who loved to listen to stories of the supernatural. Part of the lasting attraction of his stories is the way in which events of real life are combined with elements of the supernatural. Following is an example of a short anecdote.

THE STREAM OF CASH

A certain gentleman's servant was one day in his master's garden, when he beheld a stream of cash flowing by, two or three feet in breadth and of about the same depth. He immediately seized two large handsful, and then threw himself down on the top of the stream in order to try and secure the rest. However, when he got up he found that it had all flowed away from under him, none being left except what he had got in his two hands.

["Ah!" says the commentator, "money is properly a circulating medium, and is not intended for a man to lie upon and keep all to himself."][10]

The mixture of fantasy and realism in P'u's stories made them very dramatic and excellent material for the storytellers. The style is well shown in the following story.

THE THUNDER GOD

Yo Yün-hao and Hsia P'ing-tzu lived as boys in the same village and, when they grew up, read with the same tutor, becoming the firmest of friends. Hsia was a clever fellow and had acquired some reputation even at the early age of ten. Yo was not a bit envious, but rather looked up to him, and Hsia in return helped his friend very much with his studies, so that he, too, made considerable progress. This increased Hsia's fame, though try as he would, he could never succeed at the public examinations, and by-

and-by, he sickened and died. His family was so poor they could not find money for his burial whereupon Yo came forward and paid all expenses, besides taking care of his widow and children.

Every peck or bushel he would share with them, the widow trusting entirely to his support; and thus he acquired a good name in the village, though not being a rich man himself, he soon ran through all his own property. "Alas!" cried he, "where talents like Hsia's failed, can I expect to succeed? Wealth and rank are matters of destiny, and my present career will only end by my dying like a dog in a ditch. I must try something else." So he gave up book learning and went into a trade, and in six months he had a trifle of money in hand.

One day when he was resting at an inn in Nanking, he saw a great big fellow walk in and seat himself at no great distance in a very melancholy mood. Yo asked him if he was hungry and on receiving no answer, pushed some food over towards him. The stranger immediately set to feeding himself by handfuls and in no time the whole had disappeared. Yo ordered another supply, but that was quickly disposed of in like manner; and then he told the landlord to bring a shoulder of pork and a quantity of boiled dumplings. Thus, after eating enough for half a dozen, his appetite was appeased and he turned to thank his benefactor. "For three years I haven't had such a meal."

"And why should a fine fellow like you be in such a state of destitution?" inquired Yo, to which the other only replied. "The judgments of heaven may not be discussed." Being asked where he lived the stranger replied, "On land I have no home, on the water no boat; at dawn in the village, at night in the city."

Yo soon prepared to depart, but his friend would not leave him, declaring that he was in imminent danger, and that he could not forget the late kindness Yo had shown him. So they went along together, and on the way Yo invited the other to eat with him. But this he refused, saying that he only took food occasionally. Yo marveled more than ever at this, and next day when they were on the river a great storm arose and capsized all their boats, Yo himself being thrown into the water with the others. Suddenly the gale abated and the stranger bore Yo on his back to another boat, plunging at once into the water and bringing back the lost vessel, upon which he placed Yo and bade him remain quietly there. He then returned once more, this time carrying in his arms a part of the cargo, which he replaced in the vessel, and so he went on until it was all restored.

Yo thanked him, saying, "It was enough to save my life, but you have added to this the restoration of my goods." Nothing, in fact, had been lost, and now Yo began to regard the stranger as something more than human. The latter here wished to take his leave, but Yo pressed him so much to stay that at last he consented to remain. Then Yo remarked that after all he had lost a gold pin, and immediately the stranger plunged into the water again, rising at length to the surface with the missing article in his mouth and presenting it to Yo with the remark that he was delighted to be able to fulfill his commands. The people on the river were much astonished at what they saw.

Meanwhile Yo went home with his friend and there they lived together, the big man only eating once in ten or twelve days, but then displaying an enormous appetite. One day he spoke of going away, to which Yo would by no means consent. As it was just then about to rain and thunder, he asked him to tell him what the clouds were like, and what thunder was, and how he could get up to the sky and have a look, so as to set his mind to rest on the subject.

"Would you like to have a ramble among the clouds?" asked the stranger, as Yo was lying down to take a nap. Upon awaking from his nap, Yo felt himself spinning along through the air and not at all as if he was lying on a bed. Opening his eyes, he saw he was among the clouds and around him was a fleecy atmosphere.

Jumping up in great alarm, he felt giddy as if he had been at sea, and underneath his feet he found a soft, yielding substance unlike the earth. Above him were the stars and this made him think he was dreaming. But looking up he saw that they were set in the sky like seeds in the cup of a lily, varying from the size of the biggest bowl to that of a small basin. On raising his hand he discovered that the large stars were all tightly fixed; but he managed to pick a small one, which he concealed in his sleeve; and then, parting the clouds beneath him, he looked through and saw the sea glittering like silver below. Large cities appeared no bigger than beans— just at this moment, however, he bethought himself that if his foot were to slip, what a tremendous fall he would have.

He now beheld two dragons writhing their way along, drawing a cart with a huge vat in it, each movement of their tails sounding like the crack of a bullock-driver's whip. The vat was full of water and numbers of men were employed in ladling it out and sprinkling it on the clouds. The men were astonished at seeing Yo. A big fellow among them called out, "All right, he's my friend," and they gave him a ladle to help them throw the water out.

Now it happened to be a very dry season, and when Yo got hold of the ladle he took good care to throw the water so that it should fall on and around his own home. The big stranger then told him that he was an assistant to the God of Thunder, and that he had just returned from a three years' punishment inflicted on him in consequence of some neglect of his in the matter of rain. He told Yo that they must now part and taking the long rope which had been used as reins for the cart, bade Yo grip it tightly that he might be let down to earth. Yo was afraid of this, but on being told there was no danger he did so, and in a moment whish-h-h-h— away he went and found himself safe and sound on *terra firma*. He discovered that he had descended outside his native village, and then the rope was drawn up into the clouds and he saw it no more.

The drought had been excessive that year, and for three or four miles round very little rain had fallen, though in Yo's own village the water-courses were all full. On reaching home he took the star out of his sleeve and put it on the table. It was dull-looking like an ordinary stone, but at night it became very brilliant and lighted up the whole house. This made him value it highly, and he stored it carefully away, bringing it out only when he had guests, to light them at their wine.

The stone was always thus dazzling bright, until one evening when his wife was sitting with him doing her hair, the star began to diminish in brilliancy and to flit about like a fire-fly. Mrs. Yo sat gaping with astonishment when all of a sudden it flitted into her mouth and ran down her throat. She tried to cough it up, but couldn't, to the very great amazement of her husband.

That night Yo dreamt that his old friend Hsia appeared before him and said, "I am the Shao-wei star. Your friendship is still cherished by me and now you have brought me back from the sky. Truly our destinies are

knitted together and I will repay your kindness by becoming your son."
Now Yo was thirty years of age but without sons; after this dream, however, his wife bore him a male child and they called his name Star. He was
extraordinarily clever and at sixteen years of age took his master's degree.[11]

Pu's stories had many imitators, and a further collection purporting
to be by the same author and called *The Last Tales of Liao Chai* (*Liao
Chai Chih I Shih I*) was published, but it is inferior in style and is
thought to have been written by someone else. In the succeeding century other collections imitating the *Liao Chai* were given such titles as
The Story-teller's Clapper (*Hsieh To*) and *Strange Tales from a Glow-
worm's Window* (*Ying Ch'uang I Tsao*) but none equaled it in popularity.

The Dream of the Red Chamber

At the end of the Ming dynasty in the early seventeenth century, there
was another class of novel besides the historical romances and *The
Pilgrimage to the West,* previously described, which became very popular. These were realistic romance stories reflecting contemporary life.
Many were exceedingly frank about sexual matters and, as there was
no censorship at the time, they were published and circulated freely.
Later, with Ch'ing dynasty censorship, many such stories were suppressed and some disappeared altogether, isolated copies coming to
light only in recent times in Japan. Less licentious, but just as popular
as the Ming examples, were the short story romances included in the
Liao Chai. Following this trend is the eighteenth-century novel *The
Dream of the Red Chamber* (*Hung Lou Meng*),[12] perhaps the most universally known of all Chinese novels. As usual, it was published an-
onymously and circulated widely in manuscript copies before it was
finally published in 1791. The identity of the author has only comparatively recently been established, largely owing to the researches of the
writer Hu Shih, in his nine essays on *Hung Lou Meng,*[13] although there
is still some controversy on the subject.

According to these theories the book was written by Ts'ao Hsüeh-
ch'in, whose grandfather and father in turn were in charge of the Nanking Silk Bureau, an important and lucrative official position, in the
reign of the Emperor K'ang-hsi (1662-1723). Ts'ao's father was also a
poet and left a number of books of poetry and two plays. The family
was originally very wealthy, but later lost official favor and became impoverished. Ts'ao was born around 1719 and, when he was about ten
years old, the family had to leave their grand Nanking residence and
move to Peking. Ts'ao himself, although a good scholar, was extremely
poor in later life, and, as his friends recorded, sometimes did not even
have enough to eat. His own son died young; he too became ill and,
without a doctor's care, died of grief in 1762 when only about forty-
three years old.

Ts'ao's novel is thought to be largely based on the events which happened to his own family. He completed eighty chapters during his lifetime and manuscript copies were circulated. The earliest extant manuscript copy is dated 1754 and a few others belonging to the same decade have survived. The novel was finally published in 1791, but with one hundred twenty chapters. In a revised edition of 1792, the title was changed from *The Story of the Stone* to *The Dream of the Red Chamber,* by which title it has been more popularly known. It has been translated into German and more than once into English, although none of the earlier versions is a complete translation, some chapters being given in summary only. The latest English translation by David Hawkes reverts to the original title, *The Story of the Stone,* and the complete novel is at last available in English.[14]

Characters in the Story. The novel is a sad love story reflected in the fortunes of the formerly noble Chia family and set in a city which can be identified as Nanking. The Chia family is wealthy and lives with a host of relatives and servants in a grand courtyard-style house, with large gardens surrounding it. The head of the family is Chia Cheng whose young son, Pao-yü, is the hero of the story. He is about eleven years old when the novel opens. He is very intelligent, fond of literature and of female company. He loves equally his two cousins, Tai-yü (Black Jade), who is the same age as Pao-yü, and Pao-ch'ai (Precious Clasp), one year older. The girls are both beautiful in their different ways.

As the young heir of the Chia clan (an older brother having died), Pao-yü is doted upon by his paternal grandmother, a typically powerful Chinese matriarch, and indulged by her. His father, in contrast, is very stern with him, often punishing him severely for laziness in his studies, and criticizing him for the amount of time he spends with his girl cousins. Black Jade is slender and graceful; she writes poetry but is very delicate and often ailing. Precious Clasp is pretty, much more cheerful and robust than Black Jade. Pao-yü eventually falls seriously in love with Black Jade, but his father decides that Precious Clasp is the better match, and Pao-yü is tricked into marrying her. Black Jade, who has become consumptive, falls ill and dies. Pao-yü is heartbroken and goes out of his mind for a time. Finally he recovers, passes his examinations, but in the end becomes a monk. Nevertheless Precious Clasp bears him a son and so the family line will continue.

There are thirty main characters in the book and some four hundred minor ones. The reader needs a family tree at hand to remember who all the relatives are and who are their maidservants, many of whom play quite an important part in the story. The book is a vast panorama of eighteenth-century life in a wealthy Chinese household,

> one of the best documents for a study of the extended family system, its structure, organization and ideals, such as clan solidarity and honor,

respect for old age, parental authority, filial obedience, sex relationships, the position of women, and the role of the concubines, maid servants and other domestic servants.[15]

Although the novel is in some ways static because almost everything happens within the maze of courtyards and gardens of the Chia residence, the different characters are so vividly drawn and so varied that it is never dull.

Old Dame Liu (Liu Lao-lao). Humorous relief is provided in the character of Liu Lao-lao (Old Dame Liu), a country cousin and a go-between, who pays periodic visits to the Chia family, bringing them presents of fresh country produce and hoping to receive in return gifts of money from her wealthy relatives. She is portrayed as having very crude speech and table manners, and her behavior at a grand feast given in her honor by the Matriarch (who is amused by her rough manners), reduces the entire family to a state of helpless laughter. In addition, the young people of the family play tricks on her, giving her a huge pair of old-fashioned ivory chopsticks embossed with gold, so heavy that she can scarcely hold them, and then offering her a bowl of soft-boiled pigeon's eggs floating in soup, notoriously the most difficult of foods for the clumsy-handed to manipulate.

Liu Lao-lao is a character much beloved by the storytellers who delight in imitating her vulgar speech and making all sorts of puns on her name. Even though children were either discouraged or forbidden to read the book (it was thought to be licentious), parents took it for granted that they would be understood when saying to a badly behaved child, "Don't be an old Liu Lao-lao!"

Plays based on famous incidents in the story. Children would know, too, about the romantic hero, Pao-yü, and his love for the tragic Black Jade. Even if they had not obtained a clandestine copy of the novel and read it for themselves by the time they were about twelve years old (as many Chinese I have spoken to did), they would hear excerpts from storytellers or see some of the plays based on famous incidents in the story.

One of the best known is a dance play, *Tai-yü Burying Blossoms* (*Tai-yü Tsang Hua*), devised for the celebrated twentieth-century actor Mei Lan-fang. In the novel one of Pao-yü's sisters is made an imperial concubine. Her father, in order to entertain his daughter in a grand manner befitting her new rank when she returns home on a visit, has beautiful new gardens laid out on their estate, with fine courtyards for the cousins to live in. One evening Black Jade is very upset because, on going to visit Pao-yü's rooms, the door is locked in her face. Inside she can hear the laughter of Precious Clasp. She returns to her own room weeping bitterly, being reminded of her past lonely life as an orphan before she came to live in the Chia household. The next day Pao-yü comes across her all by herself in a corner of the garden burying fallen flowers. As she rakes she will not speak to Pao-yü, but sings a plaintive song reminding him how in the springtime they had buried the fallen peach blossoms together. She asks who will bury her when she dies. They eventually make up their lovers' quarrel when Black Jade learns that Pao-yü did not know of her visit the evening before and that it was only a trick played by the maid to shut her out.

Besides the forty chapters not written by Ts'ao himself, many other sequels to the novel were published during the nineteenth century, often giving the story a happier ending. At this time the novel was thought by critics to have a hidden meaning and that it was a veiled account of the life of an important official, some saying of a former prime minister, some even of a former emperor, and that the ending therefore should point a moral. That the author himself says in the first chapter that it is a true picture of the times was disregarded by commentators until recently. In the latest translation, David Hawkes accepts without question that Ts'ao is the author and that the novel is partly autobiographical.

Flowers in the Mirror

Another Ch'ing dynasty novel which continued to be quite popular with young readers up to the time of the People's Republic was *Flowers in the Mirror (Ching Hua Yüan)* by Li Ju-chen and which has been translated into English. Li, born in 1763, was a gifted scholar and calligrapher, but spent his time studying phonology, astrology, and divination rather than the required studies for the higher examinations in which he did not succeed. He remained a poor and disappointed man, writing for his own amusement. *Flowers in the Mirror*, which he never finished, is long and discursive, both a fantasy and a social satire. Hu Shih wrote of it, "This novel deals with the women problem. The author believes that men and women should have equal opportunities, equal education, and equal political rights."[16]

The novel is set in the reign of the Empress Wu who usurped the throne from her own son in the early T'ang dynasty, reigning from 684 to 705. The Empress drinks too much wine one night and issues a command that all the flowers on earth shall be in bloom by the next day. The Fairy of the Hundred Flowers and her ninety-nine subordinates dare not disobey, but for this they are sent away from heaven to become incarnate on earth as a penance.

Tang Ao is the father of the incarnate Hundred Flower Fairy. He is suspected of treason by the Empress who causes him to be dismissed from his scholarly rank and office. He then decides to forsake the world and goes on a long journey in search of immortality, accompanied by his brother-in-law, a merchant. On the way they pass through a number of fantastic lands where everything is strange: the Country of Gentlemen, the Country of Women, the Country of Two-faced People, and so on.

In the Country of Women it is the women who are talented and pass the imperial examinations while the men stay at home, an idea which was somewhat revolutionary between 1818 and 1820 when the book was written. Along the way Tang Ao also meets a number of flower spirits incarnate whom he is able to help. As a reward for his good deeds, on reaching his journey's end, he finds the herb of immortality and disappears.

When Tang Ao does not return, his daughter, the Fairy of the Hundred Flowers, sets out to find him. She too passes through strange places in her search. Eventually she reaches mountain country where a woodcutter gives her a letter from her father, who says that they will meet again when she returns home to take an examination the Empress is holding for talented women. She passes the Lamenting Fallen Flowers Pavilion where she sees a stone tablet inscribed with one hundred women's names. Her own is eleventh on the list. She goes home, passes the examination, and attends a great feast held for the successful candidates. In the final section of the novel the women join the fight to restore the legitimate T'ang dynasty. The new Emperor is installed but the Empress is still honored, and another examination for women is set for the following year. The story then ends abruptly.

Li's friends urged him to publish the hundred chapters he had already written and in 1828 he did so. But he died in 1830 without ever finishing it. A year later an edition with one hundred and eight illustrations was published which became very popular and in 1883 another well-known edition illustrated with lithographs was brought out. It was the pictures and the accounts of the strange countries which fascinated young readers more than the implied satire, just as it was the grotesque pictures in the *Book of Mountains and Seas* which had such an attraction for the young Lu Hsün.

Story on the Willow Pattern Plate

Before this chapter is closed, brief mention should be made of the *Story on the Willow Pattern Plate*, the Chinese "legend," illustrations of which have gained such remarkable popularity in the West as a decorative motif on china. The design was first engraved by the famous English potter Thomas Minton, about 1790, at the height of the "Chinoiserie" vogue in Europe. Presumably taken from a Chinese illustration, nothing seems to be known about the source of Minton's inspiration. Later copies of the Minton design were produced in Canton for re-export to Europe. The story, as it has developed, is told at considerable length in Williams's *Outlines of Chinese Symbolism* and for young people in Leslie Thomas's *The Story on the Willow Pattern Plate*, but no exact Chinese source for the story is known.

Notes

1. Wu, *The Pilgrimage to the West* (*Hsi Yu Chi*).

2. Quoted in Lu, *A Brief History of Chinese Fiction*, pp. 216–17.

3. Lu, *A Brief History of Chinese Fiction*, p. 218.

4. *Monkey Subdues the White Bone Demon.* The original Chinese edition from which the enlarged illustrations in the English-language edition are taken, was published in Shanghai in 1972 and illustrated by "The Creative Writing Group."

5. *The Monkey King, Sun Wu-kung. A Picture Story from the Cartoon Film, Uproar in Heaven.*

6. *Stories Old and New* (*Ku Chin Hsio Shuo*). Various partial translations are listed in the bibliography compiled for this present work.

7. Birch, *Stories from a Ming Collection*, p. 8.

8. Chang, *Chinese Literature: Popular Fiction and Drama*, pp. 205–61. "Madam White Forever Confined under Thunder Peak Pagoda" ("Pai-Niang-tzu Yung Chien"), chap. 28 of *Popular Words to Admonish the World*, is the source for the condensed version given here.

9. T'ien, *The White Snake. A Peking Opera.*

10. Giles, *Strange Stories from a Chinese Studio* (*Liao Chai Chih I*), p. 331.

11. Ibid., pp. 253–57.

12. *The Dream of the Red Chamber* (*Hung Lou Meng*). Details of translations are given in the bibliography for this work.

13. These essays are reprinted in Hu, *Collected Works*, vol. 3, sec. 5.

14. Hawkes, *The Story of the Stone: A Chinese Novel by Cao Xueqin.*

15. Liu, *An Introduction to Chinese Literature*, p. 238.

16. Quoted in Lu, *A Brief History of Chinese Fiction*, p. 332.

Wood-cut by Huang Yung-yü a contemporary twentieth-century Chinese artist

The Twentieth Century and Development of a Modern Colloquial Literature for Children

7

It was only in the twentieth century that the special educational and recreational needs of children were recognized and provision made for them in China. Until then, as has been shown thus far, children were treated as little adults and had to make do with what they could cull from the popular literature and entertainment of the times, which fortunately was abundant and readily available to everyone. With the many profound changes that were taking place in Chinese society the special needs of children were at long last destined to be realized.

Introduction of Western-style Education

At the turn of the century there was considerable unrest brought about by internal revolts against the effete Manchu imperial rule and by the pressures of foreign incursions into Chinese affairs. As early as the eighteen sixties, the government had been forced to recognize the need for some change in the education system, but radical changes were slow to come about.[1]

Educated Chinese who could speak one or more foreign languages were essential for the establishment of a diplomatic service to treat with foreign governments. The modernization of the equipment of the armed forces, the building and maintenance of railroads, the installation of a telegraphic system, all demanded large numbers of trained technicians and engineers. No Chinese textbooks for modern technical subjects existed at that time, so that western language manuals had to be used and rapid courses in English, French, German, and Russian introduced. Diplomatic foreign language schools were established in Peking, Shanghai, and Canton. Besides languages, mathematics and astronomy were taught. In addition a Navy Yard and Technical School were opened at Foochow in southeast China.

By the eighteen eighties a Telegraph School, a Naval Academy, and a Military Academy were established in Tientsin and a School of Western Studies opened in Canton with instruction given in mining, chemistry, plant science, and international law. In 1887 "foreign learning" was admitted as an alternative subject in the imperial examinations. In addition, in the eighteen seventies, the government began sending well-educated Chinese to study abroad in America and in England, France, and Germany. After China's defeat in the Sino-Japanese War of 1894 many students went to study in Japan, realizing that the growing power of their neighbor was due to the willingness shown by the government there to adopt western technology. By 1950 more than a hundred thousand Chinese had studied abroad. Some students went to the Soviet Union after the Revolution there, but more for political than for scholastic study.

Missionary Schools

All these educational innovations were for adults, but the demand for the ability to speak foreign languages helped the phenomenal growth during the later nineteenth and early twentieth centuries of schools at all levels founded by the various missionary societies working in China, schools in which much of the teaching was in English. Prior to 1950 there were sixteen missionary-founded universities in China, three of which were Catholic and the rest under the sponsorship of Protestant missions of various denominations. In addition, hundreds of secondary schools under the same auspices were established. Catholic missions, in particular, penetrated far into rural China and statistics show that they organized some fifteen hundred primary schools in cities and over two thousand village primary schools. In addition there were a number of mission-sponsored hospitals with teaching schools attached. Magazine and newspaper publishing grew rapidly, especially in Shanghai with its large international population.

Graduates from the missionary schools and colleges, growing up with a knowledge of a second language, were most frequently among those selected to study in the technical schools in China and to go abroad for further education. Their influence over the years on the new China has been profound. Many of the contemporary leaders were educated in Christian colleges and then studied abroad.

Government Schools

Educational reform had been going on in this pragmatic way for some four decades when, following the civil strife and foreign intervention after the Boxer Rebellion of 1901, more drastic reforms were introduced. Important government regulations for the reform of primary and secondary education were introduced in 1904 when the nearly two thousand-year-old system of civil service examinations was finally abolished. Then, after the death of the powerful and reactionary Empress Dowager in 1908, and the establishment of the Republic in 1912, reforms became more widespread. Gradually the pattern of primary and secondary education in government sponsored schools began to conform more closely to the American system, with six years of primary school, three years of junior middle (high) school and three years of senior middle (high) school. A similar pattern continues in Taiwan today.

Language Reform Movement

Another far-reaching change in education was introduced through the language reform movement, which dates from 1915. A campaign began to introduce *pai-hua*, the everyday spoken, colloquial form of the language as a written form instead of the current highly artificial classical written form, *wen-yen*. The language reform movement, the literary or cultural revolution, or the Chinese renaissance as Hu Shih, one of its chief proponents, has called it, is closely linked with the political developments in China during the period of World War I and the four years following. Since Japan's victory over China in the 1894–1895 war over Taiwan, her demands for concessions in China similar to those which had been enforced by Britain, Germany, and France had become more and more arrogant. With the weakening of the influence of the European countries engaged in World War I, Japan issued her infamous "Twenty-one Demands" on 18 January 1915. In May, Japan followed this with an ultimatum to China and on 25 May, amidst growing public unrest, a Sino-Japanese treaty was signed acceding to the demands. This was the signal for the beginning of what was to become a highly organized and popular protest movement against the abject attitude of the government.

On the surrender to the demands of Japan, Chinese students studying there protested by returning home en masse. Among them were a number of young men who had taken temporary political asylum there because of involvement in revolutionary activities at home, one of whom was Ch'en Tu-hsiu who had already helped to establish a revolutionary newspaper in Shanghai. While in Japan he had assisted in editing a liberal magazine and now, back in Shanghai, he founded the *New Youth Magazine* (*Hsin Ch'ing Nien*), which was to become one of the most influential magazines of the century. The first number appeared in September 1915, with all the contributions written in the vernacular. It quickly attracted to its columns leaders of the language reform movement, among whom was the distinguished scholar Hu Shih, then studying for his doctorate at Columbia University in New York. His now famous letter advocating literary reforms appeared in October 1916, followed by his articles, "Some Tentative Proposals for Literary Reform," "On the Genetic Concept of Literature," and "On a Constructive Revolution in Literature," all published in *New Youth* in the next two years.[2]

The May Fourth Movement

In January 1919, during the Paris Peace Conference following the World War I armistice of 11 November 1918, Japan made public a secret treaty which had been signed between her, Britain, France, and Italy in 1917, granting her concessions in the province of Shan-tung in northeast China. It was also revealed that the United States recognized Japan's "special interests" in China, and on 30 April in Paris, Woodrow Wilson, Lloyd George, and Georges Clemenceau announced their agreement to Japan's demands. Peking student groups immediately organized the mass protest which is known to history as the May Fourth Movement. On that day more than three thousand college students demonstrated against the government's acceptance of the treaty, some houses of government officials were burnt, and some scores of students were arrested.

This spontaneous demonstration was followed by similar protests in Shanghai and elsewhere and the protestors were now supported by thousands of workers, many of whom went on strike. Mass arrests were made and by June over a thousand students were in custody. At the end of the month the Chinese delegation at the Paris Peace Conference refused to sign the treaty and walked out. In December the leaders of the revolt published a manifesto in *New Youth*. A further political development was the Nine-Power Treaty signed at the 1922 Washington Conference agreeing on an open-door policy in China and that Japan should be restrained from encroachments in China. This treaty was to prove futile so far as China was concerned, as events of the following decade showed.

A direct result of the May Fourth Movement was the further educational reforms introduced by the government in an effort to placate the rebellious students. In 1920 the government ordered vernacular language teaching in all primary and secondary schools and introduced coeducation in colleges and universities. The women's suffrage movement was also active but equality in voting rights was not finally gained until 1947.

Lu Hsün and His Brother, Chou Tso-jen

The one name which is always connected with advocating the need for a new literature for young people is that of Lu Hsün, the pen name of Chou Shu-jen. There is no doubt that Lu Hsün was intellectually dedicated to this cause, but he did far more to analyze what was wrong than he was able to do to help to put things right. As a writer and a master of the new style, he has already gained a lasting place in the history of Chinese literature. Writers who are politically engaged often sacrifice the quality of their writing in the interests of propaganda for the cause they are supporting. But about Lu Hsün it has been said,

> It was China's good fortune to produce one man of genius who was able to combine the most profound sympathy for and engagement in his country's plight with an extraordinary detachment and objectivity, who managed to express himself in a language and style newly based on the common speech, but cunningly wrought with an artistry drawn from a centuries old literary tradition.[3]

Although Lu wrote little for children, some of his essays and prefaces to his translations draw attention to the outstanding need for suitable children's books. His own son was not born until late in his life when he was already sick, suffering from tuberculosis. Had he lived longer to see his son growing up, perhaps he would have been inspired to write stories for him.

Lu Hsün was born in 1881 in the small historical town of Shao-hsing (famous for its wine) in Chekiang province south of Shanghai and the great Yangtze River. His grandfather and father were minor government officials, but in 1893 his grandfather was accused of bribery and from this date the family fortunes declined drastically. In addition, Lu Hsün's father became seriously ill and died in 1896. His mother, a country woman, was a strong character and a dominating influence in Lu Hsün's life. He derived his pen name from her family name which was Lu. She had taught herself to read and she struggled hard to keep the family together during these difficult times (there were three younger sons, but the youngest died in 1898). Lu Hsün frequently stayed with his mother's family in the country, his experience of country life providing him with the background for many of his later stories and essays.

Lu Hsün attended the clan school maintained by the Chou family and received the typical classical education given to boys at this time, but had to leave that school in 1893 because of the family's financial troubles. The next year he was sent to a private school in the town, "The Three Flavour Study," so vividly described by him in his reminiscences which have already been quoted. He stayed on in his birthplace until he was seventeen years old, at which time he gained entry to a recently established state-supported naval academy in Nanking. He transferred to the similarly supported School of Railways and Mines, then run in connection with Kiangnan Army Academy, graduating from there in 1901. His studies in science had brought him in contact with western philosophy for the first time, and he avidly read Darwin, Huxley, and many other western authors in translation, becoming familiar with the philosophy of evolution. His introduction to western democratic and philosophic ideas made him bitterly resent his country's abject surrender to foreign powers following the Boxer Rebellion.

The year after graduation Lu obtained a government grant to study in Japan. At first he decided that he could best serve his country as a doctor and in preparation he spent two years in Tokyo on language study, Japanese and German, and other general subjects. During this time he contributed a number of articles on western science to Chinese student journals. In 1904 he entered the Sendai Provincial Medical School but stayed there less than two years. He gives his own account of the event which changed his entire life in his preface to *Call to Arms,* his first collection of short stories. In it he writes that by chance he saw a film of a scene in the Russo-Japanese war which had broken out. A Chinese who had been arrested as a spy for the Russians was bound and about to be executed as a warning to others, while a crowd of able-bodied Chinese was standing around, apathetically watching the ghastly event unfold. Angered and sickened by this scene, Lu determined that nothing could save China but a complete change in the outlook of the people. He would become a writer, address himself to the masses, and spend his life working for this cause.

Returning home briefly to go through an arranged marriage, Lu Hsün then went back to Tokyo, accompanied by his younger brother, Chou Tso-jen. The brothers, together with some other like-minded Chinese students, tried to publish a journal, but it came to nothing. Lu Hsün wrote a number of articles on western progressive ideas and translated some Russian and East European short stories into classical Chinese through the medium of German and Japanese translations, the only foreign languages he knew, and through English, which his brother studied. Lu Hsün also translated Jules Verne's *From the Earth to the Moon* (*De la Terre à la Lune*) as *Yüeh Chieh Lü-hsing Pien-yen* in 1903 and his *Voyage to the Centre of the Earth* (*Voyage au Centre de la Terre*) as *Ti Ti Lü-hsing Chi* in 1907, saying in his preface to the former,

> Scientific novels are as rare as the horn of a unicorn. This is one of the reasons for the decline in knowledge in our country. If we wish to make good this deficiency in modern translations and lead the Chinese masses forward, then we must make a beginning with science fiction.[4]

In 1909 Lu Hsün returned to China and became a school principal in his native province. In 1912 he was offered a position in the Ministry of Education in Nanking, moved with the government to Peking, holding various positions in the Education Ministry with only brief interruptions until 1926. At this period of his life he concentrated on studying the history and legends of his native district and the development of fiction in ancient Chinese literature. His *Brief History of Fiction* and *Outline History of Chinese Literature* remain standard works. He also published several collections and studies of ancient tales, but these were in no sense retold for young readers, as his comments often were satirical.

In Japan Lu Hsün had become acquainted with Ch'en Tu-hsiu, the editor of *New Youth*, as well as with several other young Chinese intellectuals who were enthusiastic exponents of literary reform. One of them persuaded him to write for the magazine and, in April 1918, one of his best known stories, "Diary of a Madman" ("K'uang Jen Jih Chi"), was published in it. The title and style of this story were inspired by Gogol and, as the first example of the new Chinese imaginative literature, wholly western in manner, it has had a tremendous influence on other writers. It was later included in a collection *Call to Arms* or *The Outcry* (*Na Han*). This, and a second collection, *Hesitation* (*P'ang-*

huang), contain his best fictional work.[5] His masterpiece is considered to be "The True Story of Ah Q" ("Ah Q Cheng Chuan"),[6] a satiric tour de force in which Lu Hsün lampooned what he considered the pathetic defeatism of his fellow countrymen.

Some of Lu Hsün's writings are more autobiographical sketches than short stories and describe with wry humor scenes in his native city and the surrounding countryside he had known and loved when young. These childhood reminiscences are often included in textbooks and other selections of his work made for young people. One is called simply "My Old Home" ("Ku Hsiang"), an account of a return visit made to help his mother move with him to Peking. In it Lu Hsün eloquently describes both his nostalgic memories of a boyhood peasant friend who worked in a watermelon field and the disenchantment he feels on meeting that friend again in adult life. In contrast with this tender reminiscing is his satirical and humorous description in the same piece of the grasping bean-curd seller they used to call "'Bean-curd Beauty" because she powdered her face.

Another charming story, "Village Theater" ("She Hsi"),[7] in the same setting, tells of a visit to a traveling theater in a village two miles down the river from his grandmother's house. Because the family had not allowed enough time to hire a boat to get to the theater, Lu Hsün was nearly in tears with disappointment; but eventually he and his cousins managed to borrow a relative's boat and, despite the misgivings of the older members of the family, were allowed to row themselves to the village to see the play. With the vivid descriptions of rowing along the dark river, at long last seeing the lights of the temporary open-air theater come into view, their mixed boredom with the long, sung passages of the play and enchantment with the clowns, their reluctant admission that they were all too sleepy to stay any longer, the delicious taste of the stolen beans they cooked on the way home, one might almost have been in the party oneself. The combination of a deep and sympathetic understanding of the mind of a child and penetrating satire is one of the outstanding features of his writing.

In 1924 Lu Hsün was one of the original sponsors, again with his younger brother, of another literary society, which published a magazine called *Brief Discourses* (*Yü Ssu*). Throughout his life he continued to publish translations, mostly works of Russian or other East European writers, but many of the original stories were not of outstanding literary merit. He assisted in 1925 in forming the Wei-Ming Society to encourage the publication of reliable translations, chiefly from the Russian, and in 1934 he was one of the founders of *Translation Magazine* (*I-wen*).

In 1922 he had published a translation of a book of fairy tales and a fairy tale drama which a Russian friend of his, Vasalii Iakovlevich Eroshenko, who was at that time teaching in Peking, had published in Japanese. But in the preface he wrote, although the author intended the original for the children of the workers, this Chinese translation will unfortunately not be read by children of Chinese workers, because those children will not be sufficiently well educated to appreciate it. Even children who have had schooling will find it difficult because they have as yet no background in this kind of story.

In the preface to another translation of stories by the same author, he does say that besides offering the story as a model for Chinese writers as the sort of story children enjoy, by writing it in the simplest style possible he hopes that children of eleven upwards will be able to read the stories for themselves.

During the nineteen twenties the government in Peking had fallen under the control of a powerful and reactionary pro-Japanese warlord, and in 1926 there occurred the 18th March Incident which Lu Hsün described as "the blackest day in Chinese history." On that day the acting prime minister ordered the police to fire on thousands of students demonstrating against new Japanese aggression in front of the Department of State building, and forty-seven were killed, among them some of Lu Hsün's own students whom he had been supporting in their protests. Lu Hsün now was regarded as a dangerous radical and with many others had to leave Peking in a hurry. He went first to Amoy, where he was not happy, and then to Canton where he taught at Sun Yat-sen University.

Now acclaimed as one of the finest creative writers in the country and the new monthly magazine he founded, *The Torrent* (*Pen-liu*), having become nationally well known, Lu Hsün was also increasingly suspect to the right-wing Kuomintang, whose successful coup d'etat took place in 1927. It was at this time that he seriously began to study Marxism. Fiercely independent in thought (and a pungent critic of social ills), he at times clashed with other groups of radical writers because of his caustic comments on so-called revolutionary literature. But, although never a Party member, his sympathies were increasingly with communist writers and artists and he became a member of the China League of Left-wing Writers (Chung-kuo Tso-i Tso-chia Lien-meng). He only remained in Canton for one year and with a former student of his, Hsü Kuan-p'ing, now his common-law wife, he went to Shanghai where he continued to live until his death in 1936. On several occasions he bravely sheltered "wanted" radical writers and had to move from place to place himself to escape arrest.

Lu Hsün now concentrated on writing articles for newspapers and magazines sharply critical of the reactionary trends of the government and of the social evils of his time, but he wrote no more stories. One typical short article, "Shanghai Children," is quoted in full to illustrate his pungent style and his concern for the better education of children:

Last year, because of the fighting, the neighbourhood round North Szechuan Road outside the International Settlement was quiet for many months. This year it is as lively as ever again: the shops have moved back from the French Concession, the cinemas have been open for some time, and in the parks you often see lovers strolling hand in hand, which was not the case last summer.

Walk into any lane in the residential district, and you will see buckets of night-soil, portable kitchens, flies swarming in all directions and children milling around, some engaged in active devilry, others swearing like experts—a microcosm of utter chaos. On the main roads, however, your eyes are caught by the splendid, lively foreign children playing or walking —you see scarcely any Chinese children at all. Not that there are none, but with their tattered clothes and lack-lustre expression they pale into insignificance beside the others.

The main run of Chinese families seem to have two ways only of bringing up children. The first is to let them run wild without any control, allowed to swear or even fight. Standing before or inside their own gates they are petty tyrants, conquerors; but outside they are like spiders without a web—quite incapable of anything. The second is to treat them with invariable harshness, scolding or beating them till they shrink into their shells and become slaves or marionettes, whereupon their parents praise their "obedience " and preen themselves on the success of their training. When these children are let out, they are like small birds freed for a moment from a cage. They can neither fly, sing nor hop.

At last China too has picture books for the young, the chief characters in which are naturally children. But most of the boys and girls in these books look either savage or stupid. If not actual hooligan types or juvenile delinquents, they are "good children" with bent heads, round shoulders, downcast eyes, and completely blank expressions. This is due in part to the artists' limitations, but still these drawings are based on real children and serve as models for them too. If we look at pictures of children of other lands, the English seem well-behaved and quiet, the German boisterous and proud, the Russians sturdy and warm-hearted, the French smart, the Japanese intelligent—none of them show any trace of this Chinese listlessness. The spirit of a land can be seen not only from its poetry, but also from its pictures, including those children's pictures which are generally disregarded.

Stupidity and lethargy are enough to make men decadent. The child's environment determines the future man. Our moderns talk of love, of small families, of independence and of pleasure; but very few raise the question of children's education, at home or at school, and of social reform. The men of old merely knew how to be "horses and oxen for their sons and grandsons." That was wrong, of course, but we must admit that it is even more wrong to think only of the present and forget the future, "letting our sons and grandsons remain horses and oxen."[8]

The mention of picture books for children recalls Lu Hsün's lifelong interest in the graphic arts. He himself had a minor talent in drawing and his childhood reminiscence of his excitement when his old nurse found and gave him a copy of *The Book of Mountains and Seas* with its grotesque wood-block illustrations has already been quoted.

Wood-block printing was an ancient, traditional art in China, flourishing there long before it came to Europe, but with the introduction of twentieth-century mechanical techniques, its quality was rapidly declining. Lu Hsün became interested in examples from the new school of revolutionary Russian artists and in the minor renaissance occurring in wood-block illustration in Europe, particularly in England and Germany. He published two collections of foreign woodcuts and, when the Eighteen Club of woodcut artists was founded in Shanghai in 1929, he encouraged them as much as possible. They had their first exhibition in the Chinese YMCA in 1931, Lu Hsün writing the introduction to their catalog. More than this, in August 1931 he started a class in woodcut technique with a Japanese teacher paid at his own expense and with himself as interpreter, to encourage artists in this medium. In 1934 he published a collection of the work of these young Chinese artists.

In his last years Lu Hsün also continued translating and published some stories from Gorky and Chekov, but again he says in his preface to the former, "although the writer calls the stories 'fairy tales,' they were not intended for children." And, in spite of his urging, not many of the first generation of writers in the new style thought about writing for children. After his death in 1936, a committee was formed with his wife as a member to edit his complete works which were published in twenty volumes in 1938. Quoted with appreciation in 1942 by Mao in his *Talks at the Yenan Forum on Literature and Art,* Lu Hsün became canonized by the Communist Party and through the nineteen sixties more than two million copies of his work have been sold.

What then of Lu Hsün's contribution to children's literature? The literary reform movement, of which Lu Hsün as a writer is a shining star, has revolutionized Chinese literature and with it the whole approach to fiction and to stories for children, both forms which previously had been despised and avoided by the intellectual elite. His encouragement of the revival of woodcut illustration also led to much more attention being given to picture books for children. His major contribution rests in his deep insight into the mind of the child, shown in the reminiscences of his own boyhood and his passionate desire for a new and more equitable society. Significantly, he had studied medicine, intending to become a doctor and, like some doctors, he paid more attention to diagnosing the ills which beset his country than to prescribing cures. The decorative calligraphy in figure 17 is a couplet written by Lu Hsün himself, yet another example of a modern writer using this traditional literary form to make a statement of significance.

Chou Tso-jen. Chou Tso-jen, the elder of Lu Hsün's remaining two younger brothers, born in 1885, was educated in much the same way as his older brother and eventually joined him in Japan in 1906. There he studied modern and classical Japanese, English, and classical Greek. Chou became very interested in European literature and published a history emphasizing the common Greek and Latin origins. He began publishing translations in Shanghai as early as 1908, including among

Figure 17. Fierce-browed, I cooly defy a thousand pointing fingers,
Head bowed, like a willing ox, I serve the children

A couplet in Lu Hsün's handwriting, from *Chinese Literature*, 1967, 1, a volume commemorating Lu Hsün.

these popular works like H. Rider Haggard's which would appeal to young people. He returned to China in 1912 with his Japanese wife.

In 1917 Chou became a teacher at National Peking University, associating there with the group involved in the language reform movement. He became an enthusiastic supporter of the movement and began writing in the vernacular, publishing poems as well as essays in *New Youth Magazine*. He also continued to publish many translations, always using the new vernacular, of Japanese works and from Japanese translations of Russian and other East European literatures. Some of his earliest publications in the new style were short pieces for children, but these are more or less forgotten now.

In 1932, among a collection of essays, Chou published "Children's Literature" ("Erh-t'ung ti Wen-hsüeh"), a reprint of a speech he made in Peking in October 1920. In it he echoed much of what his brother was saying, that although there was little literature actually written for children, many good stories existed in the oral tradition which should be rewritten in a form appealing to them. He also urged more translation of good stories for children from other countries and lamented the lack of good illustrators for children's books. The talk ended with a discussion of the use of literature in primary schools.

Early Vernacular Writers

Although Lu Hsün and his brother Chou Tso-jen were responsible for so much research into the fairy tales, myths, and legends of other countries and urged their fellow writers to use the translations they made as models for the creation of a genuine vernacular literature for China's children, among the twenty or more outstanding imaginative writers of the first few decades of the language reform movement, only five published work expressly for children and this was a comparatively minor part of their work.[9]

Yeh Shao-chün. Yeh Shao-chün, a founding member with the Chou brothers of the Literary Research Society (Wen-hsüeh Yen-chiu Hui), was born in 1894 in Soochow in central China, the son of a rent collector. He was educated at a traditional primary school and at one of the new western-style middle schools where he studied western languages. Unable to afford a university education, Yeh became a primary school teacher and later taught in a variety of schools and colleges. These experiences formed the background for many of his stories with a schoolmaster and teen-agers as characters.

He published six books of short stories, among them two for children. In *The Statue of an Ancient Hero (Ku-tai Ying-hsiung ti Shih-hsiang)* there are nine stories, among them "The New Robe of the King," based on Anderson's "The Emperor's New Clothes." There is an animal fable, "The Silkworm and the Ant," and other stories, all with a somewhat forceful moral. His other collection for children, *The Scarecrow (Tao Ts'ao Jen)*, has twenty-three stories, most of which are didactic in tone, strongly reflecting the social injustices of his time. In contrast, the occasional simple stories he wrote, like "The Little White Boat," seem too bland and pretty.

In 1937 Yeh moved to Shanghai and then, after the Japanese occupation of the city, made his way to Free China in the far west of the country. He retained the respect of both the Nationalists and the Communists and, after the establishment of the People's Republic, continued to hold educational appointments, but published no more stories.

Lao She. Lao She (often romanized Lau Shaw), the pen name of Shu Ch'ing-ch'un, is among the modern Chinese writers whose names are well known abroad mainly because of the American translation of his novel, *Rickshaw Boy*, which gained best-seller success even though it was an unauthorized translation and the ending was bowdlerized.

Lao She, who was born in Peking in 1899, was only two years old when his father was killed in the Boxer Rebellion. He went to primary school and to Peking Normal School and, at the early age of seventeen, taught at a municipal primary school. He was given the opportunity to study the new educational methods and was appointed supervisor of education for a Peking school district. Later he resigned this position and taught Chinese literature in high schools until eventually he had saved enough to support himself and his mother while he attended Yenching University.

In 1924 Lao She was able to go to England where he taught Chinese at the School of Oriental and African Studies at the University of London. He read deeply in English literature and his study of Dickens inspired his first novel, *Lao Chang's Philosophy* (*Lao Chang-ti Che-hsüeh*) which was serialized in the *Short Story Monthly* (*Hsiao-shuo Yüeh-pao*) in Shanghai. He remained in England for three years, publishing two other novels which were serialized in the same magazine. He also spent three months on the Continent and then returned to China, stopping for some months in Singapore. There he taught Chinese in a middle school and published another novel, adding to his growing reputation as a comic writer and a defender of the underdog. While in Singapore he also wrote a story for children, *Hsiao P'o's Birthday* (*Hsiao P'o-ti Sheng-jih*). This is a long tale about a group of children that reflects the multiracial character of Singapore. Hsiao P'o is about seven years old and he and his three Chinese friends play games with twin sisters who are Malayan and with three Indian children. Their school life and Hsiao P'o's many fights to protect the girls and smaller children are described. His birthday treat is a visit with his father and his brother and sister to the Botanical Gardens where they love to watch the monkeys. In the afternoon they go to their first movie. The story is something of a failure. The language and style make it suitable for twelve- and thirteen-year-olds, yet the story itself, about younger children, has no sustaining plot to hold the interest of these older readers.

On returning to China Lao She taught at several universities and continued to write and publish more novels and short stories. In 1937 he completed the book which was acclaimed as his masterpiece, *Camel Hsiang-tzu (Lo-t'o Hsiang-tzu)*, the one translated as *Rickshaw Boy.* First published in the magazine *Cosmic Wind (Yu-chou Feng)*, edited by Lin Yü-t'ang, it is the story of the corruption and doom of a strong and good-natured rickshaw puller in Peking, known as "Camel" Hsiang-tzu. Its publication in book form was held up by the outbreak of the Sino-Japanese War that same year, finally appearing in 1939.

Lao She went to Free China during the war years and wrote a number of plays with patriotic themes, his reputation as a writer increasing all the while. He also wrote ballads for recitation with drum accompaniment (ta-ku), a folk-art form which had become popular again in the war years, particularly with students. After the war he went to America and stayed for three years, during which time he published his well-known trilogy, *Four Generations under One Roof (Ssu Shih T'ung T'ang)*, the final volume appearing in 1957. A story of Peking under eight years of Japanese occupation, it was translated in an authorized though abridged form by Ida Pruitt as *The Yellow Storm.* Others of his stories were translated by Helena Kuo.

When the People's Republic was established, Lao She returned again to China and was acclaimed "the People's Artist" by the Mayor of Peking. He was responsible for the Peking dialect version of the revival of the old play *Fifteen Strings of Cash (Shih-wu Kuan)* which became so popular throughout the country in 1956. He served on numerous literary committees under the new regime and published more plays, including one for children, *Pao Ch'uan*, the name of a character in the play. It will be readily seen that although teen-agers are likely to explore the famous Lao She's writing, apart from one or two pieces he did not attempt to write specifically for children.

Chinese Writers in English

China's increased cultural contact with the West during the nineteen twenties and thirties had a two way effect, and general interest in China and things Chinese grew accordingly. Writers like Lao She, who lived and taught abroad for considerable periods, introduced the work of the new school of young Chinese writers to a much wider audience. Among the Chinese who studied in England and America there were gifted writers who became so fluent in English that they developed their own inimitable style in their adopted language. Outstanding among such writers were Chiang Yee and Hsiung Shih-i in England and Lin Yü-t'ang in America. S. I. Hsiung, the editor and translator of the classical plays *Lady Precious Stream* and *The Western Chamber,* has already been mentioned.

Chiang Yee. Chiang Yee and Lin Yü-t'ang earn passing mention here because there are few detailed portrayals of the life of children in stories by Chinese writers and the vivid accounts in the work of these two writers are useful for comparative purposes. Chiang Yee, born in 1903, as a young man served as a district magistrate in his native Kiangsi province in central China. He went to England in the early thirties, originally intending to study science. But he soon gave that up and, like Lao She, became a lecturer at the School of Oriental and African Studies in London.

Adopting the English pen name of "The Silent Traveller," Chiang Yee wrote and illustrated a number of charming travel books, among them *The Silent Traveller in London*. He published *A Chinese Childhood* in 1940, an autobiographical book, written with a wry sense of humor, about his growing up in a large Chinese household, with the traditional festivals the only exciting events interrupting life's leisurely pace. Besides his "Silent Traveller" books, Chiang Yee wrote and illustrated a number of picture books for children, again with his intriguing touches of humor, but, as the text was written in English, this is not the place to discuss them.

It is interesting and a little sad to note that Chiang Yee's interest in books for children was such that his son was educated as a printer, and they originally had intended to go back to China to begin a publishing business, specializing in illustrated books for young people, had political events not prevented them. After World War II, Chiang went to live in America and taught at Columbia University in New York. Eventually he was able to pay a visit to his family left in China for all these years and died in Peking in 1978.

Lin Yü-t'ang. Lin Yü-t'ang, born in 1895, came from a Christian family from Fukien province in southeast China, and, after attending college in Shanghai, he entered Harvard in 1919; he also studied in France and Germany. On his return to China he began to write; he also taught at several universities. He was a regular contributor to the magazine *Brief Discourses (Yü-ssu)* and founded several new magazines himself, among them one specializing in satire and humor, a great innovation at that time in China. He was responsible with a group of young writers for an English-language magazine published in Shanghai, *T'ien-hsia Monthly*, with the aim of making known as much "new" Chinese writing as possible to an English-speaking international audience.

In 1939 he published his best-known novel in English, *Moment in Peking*, a panorama of the life of an extended family living in a typical courtyard-style house in Peking, with a multiplicity of relatives and servants. Mulan, the heroine, is only ten years old when the story opens; she has two younger sisters, one adopted, and also a brother. The novel traces the transition in family life from the time of the old imperial China at the turn of the century, through the establishment of the Republic in 1912, to the modernization of city life and the outbreak of the war with Japan in 1937. Although a fictional account, the detailed descriptions of the life of children, both served and serving, in a prosperous Peking household are vivid and convincing. Lin returned to China from America during World War II, but came back to the United States. He died in Taiwan in 1976.

Translators from European Languages

Writers in the new style may not immediately have followed the path which Lu Hsün and his brother hoped they would in creating a true vernacular literature for children, but the translations which the brothers and other writers published did strongly influence the writing of the period. This influence on style, freely acknowledged by many writers, in turn created a taste for western literature among the general reading public. By the end of the nineteen thirties some two hundred translations of western novels had been published, the greater number being English and American, then French, German, and Russian, as well as a few from Norwegian, Polish, Hungarian, Danish, and other literatures. Many translations from twentieth-century Japanese writers were also published, but these were in a different category, expressing as they did a more familiar pattern of living which had its roots in Chinese culture.

Lin Shu. Ironically, Lin Shu, a pioneer translator and a strong influence on a number of writers, became a bitter opponent of the language reform movement. He was born in 1852 in Fukien, in southeast China. His family had been fairly prosperous farmers but were seriously impoverished at the time of his birth. His mother, who early recognized her son's outstanding abilities, was from a scholar-gentry family. Eventually the help of an uncle enabled Lin to attend the local primary school. When he was ten years old his father obtained a position as secretary to an official in Taiwan and the family finances improved somewhat. Lin joined his father in Taiwan when he was fifteen and while still very young married a girl from his native town. His father died when he was eighteen, but his father-in-law continued to support his education.

By the time he was thirty years old, Lin had passed the first two degrees in the imperial examinations but failed altogether seven attempts to pass the highest degree examination in Peking. This period was one of great personal sorrow as well as disappointment, for his mother died and he lost two of his children through tuberculosis. A friend, recently returned from studying in France, in order to help Lin take his mind off his troubles, suggested that they should translate *La Dame aux Camélias* by Alexandre Dumas fils. The friend wrote down a rapid vernacular translation which Lin promptly turned into what all critics agreed was "elegant classical Chinese," and another friend published the work in 1899. It was an immediate success and thousands of copies were sold.

Lin turned to schoolteaching, first in Hangchow and then in Peking. He was sympathetic with the ideals of an abortive reform movement to introduce changes in government and a constitutional instead of an autocratic monarchy. He wrote poems in the vernacular on themes of educational and social reform. In 1901 he translated Harriet Beecher Stowe's *Uncle Tom's Cabin,* again with a collaborator. He was appointed to the Translation Bureau of the Imperial University (later Peking University) and in 1905 he became a teacher of Chinese literature in the same university, and eventually Dean of the School of Letters.

Lin's ignorance of any foreign language made him not only dependent on collaborators for initial versions of stories he was translating, but for the choice of work too. Popularity seems to have been the guiding principle, with the result that not always the best writers nor the best examples of their work were chosen. Lin also was unable to check his versions with the originals, and critics have therefore described his translations as "imaginative adaptations" rather than literal translations.

> He possessed a mastery of the classical language and an ability to portray in rich and subtle language the mood and setting of his characters which resulted in a paradoxical situation; the alterations and omissions often had the effect of improving the text for Chinese readers, who were able to feel that they were reading an elegant classical Chinese tale which recounted the strange but interesting lives of the people of the West.[10]

Between 1904 and 1914 Lin translated fifty novels which were then published in a collected edition of ninety-seven volumes by the Commercial Press.[11] A glance at some of the titles will show how wide their appeal would be to young people. In 1904 he translated Aesop's *Fables,* Charles Lamb's *Tales from Shakespeare,* and H. Rider Haggard's *Joan Haste.* In the following year he translated *Ivanhoe* by Sir Walter Scott, *Robinson Crusoe* by Daniel Defoe, and a more popular Haggard book, *Allan Quatermain.* Jonathan Swift's *Gulliver's Travels* and Washington Irving's *Tales of a Traveller* were published in 1906, and Chinese readers were introduced to Sherlock Holmes in Arthur Conan Doyle's *A Study in Scarlet.* Lin also translated the same author's *Micah Clarke.*

In the next two years his versions of several of the novels of Charles Dickens brought Lin even wider acclaim. *Nicholas Nickleby* was followed by *Oliver Twist, David Copperfield,* and *Dombey* and Son. Arthur Waley, a master translator of Chinese into English, writing in the *Atlantic Monthly* (November, 1958) about Lin's "reverse-way" translations, said, "Dickens, inevitably, becomes a rather different, but to my mind, a better writer. All the over elaborations, the over statements, the uncurbed garrulity disappear." Of course, a translator's duty to his author is to get as close to the original as possible, but the appeal of Lin's versions cannot be gainsaid. Lin himself said that Dickens was the equal of the best Chinese writers of the past. In addition to the writers mentioned, he also translated from Fielding, Goldsmith, H. G.

Wells, Balzac, and Tolstoi and wrote prose versions of four of Shakespeare's plays and of the *Iliad* and the *Odyssey*, as well. An extraordinarily prolific writer, Lin also produced a number of original works —novels, short stories, essays, poems, and widely used textbooks of literature.

The influence of Lin's work was very great, giving a wide Chinese audience, including teen-agers, a much greater knowledge of the literary achievements of the West, of its varied customs and societies, introducing new ideas on the kinds of subjects that could be treated in novels. After the founding of the Republic in 1912 his position as a leading writer in the previously admired classical style began to change. A new generation of students was demanding new teachers who were in sympathy with the aims of what was to become the language reform movement. Eventually Lin had to resign his position at Peking University. This exacerbated his feelings and he wrote several articles bitterly attacking the general use of the vernacular for literary purposes, saying that the abandonment of the traditional style would destroy Confucian principles. He died in 1924.

Yen Fu. Brief mention must also be made of Yen Fu, whose translations of the works of Herbert Spencer, John Stuart Mill, Adam Smith, Thomas Henry Huxley, and others are acknowledged to have had a profound effect on the thinking of the new generation of writers, including Lu Hsün, Hu Shih, and Mao Tse-tung himself. A fellow provincial of Lin Shu, he was born in Foochow in 1854. The son of a practitioner in Chinese medicine, he early showed great intelligence and for that reason his classical education began at the age of five with a private tutor. His father died when Yen was only ten and the family could no longer afford his tutor, but he gained first place in the entrance examination at the nearby Ma-chiang Naval Academy which provided him with free board and tuition, giving support to his family. He had the choice of instruction in French or English and chose the latter. After graduation and two years' practical experience in the Navy he was one of the earliest Chinese scholars to be sent to England in 1877. He studied at Greenwich Naval College and although his class work was excellent, he neglected the practical side of his training in favor of studying the English form of government. This included studying the philosophical and scientific works which Yen later translated because he thought these works would provide the clue to a system of government he much admired and to the secret of the power and prosperity of the West.

On his return to China, Yen's western training did not qualify him for any high government post and he failed later attempts to qualify for the higher degree in the traditional imperial examinations. He held various positions in higher education, but teaching and administration did not satisfy him. He concentrated his energies instead on translating and commenting on the English philosophical, sociological, and economic works he had studied. He wrote in elegant classical Chinese and the expressions he coined to convey the meaning of "natural selection," "evolution," "struggle for existence," and similar ideas were immediately adopted into the language. His translations of Mill's *On Liberty* and Smith's *The Wealth of Nations* and Huxley's *Evolution and Ethics* are classics in their own right and his work greatly influenced the twentieth-century revolution in Chinese thought.

Later Vernacular Writers

Of the three remaining well-known modern writers in the vernacular who attempted to write for young people, two, Ping Hsin and Chang T'ien-i, were comparatively successful. The third, Shen Ts'ung-wen, is mentioned because the one book he wrote for younger readers reflects the strong influence of western literature on the "new wave" of Chinese writers.

Ping Hsin. Ping Hsin, the pen name of Hsieh Wan-ying, is better known in the West than many other modern Chinese writers, for she studied at Wellesley College in America and subsequently traveled abroad a great deal to Europe and America; later as a semiofficial cultural ambassador for the People's Republic she went again to Europe, and to India, Egypt, and Russia. She was born in the coastal province of Fukien in southeast China, her father being an officer in the Chinese Naval Service. Because of this the family moved quite frequently and Ping Hsin was educated at home before returning to live with her grandparents in her native city in order to attend Foochow Normal School. In 1913 the family moved to Peking and Ping Hsin entered the Bridgman Academy, a missionary school there. She and her mother became Christians.

After graduating from that school, Ping Hsin attended Peking Union College for Women (later known as Yenching University); there she became involved with the group of young people advocating language reform and, although of a retiring nature, took part in some of the political activities of the group. She eagerly read the new magazines and the many new translations from European languages being published. She had already tried writing stories while at school; now she began writing in the vernacular, publishing her first book of poems and a collection of short stories in 1923. In the same year she graduated from Yenching, went to the United States, and entered Wellesley College. There it was discovered that she was suffering from tuberculosis, for which illness she had to spend six months in a sanitorium.

While in the sanitorium Ping Hsin wrote *Letters to Young Readers* (*Chi Hsiao Tu Che*)[12] which were published first in the literary supplement of a newspaper, where they proved to be extremely popular, and later were published in book form. Dedicated to her mother, whom she loved deeply, the *Letters* are written in a simple, rather ingenuous style, their themes being the love of nature, the love of animals, love in general, and escape from the world. She graduated with an M.A. in 1926, having written a number of stories during her university years which are considered her best work.

Ping Hsin then returned to China and taught at her old university in Peking. She married in 1929 and in 1936 she and her husband, who had also studied in America, paid a return visit there and to Europe, going back via the Soviet Union to China. During the war years she and her husband went to Free China. She published a number of essays, portraits of prominent Chinese women, and *More Letters to Young Readers* (*Hsü Chi Hsiao Tu Che*). After the war she and her husband taught at Tokyo University and with the establishment of the People's Republic they returned to China. Ping Hsin became a member of the All-China Federation of Literature and the Arts (Ch'üan Kuo Wen-hsüeh I-shu Chieh Lien-ho Hui) and the Union of Chinese Writers (Chung-kuo Tso-chia Hsieh-hui). Two volumes of her stories for children were published in 1950, *T'ao Ch'i's Summer Dairy* (*T'ao Ch'i-ti Shu-ch'i Jih-ch'i*) and *Indian Fairy Tales* (*Yin-tu T'ung-hua Chi*). *T'ao Ch'i's Summer Diary* is a simple story about the summertime adventures of T'ao Ch'i and another boy and a girl in a youth team.

It was between the years 1953 and 1958 that Ping Hsin undertook her semiofficial travels abroad, engaging in juvenile propaganda for the government. She also contributed to the new magazines being published for children and published a final collection of her essays in 1964, but her later work was never as popular as her early writing. Often criticized as being too sentimental, in her early stories like *A Year Away from Home* (*Li Chia-ti I Nien*), describing the loneliness of a thirteen-year-old boy, and *Since Her Departure* (*Pieh Hou*), the story of a thirteen-year-old orphan, she was able to capture the poignant feelings of adolescents.

Chang T'ien-i. Chang-T'ien-i is the most successful of the first generation of outstanding writers in the modern style who have seriously turned their attention to literature for children, but he only achieved renown in this field after the Communists had come to power. The fifteenth and youngest son in a family from Hunan province, in which the grandfather, father, and uncles were scholar-officials, he was born in Nanking in 1907. When he was seventeen years old, the family moved to Peking. He did not go to a university but mixed with the group of young writers concerned with language reform and determined to be a writer himself. After some articles had been accepted by newspapers, Chang was successful in having his first short story published in *The Torrent* (*Pen-liu*), the monthly magazine edited by Lu Hsün, who encouraged him in his writing. During the nineteen thirties he wrote all together four novels and six volumes of short stories. It is on these works that his reputation as a modern vernacular writer still rests.

During World War II Chang moved to Free China, teaching for a while and publishing a further collection of three stories in 1943. He developed tuberculosis and had to go into a sanitorium and rest for a few years. Before the war he had already published a few stories for children, including *A Strange Place* (*Ch'i-kuai ti Ti-fang*) in which a country boy goes to a big city to stay with his father who works as a gardener in a large house belonging to a foreigner. Everything there is strange. He is not allowed to play naturally with the "young master" of the house whom he regards as a coward, but must allow himself to be attacked by the foreign boy. Unhappy with his father's subservient position and his own, he longs to return to the freedom of his simple country life again.

Chang specialized in children's literature after the establishment of the People's Republic. He attributed his success to his understanding of children and claimed that the best way to learn about children is from the children themselves. To accomplish this he regularly visited children in their schools and went for walks with them, thereby discovering what appealed to them and what would help them in their development.

In 1952 Chang published *The Story of Lo Wen-ying* (*Lo Wen-ying ti Ku-shih*), bound with two other stories, "Going to See a Movie" ("Ch'ü k'an tien-ying") and "We and They" ("T'a-men ho wo-men"), all written with a strong moral point of view, but in a vigorous, humorous style that has a definite appeal. The title story is about a young boy who wanted to join the Pioneers but had to do better at school before he could be admitted. It is reported that in China the story of Lo Wen-ying now is often quoted to children who want something badly but who must work harder in order to get it. Chang continued to write stories and one-act plays for children during the fifties and sixties and also served on a number of literary committees.

Shen Ts'ung-wen. Shen Ts'ung-wen, born in 1903 in western Hunan province, is well known for the stories he wrote for adults of the life of ordinary soldiers and of the Miao people, a minority group living in western China. His one book for young people, *Alice's Adventures in China* (*A-lissu Chung-kuo Yu-chi*), published in two volumes in Shanghai in 1928, can only be called a curiosity. The author himself acknowledged in the preface that the book was a failure. He had attempted to satirize the corruption and the social evils of his time, using a humorous style to appeal to teen-agers, but he said he realized that the state of affairs in his country were too heartbreaking for that kind of treatment.

Publishing in the Republic

Although the most famous writers of the twenties and thirties did not write much specifically for children, this does not mean that the new generation of children growing up in the Republican era were completely without books designed for them. That need was met by the newly founded publishing houses, whose primary business was to provide for the greatly increased demands for textbooks to accompany the educational reforms taking place, especially the "foreign learning" texts, which were often bilingual.[13]

The Commercial Press. The Commercial Press (Shan Wu Yin Shu Kuan) was the most important of the new publishing houses. Established in 1897 in Shanghai, by 1902 it was a flourishing concern with branches in Peking and Hong Kong. It was the general practice of the larger publishing houses in China to control their own chain of bookstores, selling their own publications but also stocking books and journals produced by smaller publishers and importing large quantities of books from overseas as the demand for English, American, and other foreign language publications grew. The Commercial Press was operating thirty-six bookstores in 1930, with shops in all the major cities of China and by this date had published more than eight thousand titles. The Commercial Press suffered very severe damage at the outbreak of the Sino-Japanese war in 1937 when its headquarters in Shanghai was totally destroyed. The establishment in that city included a large translation unit, a large reference library, research and editorial offices; all these, together with a stock of nearly half a million books and periodicals, were lost. The firm managed to recover from some of its losses after World War II and reopened its publishing houses in Shanghai, Peking, and Hong Kong. After the establishment of the People's Republic, the main business moved to Taiwan and the Hong Kong house continues. The section left in China was absorbed into the Communist government reorganization of publishing after the 1950 First National Conference on Publishing, but not without drastic revision of its publishing program and the resulting destruction of many of the fifteen thousand titles it had in stock.

China Book Company and Other Publishers. The most important rival of the Commercial Press was the China Book Company (Chung-hua Shu Chu), often called the "Chung-hua" in English also. Wherever one found a Commercial Press bookshop in China, there was almost certain to be a Chung-hua bookstore within a stone's throw. Numbers of other smaller publishing houses were opened, many of these operating their own bookstores. A 1949 survey shows that there were more than three hundred publishing houses in China, with at least two-thirds of them centered in Shanghai.

Publishing Children's Books

The usual procedure for the publishing houses was to commission books for children, paying the authors and illustrators an outright sum instead of royalties for their work. Again, if an author or an artist had an idea for a book, it would be submitted to a chosen publisher, but still would be paid for outright. This meant that publishers could reprint a work as many times as they wished or reuse its illustrations without any extra payment.

Serial picture books were extremely popular, especially those illustrating the well-known scenes from historical tales like those from *The Romance of the Three Kingdoms*, *The Tale of the Marshes*, and *Monkey* already described. The books appeared in numerous editions from different publishers at a very cheap price, but the standard of illustration on the whole was very high. The long tradition of calligraphic line which underlies all Chinese art assures that a number of competent illustrators are always available, even though they might regard such commissions as hack work.

Publishers' Series for Children

Printing and publishing flourished also in Hong Kong and besides the Commercial Press and the Chung-hua Book Company, many other publishers had outlets there. After the Communist government was established, a number of publishers moved their entire businesses from Shanghai to Hong Kong. Publications for children from these houses consisted mostly of popular series. In print are *Selection of World Juvenile Literature* (*Shih-chieh Shao-nien Wen-hsüeh Hsüan Chi*), *Biographies of People of World Renown* (*Shih-chieh Wei Jen Chuan Chi*), *Youth Knowledge Series* (*Ch'ing-nien Chih-shih Ts'ung-shu*), *Oriental Juvenile Literature* (*Tung-fang Shao-nien Wen K'u*), and other similar series.

Children's Magazines

The Shanghai publishing houses also catered to the growing demand for suitable reading for children by sponsoring a number of magazines. *Little Friends* (*Hsiao P'eng-yu*) and *Boy's World* (*Erh-t'ung Shih-chieh*) were among the most popular. Several similar magazines continue to be published in Taiwan and Hong Kong. The Children's Book Centre (*Erh-t'ung Shu-pao Chung-hsin*) an indigenous Hong Kong company, is organized by Mrs. Lau Wai King, herself an active writer for children and editor of a magazine, *Children's Weekly* (*Erh-t'ung Chou-k'an*). Her company has over fifty titles for children in print. Another children's magazine currently published in Hong Kong is *Children's Paradise* (*Erh-t'ung T'ien-t'ang*), edited by the artist Lo Koon-chiu.

Cartoon Strips

There were a few cartoon strips with child characters published in Shanghai newspapers in the nineteen twenties and thirties. One of the most popular and successful was by Chang Lo-p'ing who created the character San Mao ("Three Hairs"), an appealing seven-year-old urchin used as a vehicle for satirical social comments on the contrast between the world of the rich and the world of the poor. Although not drawn for children, the cartoons were certainly followed by them. A book of Chang Lo-p'ing's collected drawings was republished in 1959 in Shanghai by the Young People's and Children's Press.[14]

One of the best portrayers of children of the period was Feng Tzu-k'ai, who was born in 1898. After studying in Japan he taught at several art schools in Shanghai and joined the editorial staff of the K'ai-ming Book Company. He used a traditional, bold, free brush stroke but was a pioneer in drawing people directly from life, filling many sketch books with drawings made on the spot from scenes around him. His lively drawings were published in newspapers and two books of his sketches of children were published by his company in 1925 and in 1927, *Sketches of Children (Erh-t'ung Man-hua)* and *A Collection of Sketches by Feng Tzu-k'ai (Tzu-k'ai Hua-chi)*, a book republished in 1950.[15] His delightful and spontaneous drawings of children, examples of which are shown in figure 18, inspired the "Little Pear" books of Eleanor Lattimore which became so popular in the United States, the first one published by Harcourt in 1931. Feng was also well known for an illustrated edition of Lu Hsün's famous anti-hero *Ah Q*, originally published in 1939.

Publishing for Children in the People's Republic

The total change in the publishing world of books for children since the establishment of the People's Republic in 1949 is but one reflection of the revolution in education for the masses which has taken place and which can only be very briefly summarized here to complete the perspective of twentieth-century developments. The New China Book Publishing Company (Hsin Hua Shu Ch'u), which Mao Tse-tung established in 1942 after the Long March to Yenan to take care of the publishing program of the Communist Party, has continued to be the main printing, publishing, and distributing organization with its activities expanded on a nationwide scale. It functions under the Bureau of Publication, a Division of the Committee of Cultural and Educational Affairs.

In addition to the main New China Book Publishing Company, the reorganized Commercial Press, and the Chung Hua Book Company, many specialized and regional publishing concerns have been set up, among them the Workers' Publishing House and several specializing in publishing for young people. The China Youth Press (Chung-kuo Ch'ing-nien) and the China Youth and Children's Press (Chung-kuo Shao-nien Erh-t'ung) are two of the most important. There are regional and minority group publishing houses for youth as well, the Southwest China Youth Press (Hsi-nan Ch'ing-nien) being an example. There is a special section of the Chinese Writers' Union for writers for young people, but the work of many nonprofessional writers is also published.

Figure 18. Two drawings of children
from *Sketches by Feng Tzu-k'ai.*

There are many examples too of cooperative writing by groups of people—the Chinese edition of the serial picture book, *Monkey Subdues the White-bone Demon,* previously discussed, is by a "Creative Writing Group."

The number of books published each year for children grew steadily throughout the fifties, reaching a peak in 1961, since when the annual total published has declined slightly. About three thousand titles (excluding serial picture books) were published annually up to the time of the Cultural Revolution. The number of copies of these publications distributed is staggering. Of the ever popular serial picture books, used extensively for the newly literate as well as for children, published between 1950 and 1960, twenty thousand different titles were produced, with first printings of two hundred thousand copies. All together in that decade six hundred million copies were distributed. Not all the picture books are propaganda works about labor heroes or peasants outwitting wicked landlords. Retellings of classical historical stories from *The Romance of the Three Kingdoms,* hero stories from *The Tale of the Marshes,* and stories of the well-known plays and films are often the most popular.

The distribution system organized by the government is excellent. The New China Book Publishing Company has over three thousand branches and subbranches and in the more isolated villages bookstands are set up in the village store or commune headquarters. Every book published is available through mail order to every part of China and the bookstores have to pay the postage. The Post Office provides special order forms so that ordering procedures are simple. Peking now has ninety bookshops and the largest reports ten thousand customers each day. Average prices run to the equivalent of between forty U.S. cents and one dollar forty cents. Secondhand bookstores still exist in the big cities and do a lively trade, although they are not officially encouraged. The new magazines for children also enjoy a large circulation. There is a new *Little Friends* (*Hsiao P'eng-yu*) for primary school children, the *Children's Times* (*Erh-t'ung Shih-pao*) for the next age group, and *Youth Literature* (*Ch'ing-nien Wen K'u*) for middle school boys and girls.

After a time it was decided that the initial pruning of the stocks of the Commercial Press and the Chung-hua Book Company had been too radical, and many of the classics and earlier works are back in print again. Most of the popular translations from Western authors published before 1950, such as *The Arabian Nights, Treasure Island, Robinson Crusoe, Gulliver's Travels, Huckleberry Finn,* and the like, are available once more. The Foreign Languages Press publishes translations of Chinese books for young people overseas in many languages, with the greatest number in English, and many in French, German, Indonesian, Japanese, Spanish, and Esperanto. In its first decade it distributed over four-and-a-half million books to seventy-one different countries. The popular multilingual illustrated journals like *People's*

China and *China Pictorial* are widely read by young people in many countries.

Schools

This increased publishing program for young people parallels the remarkable progress which has been made since 1950 toward the goal of providing at least primary education for every child in China. Children now start primary school at age seven instead of six, lower primary education lasts for four years and upper primary for two. Middle and high schools are established only in towns, and entry is more selective. The great distances country children would have to travel means that they would have to be boarders at the school, and this is also a limiting factor.

Kindergartens and Nursery Schools. The provision of kindergartens and nursery schools is becoming more and more widespread. Usually organized by village and urban communes under guidelines from the Ministry of Education, these not only benefit the children, they enable numbers of young mothers to work outside the home. In kindergarten the children learn to speak the National Language through group recitation and singing, while dancing and games provide physical activity. In addition they have elementary lessons in nature study and in personal cleanliness and hygiene.[16]

By the time children have completed the first four years of primary school they have progressed through eight graded language textbooks, one for each of the two-semester school years; they can read two thousand, seven hundred and fifty characters and know something of the *pin-yin* system[17] of romanization as well. Most primary schools have libraries and children are encouraged to read and, in turn, to help illiterate parents to read, especially with the aid of the generous supply of serial picture books.

Public Libraries

The post-1950 growth in the provision of libraries has also been phenomenal, but the foundation of a modern national library organization in China began with the general reforms in education of the Republican era.[18] Traditionally, as has been described earlier, every dynasty had maintained an imperial library and scholars were entrusted with advising the emperor on texts to be collected, edited, recopied, or printed. Besides the imperial library there were several outstanding provincial libraries with historic collections and numberless private libraries, the collecting of rare and esoteric works and the possession of a good working collection of the classics, philosophy, and belles lettres having been the mark of the true scholar.

In 1908 the Ministry of Education promulgated rules and regulations governing public libraries, the Metropolitan Library of Peking was founded, and sixteen provincial libraries were established or expanded. American missionaries were responsible for founding the Boone Public Library in Wuchang in central China in 1911 and, a decade later in the same city, Boone University which inaugurated the Boone School of Library Science with courses in library service for children. In 1915 new rules governing libraries were introduced and, from 1916 onward, all books published had to be registered with the Ministry of Education and a copy of each work presented to the Metropolitan Library in Peking.

In 1920 Peking Normal College began offering summer courses in library science. Several other universities quickly followed suit in the next year or two, and in 1922 a Training School for Librarians was established in Canton. Provincial library associations were encouraged from 1920 onward, and in 1925 the Library Association of China was founded with advice from a representative of the American Library Association. In 1929 the National Library of Peking was established with the amalgamation of two existing libraries. By 1936, besides the growing strength of university and research libraries, there were thirty-three provincial libraries, eight large municipal libraries with children's rooms, over two thousand five hundred school and college libraries, and nearly one thousand mass education libraries also with children's rooms.

The sad story of events occurring in China with the outbreak of the Sino-Japanese War in 1937 is repeated once more in the fate of this promising growth of public libraries and library provision for children. By the end of the war in 1945 fewer than one-fifth were still functioning. During the wartime establishment of a temporary capital in Chungking in western China, another National Central Library was opened. Moved to Nanking in 1948, it attempted to serve school children as well as adults and provided a special children's reading room.

Since 1950 a tremendous growth in library service throughout the country has accompanied the increase in education and publishing. There is now a public library in every county, municipality, and borough of the larger cities. All have reading rooms for children with programs of storyhours, play-acting, and other activities. Augmenting this service there are over two thousand six hundred cultural club libraries, all of which have children's rooms. These club libraries, organized by the communes, take over the reader services of the public libraries in rural areas where they are frequently the only ones available.

Children's Recreational Centers

A further word must be added about the new recreational centers for children found in the larger cities, which are in the tradition of the old theater entertainment districts. Many tourists have visited the Great World in Singapore with its theaters, cinemas, restaurants, shops, and stalls of all kinds. In Shanghai there continues to be a Great World, an enormous recreation center for family groups with special theater shows, puppet shows, documentary and feature films, and storytellers, as well as educational and scientific exhibitions for young people. There are also children's "palaces"; one of the most publicized is the old mansion in Shanghai, formerly known as Marble Hall, which belonged to an international financier in the "bad old days." The writer spent a few weekends there in those bad old days when it was being used by various cultural organizations, and she cannot think of a better use of the vast palace with its huge rooms, terrace, and garden. These children's palaces, and there are twelve in Shanghai, have libraries with storytellers in attendance; gymnasiums and ping-pong rooms; rooms for model-making, dance, and singing classes; and children's shows of all kinds performed by children for an audience of children.

Notable advances have also been made in library provision for children in Taiwan, Hong Kong, and Singapore since the fifties, but as the aims, organization, and methods are different from those in the People's Republic, these require an account on their own.

Notes

1. For information about educational reforms the writer is indebted to Biggerstaff, *The Earliest Modern Government Schools in China.*

2. Article on Hu Shih in Boorman, *Biographical Dictionary of Republican China.*

3. E. G. Pulleyblank in the foreword to Huang, *Lu Hsün and the New Culture Movement of Modern China,* to which book the writer is indebted for information on the May Fourth Movement.

4. All translations from the prefaces to Lu Hsün's translations were made for the writer by Professor Tsai-fa Cheng of the Department of East Asian Studies, University of Wisconsin-Madison.

5. Lu, *Selected Works,* vols. 1 and 3.

6. Lu, *Selected Stories.*

7. Ibid.

8. Lu, *Selected Works,* vol. 3.

9. For much of the critical and biographical information about twentieth-century Chinese writers mentioned in this chapter, the writer is indebted to Hsia, *A History of Modern Chinese Fiction, 1917–1957,* and to Boorman, *Biographical Dictionary of Republican China.*

10. Article in Boorman, *Biographical Dictionary of Republican China,* where the Chinese titles for all the translated works mentioned here are given.

11. Lin, *Lin I Hsiao-shuo Ts'ung-shu (Collected Edition of Novels Translated by Lin).*

12. Copies of some of the works of Ping Hsin and the other contemporary writers mentioned in this chapter were not available to give bibliographical details.

13. For information in this section, I am indebted to: Liu, *Book Publishing in Communist China;* Nunn, *Publishing in Mainland China;* Diény, *Le Monde Est à Vous: La Chine et les Livres pour Enfants;* and Nebiolo, *The People's Comic Book.*

14. Chang, *San Mao Liu-lang-chi* (*San Mao Strip Cartoons*).

15. Feng, *Tzu-k'ai Man-hua-lien* (*A Collection of Sketches by Feng-Tzu-k'ai*) is the title of the 1950 reprint.

16. Up-to-date and detailed descriptions of nurseries, kindergartens, and primary schools can be found in Kessen, *Childhood in China*.

17. *Pin-yin* is the form of romanization devised by the Chinese as a standardized method of providing phonetic values for their written characters. In 1979 this phonetic system became mandatory in all Chinese official documents. In the past a number of systems were devised by scholars to render Chinese phonetically in their own language, English, French, German, etc. This meant that different spellings were often given to an identical Chinese word. The Wade-Giles system of romanization used throughout this book has been most commonly used for English language translations and transliteration in a wide variety of publications of all kinds on China.

18. For the information about China's libraries, the writer is indebted to T'an, *The Development of Chinese Libraries under the Ch'ing Dynasty, 1644–1911*; Chiang, "A historical sketch of Chinese libraries" in *Philobiblon* 2, pt. 2, 1948; Cheng, "Libraries in China today" in *Libri* 9, no. 2, 1959; *The National Central Library, a Record* (brochure, 1947); and *The National Library, Peking*, (brochure, 1955).

Folklore and Nursery Rhymes, Riddles and Proverbs

8

It may seem strange to describe some of the oldest literature for children last of all, but consistent scholarly efforts to collect and record original regional versions of the nursery rhymes, riddles, folk songs, and folktales which form such an important part of the history of popular literature were not made in China until the first half of the twentieth century. The aim of the language reform movement was to make the colloquial speech of the ordinary people acceptable as a written form, freeing literature from its classical bonds. As has been shown by the existing rich store of popular literature, it was part of the official policy throughout China's long history to collect and record songs, stories, and sayings from the people in the countryside, using their own colloquial language. But with widespread public attention focused on all forms of colloquial usage, it was realized that there was still a vast repertoire of songs, rhymes, and stories of all kinds which had never been written down in any form.

Modern Collections of Oral Folklore and Folk Songs

In 1918 a Folk Song Collection Bureau (Ko-yao Shou-chi Tsu) was founded which became the Folk Song Research Society (Ko-yao Yen-chiu Hui) two years later and which published a journal, *Folk Song Weekly (Ko-yao Chou-k'an)*. The society included in its manifesto the following aim:

> Now we collect and print materials to prepare the way for technical study. This is our first aim. From these sources we may select some good songs . . . and compile them into a selection of "The People's Voice." . . . The work is not only to make manifest the hidden light of the people but also to promote the development of the national poetry.[1]

Besides the literary aims of the movement, it had from the beginning a social aim as well. The majority of China's peasants were still illiterate and clung to many harmful superstitions. Their stories, songs, proverbs, and sayings would throw light on these beliefs and help educators in their eradication. Officials, teachers, and students from all over the country were invited to send contributions, the collecting to be done to very specific guidelines. The problems of collection were considerable, particularly with recording dialect speech, because there were sometimes no written symbols in existence for some of the spoken words. In these instances collectors were asked to write the sounds according to an established phonetic system or in romanized form. The collectors also were asked to make notes at source which would help to determine the exact meaning of these words. They were instructed to record the music for the songs and to write the words exactly as they heard them, however vulgar or colloquial the expressions used, and not to edit them. They were asked to make notes on time and place and setting and to give as much information as possible about the people who were singing or reciting.

The response to the society's request was enormous. Within three years some fourteen thousand folk songs had been collected, and over two thousand of these were published in the society's journal. Various comparative studies of the content of these songs were made on such subjects as the position of women as reflected in them and other social topics.

The collection of oral folktales was also enthusiastically undertaken. In 1927 the Folklore Society (Min-su Hsüeh Hui) was organized by the Institute of Philology and History of the National Sun Yat-sen University in Canton. The society published the *Folklore Weekly* (*Min-su Chou-k'an*), followed by the *Journal of Chinese Folklore* (*Min-su Tsa-chih*), which provided a classified index of the contents of the *Folklore Weekly*. In addition, the institute founded a folklore museum with a collection of folk costumes, religious symbols, musical instruments, and folk toys. In conjunction with these activities, courses in the study of folklore on western lines were instituted. Book-length national and regional collections of folklore were published, as were bibliographies of these publications. Basic works on the techniques and theory of folklore collecting were translated from English and French.

Authentic Folktale Collections

A most useful, well-annotated guide to the folktales of China, in English with titles in romanized Chinese as well as Chinese characters, *Chinese Folk Narratives: A Bibliographic Guide*,[2] has been compiled and published by Ting Nai-tung and Ting Hsü Lee-hsia. This provides an extensive list of classical literary sources, together with a fifteen-page list of the many oral versions resulting from the work of the folklore research societies just described. There is first a list of general collections, then collections classified under regions, followed by tales collected from the minority peoples of China. A comprehensive collection of folktales, the *Pai Hsin Pocket-size Series* (*Pai Hsin Hsiao Ts'ung Shu*), was edited as a multivolume series by Lin Lan, the wife of a Shanghai publisher, and first published by the Pai Hsin Book Company in 1925. She later republished the series as *Tales from the Orient* (*Tung-fang Ku-shih*) in thirty volumes and larger format in Taiwan.

A pioneer in introducing authentic oral versions of Chinese folktales to the West is Wolfram Eberhard, a German sinologist and sociologist, who undertook extensive fieldwork in China and who taught both in Chinese universities and at the University of California, Berkeley. He published his *Chinese Fairy Tales and Folk Tales* in German in 1937, translated into English by Desmond Parsons. According to the Tings' careful analysis, eighty-three of the one hundred and thirty-seven stories collected by Eberhard appear in Lin Lan's collection. Eberhard reedited a selection of seventy-nine of these tales with an index of tale types and motifs for the distinguished University of Chicago series, *Folktales of the World*, edited by R. M. Dorson, already referred to.

Use of Folklore in the People's Republic

Even before the establishment of the People's Republic, the Communists had been quick to realize the value of folklore in their peasant education programs and for propaganda purposes. From the start there were two rival schools of thought as to how best it could be used. Mao Tse-tung (who was always described as a bandit by the National Government before he came to power) encouraged cadres to use only those elements which would support the revolutionary cause—stories which made heroes of bandits fighting feudalistic authority or tales of poor peasants or downtrodden or exploited women and which made villains of officials, landlords, and others in power. Such stories were often rewritten for storytellers or made into plays for peasants and children to act for themselves or which would be performed by one of the many new traveling companies of actors or puppeteers.

Other folklorists wished to preserve a scientific approach, recording the material exactly as it was found. Once the Communists were in power, folklore collecting was encouraged on a nationwide scale, but there was a good deal of controversy about the theory and technique. At a 1959 meeting of the Chinese Folklore and Literature Research Society (Chung-kuo Min-su Wen-hsüeh Yen-chiu Hui) which had been founded to replace the earlier groups, it was stated that stories amounting to a million words had been collected but that "Folk songs are the products of the Big Leap Forward, they really express the powerful will of the people to build socialism and to march towards communism. . . ."[3] The rewriting of a northern Shensi folk song could go to such lengths as this verse from *The East Is Red* (*Tung-fang Hung*):

Chairman Mao loves the people.
Chairman Mao, he is our guide.
To build a new China, *hu erh hai ya,*
He leads us, he leads us forward.[4]

Rewritten folk songs and stories with an added moral or political twist do not form the whole picture in folklore publications after 1950. The Ting *Bibliography* lists several reliable collections, notably *Selected Chinese Folktales (Chung-kuo Min Chien Ku-shih Hsüan)*, edited by Chia and Sun, published in two volumes in 1962. In English, the Foreign Languages Press issued *Folktales from China,* a five-volume collection, also in 1962, and *Seven Sisters: Selected Chinese Folk Stories* in 1965. The latter contains eleven tales from minority peoples and only one Han-Chinese story. The title story is from the picturesque Miao people.

Comparative Versions of Folktales

The greater interest in the traditions of the minority peoples living in China engendered by the war, when so much of China's intellectual life took place in the interior, resulted in a large number of tales being culled from them. A good selection is listed under the regional and minority peoples arrangement of the Ting *Bibliography*. With the publication of the regional collections it was possible to trace the origins of many stories and to see how almost every part of China had its own version of a well-loved story. Some of the better known ones were collected into comparative editions, among them *A Collection of the Versions of the Legend of the White Snake (Pai She Chuan Chi)*, edited by Fu Hsi-hua, published in 1958. A version of this famous story has already been given. *A Collection of Versions of Meng Chiang Nü Traveling Ten Thousand Miles in Search of Her Husband (Meng Chiang Nü Wan Li Hsün Fu Chi)*, edited by Lu Kung, was published in 1955. Following is Eberhard's translation of one version of the story "The Faithful Lady Meng," often referred to in translation as "The Pumpkin Girl"[5]:

THE FAITHFUL LADY MENG

The Meng family garden and the garden of the Chiang family were separated by only a wall. One year the Mengs planted a pumpkin on their side of the wall, and the Chiangs did the same on theirs. Both plants climbed the wall, and at the top they joined together and became one plant.

After the pumpkin had bloomed luxuriantly, it developed a huge fruit, which both families wanted to pluck when it became ripe. After a long discussion it was decided that each should take a half; when they cut it open, they found an unusually pretty girl inside. The two families together looked after her and named her Meng Chiang.

This happened in the reign of the wicked, unjust Emperor Ch'in Shih Huang-ti. He was afraid at this time that the Huns would break into the country from the north and not leave him any peace. In order to keep them in check, he decided to build a wall along the whole northern frontier of China. But no sooner was one piece built than another fell down, and the wall made no progress. Then a wise man said to him, "A wall like this, which is over ten thousand miles long, can be built only if you immure a human being in every mile of the wall. Each mile will then have its guardian." It was easy for the emperor to follow this advice, for he regarded his subjects as so much grass and weeds, and the whole land began to tremble under this threat.

An ingenious scholar went to the emperor and said, "Your method of building the wall is making the whole country tremble. It is quite possible that revolts will break out before it is finished. I have heard of a man called Wan. Now since Wan means ten thousand, he will be enough, and you need only fetch him." The emperor was delighted with this suggestion, and sent for Wan at once, but Wan had heard of the danger and had run away.

Meng Chiang was now a grown-up girl. One clear moonlight night she went into the garden to bathe in the pond. In the joy of the bath she said to herself, "If a man were to see me now, I would willingly belong to him forever, whoever he was." Wan happened to have hidden in a banana tree in the garden and, hearing Meng Chiang's words, he called out, "I have seen you."

Meng Chiang became his wife. While they were happily seated at the wedding-feast the soldiers arrived and the heartless brutes seized him and carried him off, leaving Meng Chiang in tears.

In this way she was separated from Wan even before the marriage had been consummated, but in spite of this she loved him and thought of nothing else but him. She was just as attached to her memory of him as other wives to their husbands. Eventually, heedless of the fatigues of the journey, she travelled over mountains and through rivers, to find the bones of her husband. When she saw the stupendous wall she did not know how to find the bones. There was nothing to be done, and she sat down and wept. Her weeping so affected the wall that it collapsed and laid bare her husband's bones.

When the emperor heard of Meng Chiang and how she was seeking her husband, he wanted to see her himself. When she was brought before him, her unearthly beauty so struck him that he decided to make her empress. She knew she could not avoid her fate, and therefore she agreed on three conditions. First, a festival lasting forty-nine days should be held in honor of her husband; second, the emperor, with all his officials, should be present at the burial; and third, he should build a terrace forty-nine feet high on the bank of the river, where she wanted to make a sacrifice to her husband. On these three conditions she would marry the emperor. Ch'in Shih Huang-ti granted all her requests at once.

When everything was ready she climbed onto the terrace and began to curse the emperor in a loud voice for all his cruelty and wickedness. Although this made the emperor very angry, he held his peace. But when she jumped from the terrace into the river, he flew into a rage and ordered his soldiers to cut up her body into little pieces and to grind her bones to powder. When they did this, the little pieces changed into little silver fish, in which the soul of the faithful Meng Chiang lives forever.[6]

Reprinted from *Folktales of China*, Wolfram Eberhard, editor and translator, by permission of the University of Chicago Press. Copyright © by Wolfram Eberhard.

The majority of the modern recorded versions of the folktales and anecdotes referred to are not in forms intended for children, although they do provide a rich repertoire for retelling. The Tings' annotations identify the occasional volume intended for children and the names of the publishers after 1950 are some indication of the style of a collection. The China Youth and Children's Press of Peking, the Shanghai publishing house of the same name, and other similar publishers, like the China Youth Press, occur with fair frequency.

Bertha Hensman, a collector of folktales, residing in Hong Kong, has made a series of recordings on tape of tales told by older refugees from the Mainland. These she has transcribed and translated and subsequently published as *Hong Kong Tale-spinners* (1968) and *More Hong Kong Tale-spinners* (1971). She found that the storytellers were using prompt books which were still being published in Hong Kong by Wu Kuei T'ang Publishing Company. Crudely printed, the stories are divided into booklets of about fourteen pages, each one representing a session of the storyteller's time. She herself has built up a collection of some eighty sets and has found that many are variant versions from different parts of China of the tales in Lin Lan's collection.

Animal Stories

The Ting *Bibliography* notes that the modern oral collections of folktales contain many more animal stories than the older literary collections. *A Collection of Chinese Animal Tales (Chung-kuo Tung Wu Ku-shih Chi)* is an anthology of ninety-one tales about animals gathered from twenty minority peoples published in 1966.

Humorous Anecdotes and Jokes

A few very well known examples of humorous anecdotes from classical literature already have been given in their chronological place in this narrative, such as the story of Chuang-tzu's reply to the royal invitation to high office, the story of the foolish old man who moved a mountain, and the anecdote from P'u Sung-ling, "The Stream of Cash." These are good examples of the traditional kind. Many of the jokes told by storytellers from time immemorial either rely on puns and double entendre and so are difficult to record without a lengthy explanation, or they are simply explicit in sexual references and not intended for children's ears. Humorous anecdotes and jokes also feature largely in folktale collections. Lin Lan included a number in her story collections and also published some in separate collections. These are listed under appropriate headings in the Ting *Bibliography*.

Nursery Rhymes

Nursery rhymes, counting rhymes, action songs, riddles, and tongue twisters are also an important part of the folklore of a country. Curiously enough, the pioneer recorder of China's vast body of traditional folk rhyme, passed on from generation to generation by word of mouth, was an Italian, Guido Amedeo Vitale (1872–1918), who served as secretary-interpreter for the Italian Legation in Peking. A Neapolitan, he had studied Chinese at the University Institute of Oriental Studies founded in Naples by the Jesuit scholar Father Matteo Ripa. During his long residence in Peking, Vitale, who was exceptional in being interested in the life of the ordinary Chinese people, acquired an extraordinary knowledge of the vernacular language, so that he could wander about the streets and countryside and talk freely with the people he met, regardless of their varying dialects. He published his *Chinese Folklore: Pekinese Rhymes* in 1896 and his *Chinese Merry Tales* in 1901, two decades before Chinese scholars began serious study of their own national folklore. All subsequent collections of Chinese nursery rhymes with English translations owe a debt to Vitale, sometimes acknowledged, sometimes not. In the preface to his *Chinese Folklore: Pekinese Rhymes* he says that from these rhymes the reader will acquire "a small treasure house of words and phrases hardly to be met with elsewhere, a clearer insight into scenes and details of Chinese common life and the notion that true poetry may be found in Chinese popular songs." He goes on to say that the authors of the rhymes are unknown, that they are like

wild flowers which spring up, nobody knows how or when and they fade and die in the same way. . . . Composed as they are by illiterate people, they show a system of versification analogous to that of many European countries. . . . After the work of collection, came the work of explanation and translation which was not always easy.

The Chinese text is given for each rhyme, then notes on the meaning and on the occasion when the rhyme was spoken or sung, followed by a more or less literal prose translation. The book has an index of first lines romanized in alphabetical order and a subject index both to the rhymes themselves and to the extensive notes. This is very helpful in tracking down the original source in later English versions, which often appear in very free translations.

Looking through the index the reader may find examples of nearly all the familiar topics of nursery rhymes we know in English. Many of them do not translate very well, but here are a few examples paraphrased from Vitale into rhythmic lines to give some idea of their content:

Sleep, Little Flower
Little Flower is asleep,
Quietly resting
Most charming Little Flower.
    —(no. 10)

A counting, clapping rhyme begins,

Clap hands on the first day of the year,
The old lady goes out to look at the lotus lanterns;
Claps hands on the second day of the second moon,
The old lady likes to eat sugar sticks;
Clap hands on the third day of the third moon,

—(no. 48)

and so on through the year.

A pat-a-cake rhyme:

Fry the pancake,
Fry the pancake,
Toss it over,
Done to a turn.

—(no. 51)

Itinerant monks used to carry drums, the sound of which was like thunder. So boys sang:

The wind roars
The rain pours
Beating the drum
Makes thunder come.

—(no. 70)

A flower-seller's song went something like this:

Balsam so red,
Larkspur so blue,
Sweet smelling grasses
And white roses too.

—(no. 155)

Vitale collected one hundred and seventy rhymes, all from Peking, none of which had ever been written down before.

Isaac Taylor Headland, a professor at Peking University, added to the fund of recorded vernacular rhyme, choosing one hundred and thirty-nine of more than six hundred which he had collected from many parts of China and published in 1900 in his *Chinese Mother Goose Rhymes*. It is a pity that this collection has not been reprinted like Vitale's, because Headland's rhymed translations are more successful than some later attempts. Each rhyme has the Chinese text followed by the translated version and each rhyme is illustrated with an appropriate photograph of a "child in the street." These faded sepia and green prints of actual photographs of Chinese children in the streets of Peking in pre-Republican China, bundled up in their padded gowns and jackets, have a nostalgic charm and interest all their own.

Following are two of his rhymes:

The Dragon Pagoda,
It touches the sky,
The Dragon Pagoda,
Thirteen stories high.

This next one is surprisingly reminiscent of "Hickory, Dickory, Dock":

He climbed up the candle-stick
The little mousey brown,
To steal and eat tallow
And he couldn't get down.
He called for his Grandma,
But his Grandma was in town,
So he doubled up into a wheel
And rolled himself down.

E. T. C. Werner published a scholarly edition of rhymes, *Chinese Ditties*, in 1922. His book has a parallel text with extensive notes and, of special interest to folklorists, a note identifying the place where the rhyme was collected. Another collection, *Chinese Children's Rhymes*, having English text only, and with line illustrations, was made by Ruth Hsü in Shanghai in 1935. Her rhymed versions read quite well.

New Year lanterns
Are gay and entrancing,
While all around
Children are playing and dancing;
Old and young
All are welcoming
The New Year's coming.

Yet another of her rhymes on the same theme:

On New Year's day
The children go calling
Their respects to pay.
They kneel and bow
In the most proper way.
But if there's no money,
They turn around and are gone
With little delay.

Riddles and Riddle Rhymes

One or two other bilingual collections[7] listed in the bibliography for this work have been reprinted from earlier Mainland editions in Taiwan or originated there, but the best contemporary collection, though small, is Robert Wyndham's *Chinese Mother Goose Rhymes*. He has chosen and edited forty-one rhymes, mainly taken from the Vitale and the Headland collections, and made them a little more easily singable and sayable. Among these are several riddle-rhymes which have a special appeal:

My boat is turned up at both ends,
All storms it meets it weathers.
On its body you'll find not a single board,
For it's covered all over with feathers.
Daily we fill it with rice,
It's admired by all whom we meet.
You will not find a crack in my boat,
But you'll find underneath it two feet!
What is it?

Reprinted with permission of William Collins Publishers, Inc., from *Chinese Mother Goose Rhymes* by Robert Wyndham. Copyright © 1968 by Robert Wyndham.

And one turns the page to find the answer—a duck! The Chinese text for each rhyme has been handwritten by the artist, Ed Young, who has drawn attractive colored illustrations reminiscent of traditional Chinese paper cuts for each page.

There are hundreds of ordinary riddles which are passed on from generation to generation of school children. Here are a few examples taken from *China Reconstructs*[8] that older Chinese say have not changed much from their day:

Long neck and round belly
Like a chicken but doesn't run
It takes in white liquid
And gives out brown.
      Answer, a teapot.

Born without bones
And dying without trace
It has no body and no shape
It wanders through streets and cities.
      Answer, the wind.

Blood brothers, more than thirty
The younger were born before the older.
      Answer, teeth.

A creature two inches high
In red cap and white suit
When he bumps his head on the wall
He flares in anger.
      Answer, a match.

Counting Rhymes

Here are a few examples of counting and number rhymes which have been supplied with translations by a friend of the writer's.[9] An acting-counting rhyme:

> This old man is seventy-seven,
> In four more years he'll be eighty-one.
> Not only can he play the lute,
> He can also play the flute.

When reciting or chanting this, the children mime the numbers with their fingers and perform the actions of playing the lute and the flute. Another simple number rhyme goes like this:

> One, two, three, four, five,
> Metal, wood, water, fire, earth, (the five elements)
> Five times six makes thirty.
> Five times seven makes thirty-five.

Tongue Twisters

The following masterly translations of tongue twisters were supplied by the same friend. Here the romanized Chinese has been included, so that some idea of the Chinese sounds can be appreciated:

> If you can cook my cold cooked bean curd,
> (Ni huei tun wo-ti tun tung tou fu,)
> Do come and cook my cold cooked bean curd.
> (Lai tun wo-ti tun tung tou fu.)
> But if you can't cook my cold cooked bean curd,
> Ni pu huei tun wo-ti-tun tung tou fu,)
> Don't muddle cook and meddle cook and spoil
>   cook my cold cooked bean curd.
> (Pieh hu-tun luan-tun tun-huai-le wo-ti tun
>   tung tou fu.)

> There is a noodle shop facing south,
> (Yu ko mien p'u mien hsiang nan,)
> Hanging with blue cotton quilted door
>   curtains.
> (Kua shang lan pu mien men lien.)
> It is facing south with blue cotton quilted
>   door curtains,
> (Kua shang lan pu mien men lien mien pu
>   mien hsiang nan,)
> It is still facing south without the blue
>   cotton quilted door curtains.
> (Chai-le lan pu mien men lien mien pu mien
>   hsiang nan.)

Children learn characters by making rhymes about them. For instance, the character for six (六) is memorized thus:

A dot and a horizontal stroke
  (the upper two strokes)
(I tien, i heng,)
Two eyes to stare.
  (the lower two strokes)
(Liang yen i teng.)

This is a very simple example for a very simple character. The different strokes all have names and there are rhymes for characters up to fifteen or more strokes.

Cumulative Story Rhymes

One of the oldest forms of story-verse is the cumulative or chain story rhyme, like "This is the house that Jack built." Examples occur in most of the literatures of the world. Many African languages have examples and in Asia there are versions in Sanskrit, Arabic, Persian, and other languages. One of the earliest examples in China was recorded in an ancient commentary on the *Book of Songs* (*Shih Ching*) by the philosopher-writer Han Ying (fl. B.C. 150) in which anecdotes culled from history[10] are used to illustrate moral points:

> King Chuang of Ch'u was going to raise an army to attack Chin. He announced to his officers and Grand Officials, "Anyone who dares object will be put to death without mercy."
> Sun-shu Ao said, "I have heard that the son who, fearing the severity of a whipping, dares not remonstrate with his father, is not filial, and that the minister who, fearing the punishment of axe and chopping block, dares not remonstrate with his prince, is not loyal." Whereupon he went ahead and offered a remonstrance:
>
> In my garden there is an elm tree. On top of the elm tree is a cicada. The cicada is just vibrating his wings and singing his sad song, intent on drinking the fresh dew, not knowing that the mantis behind him is twisting his neck, about to seize and eat him. The mantis, intent on eating the cicada, does not know that behind him the sparrow is stretching his neck, about to peck and eat him. The sparrow, intent on eating the mantis, does not know that the boy beneath the elm tree with cross-bow and pellets is looking up about to shoot him. The boy, intent on shooting the sparrow, does not know that in front of him is a deep pit and behind him an uprooted tree. These all are occupied with the advantage before them without realizing the [possible] injury behind. It is not only animals and common people who behave like this; rulers also do the same thing. . . .
>
> That the state of Ch'u enjoyed peace was due to Sun-shu Ao's efforts.

From *Han Shih Wai Chuan: Han Ying's Illustrations of the Didactic Application of the Classic of Songs* by Han Ying. An annotated translation by James R. Hightower. Copyright © 1952 by the Harvard-Yenching Institute, Harvard University. Reprinted with permission of Harvard University Press.

"While the mantis is after the cicada, the sparrow comes from behind" ("Tang lang pu ch'an, huang ch'üeh tsai hou") is an often quoted proverb. Such anecdotes, quoted again and again from literary sources, are echoed in oral examples, sometimes rather crude, but where the repetitive patter of the lines forms their fascination. Here is one quoted by Vitale:

> The dark-skinned old woman
> Rolls on the ground,
> Scolding her husband for not buying cosmetics for her.
> But when he does buy cosmetics for her she does not use them,
> But scolds her husband for not buying hemp for her.
> When he buys hemp for her, she does not thresh it,
> But scolds her husband for not buying a horse for her.
> When he buys a horse she does not feed it,
> But scolds her husband for not buying a wardrobe for her.
> When he buys a wardrobe she does not use it,
> But scolds her husband for not buying a cord for her.
> When he buys her a cord she hangs herself
> And frightens her husband to death.

Proverbs

Are proverbs for children? When do we first learn that "All that glitters is not gold"? With the long tradition of Chinese literature, with the veneration in which it has been held, with all traditional education having been based on a thorough knowledge of the Classics, naturally proverbial sayings abound. Many such sayings have been quoted through the ages so often that they are woven into the fabric of the language. Here are a few well-known proverbs which are of particular interest when linked with their Western parallels as they have been in *Selected Chinese Sayings* by T. C. Lai, from which source they have been taken. In the book each proverb is given in Chinese characters and in romanized form, followed by a translation or an explanatory note, and where possible, an English equivalent. The similarity of a number of these is striking. In addition the original source is listed, showing an extremely wide range of literature from the *Book of Change*, probably the earliest of the classics, to the eighteenth century novel, *The Dream of the Red Chamber*. It will be noticed from the romanized versions that the Chinese saying is in the four- or six-word rhythmic phrase so characteristic of the language.

> Cities in the sea [believed to be buildings produced
>   by the exhalations of sea serpents].
> (Hai shih shen lou.)
> Castles in the air.

> What proceeds from you will return to you again.
> (Ch'u erh fan erh.)
> Tit for tat.

To see a thing once is better than hearing it a hundred times.
(Po wen pu ju i chien.)
Seeing is believing.

Like water off a duck's back.
(Shui kuo ya pei.)
[The saying is exactly as in English.]

To make the Four Seas my home.
(Szu hai wei chia.)
To feel at home anywhere.

A square handle in a round socket.
(Tsao yüan jui fang.)
A square peg in a round hole.

Heroes have similar minds.
(Yin hsiung so chien lüeh t'ung.)
Great minds think alike.

Reprinted from *Selected Chinese Sayings*, translated and annotated by T. C. Lai, Copyright 1960 by T. C. Lai.

The last proverb quoted perhaps contains an appropriate thought with which to end this brief account of the popular literature with the longest unbroken tradition in the world and certainly one belonging to more people than any other. Dynamic changes are still going on in China and, undoubtedly, once the process of complete romanization of the language is carried through, more drastic changes than any which have yet taken place in its long history will occur. It is to be hoped that the changes will be gradual enough to continue to preserve much of the marvelous legacy of the past and so enrich the future.

Notes

1. Information in this section is taken largely from R. M. Dorson's Foreword to Eberhard, *Folktales of China*.
2. Hereinafter referred to in the text as the Ting *Bibliography*.
3. *China News Analysis* 353: 1–7 (16 Dec. 1960).
4. From a greeting card issued by the Foreign Languages Press, 1973.
5. Christie, *Chinese Mythology*, pp. 96, 97.
6. Eberhard, *Folktales of China*, pp. 24–26.
7. *See* Bibliography under Ch'en Tzu-shih and Kinchen Johnson.
8. "Riddle Me This" in *China Reconstructs* (June 1957), p. 32.
9. Mrs. S. H. T'ien Macdonald, Department of Chinese, Leeds University, Leeds, England.
10. Hightower, *Han Shih Wai Chuan: Han Ying's Illustrations of the Didactic Applications of the Classic of Songs*, pp. 341, 342.

L		The Three Dynasties
E	**D**	Fu-Hsi
G	**Y**	Shen-nung
E	**N**	Yen Ti
N	**A**	The Five Emperors
D	**S**	Huang Ti, the Yellow Emperor
A	**T**	Chuan Hs'un
R	**I**	K'un
Y	**E**	Yao
	S	Shun

B.C. 2205–1766	Hsia
B.C.1765–1123	Shang
B.C. 1122–221	Chou

	B.C. 1122–722	Early Chou
	B.C. 722–480	Ch'un Ch'iu period
	B.C. 480–221	Warring States period
B.C. 221–207	Ch'in	(Shih Huang Ti, first unifier of China)
B.C. 206–A.D. 220	Han	
	B.C. 206–A.D. 9	Earlier Han and Interregnum
	A.D. 25–220	Later Han

A.D. 221–280	San Kuo period, Three Kingdoms of Shu-Han, Wei, and Wu
A.D. 280–581	Six Dynasties
A.D. 581–618	Sui
A.D. 618–906	T'ang
A.D. 907–960	Five Dynasties
A.D. 960–1126	Northern Sung
A.D. 1127–1279	Southern Sung
A.D. 1260–1368	Yüan (Mongol)
A.D. 1368–1644	Ming
A.D. 1644–1908	Ch'ing (Manchu)
A.D. 1912–1949	Republic
A.D. 1949–	People's Republic

Bibliography

Chinese names follow the traditional order with family names first, followed by given names which are connected with a hyphen when, as is usual, there are two; e.g., Mao Tse-tung, Mao being the family name.

Chinese works printed before 1900 with published English translations are listed under their romanized Chinese titles, the form in which they are most usually referred to; under their authors where known; under their translators; and under their translated titles in varying forms, i.e., the *Shih Ching* as *Book of Odes, Book of Poetry,* and *Book of Songs.* Other Chinese works discussed in the text for which no accessible English translations exist appear in the Index only. Twentieth-century Chinese books are referred to in standard form.

The simplified Wade-Giles system of romanization has been adhered to as it is the one used in all the English-language reference works cited. A note on the current official Chinese system of romanization (*pin-yin*) is given on page 138, note 17.

Chinese characters for the works included in the Classics (the Five Classics and the Four Books) may be found in Legge, *The Chinese Classics,* which is a bilingual text. Chinese characters for most of the other older Chinese works discussed in the text may be found in the index to Lu Hsün's *A Brief History of Chinese Fiction.* Chinese characters for twentieth-century writers and their principal works may be found in Boorman's *Biographical Dictionary of Republican China.*

Books marked with an asterisk (*) are recommended for further reading.

Acton, Harold, and Lee Yi-hsieh, trans. *Four Cautionary Tales.* With a preface by Arthur Waley. London, Eng.: John Lehmann, 1947.

A-li-ssu Chung-kuo Yu-chi (Alice's Adventures in China). See Shen Ts'ung-wen.

All Men Are Brothers (Shui Hu Chuan). See Buck, trans.

Analects of Confucius. See Waley, trans.

Biggerstaff, Knight. *The Earliest Modern Government Schools in China.* Ithaca, NY: Cornell University Pr., 1961 (reprinted, Port Washington, NY: Kennikat Pr., 1972).

Biographical Dictionary of Republican China. See Boorman.

Biographies of Chinese Women (*Lieh Nü Chuan*). See O'Hara.

*Birch, Cyril. *Chinese Myths and Fantasies.* New York: Walck, 1961.

_____, ed. *Anthology of Chinese Literature,* vol. 2. *From the 14th Century to the Present.* New York: Grove Pr., 1972.

_____, trans. *Stories from a Ming Collection. Translations of Chinese Short Stories Published in the Seventeenth Century.* London, Eng.: The Bodley Head, 1958.

Bishop, John Lyman. *The Colloquial Short Story in China: A Study of the San-Yen Collections.* (Harvard-Yenching Institute Studies no. 14) Cambridge, Mass.: Harvard Univ. Pr., 1956.

*Bodde, Derk, trans. and annot. *Annual Customs and Festivals in Peking as Recorded in the Yen-ching Sui-shih-chi* by Tun Li-ch'en. 2d ed. rev. Hong Kong: Hong Kong Univ. Pr., 1965.

Bonnet, Leslie. *Chinese Fairy Tales.* Illus. by H. Toothill. London, Eng.: Frederick Muller, 1973 (1958).

The Book of Lieh-tzu. See Graham, trans.

The Book of Mountains and Seas (*Shan Hai Ching*). See Schiffeler.

Book of Odes (*Shih Ching*). See Karlgren, trans.

Book of Poetry (*Shih Ching*). See Legge, trans.

Book of Songs (*Shih Ching*). See Waley, trans.

Boorman, Howard L., and R. C. Howard, eds. *Biographical Dictionary of Republican China.* New York: Columbia Univ. Pr., 1967. 4 vols.

Buck, Pearl, trans. *All Men Are Brothers* (*Shui Hu Chuan*). Trans. from the Chinese. New York: John Day, 1933, 1937.

Carter, Thomas Francis. *The Invention of Printing in China and Its Spread Westward.* Rev. by L. Carrington Goodrich. New York: Ronald Pr., 1955.

Celebrated Cases of Judge Dee (*Dee Goong An*). See Van Gulik, trans.

Chang, H. C. *Chinese Literature: Popular Fiction and Drama.* Edinburgh: Edinburgh Univ. Pr., 1973. [Contains translation of "Pai Niang-tzu Yung Chen Lei-fang-t'a" ("Madame White Forever Confined under Thunder Peak Pagoda") from chap. 28 of *Ching Shih T'ung Yen* (*Popular Words to Admonish the World*) in *Ku Chin Hsiao Shuo* (*Stories Old and New*).]

Chang Lo-p'ing. *San Mao Liu-lang-chi* (*San Mao Strip Cartoons*). Shanghai: Shao-nien Erh-t'ung Ch'u Pan She, 1959 (reprinted 1962).

Chang, T'ien-i. *Ch'i-kuai ti Ti-fang* (*A Strange Place*). Shanghai: Wen-hua Sheng-huo Ch'u Pan She, 1950.

_____ *Lo Wen-ying ti Ku-shih* (*The Story of Lo Wen-ying*). Peking: Youth Publishing Pr., 1952.

Ch'en Tzu-shih, comp. *Peiping Nursery Rhymes with English Translations* (*Pei-p'ing Tung Yao Husan Chi*). (Chinese Folklore, first series) Taipei, Taiwan: Great China Book Co., 1968.

Cheng Chi. "Libraries in China Today," *Libri, International Library Review* 9, no. 2: 105–10 (1959). Copenhagen: Munksgaard, 1959.

Chi Hsiao Tu Che (*Letters to Young Readers*). See Ping Hsin.

Ch'i-kuai ti Ti-fang (*A Strange Place*). See Chang T'ien-i.

Chia Chih and Sun Chien-ping. *Chung-kuo Min Chien Ku-shih Hsuan* (*Selected Chinese Folk Tales*). Peking: People's Literature Press, 1962. 2 vols.

Chiang Fu-tsung. "A Historical Sketch of Chinese Libraries," *Philobiblon, A Quarterly Review of Chinese Publications* 2, no. 2: 1–52 (March 1948). Nanking: National Central Library, 1948.

*Chiang Yee. *A Chinese Childhood.* London, Eng.: Methuen, 1940.

_____ *The Silent Traveller in London.* London, Eng.: Country Life, 1938.

Ch'ien Han Shu (The History of the Former Han Dynasty) by Pan Ku. *See* Dubs, trans.

China News Analysis, no. 353, 16 Dec. 1960. Hong Kong: China News Analysis.

A Chinese Childhood. See Chiang Yee.

Chinese Childhood. See Fawdry.

Chinese Children's Rhymes. See Hsü, Ruth.

Chinese Classics. See Legge, trans.

Chinese Ditties. See Werner.

Chinese Fairy Tales. See Bonnet.

Chinese Fairy Tales and Folk Tales. See Eberhard.

Chinese Folklore: Pekinese Rhymes. See Vitale.

Chinese Merry Tales. See Vitale.

Chinese Mother Goose Rhymes. See Headland, trans.

Chinese Mother Goose Rhymes. See Wyndham.

Chinese Tales of Folklore. See Lu Mar.

Ching Hua Yuan (Flowers in the Mirror). See Li Ju-chen.

Chou Shu-jen. *See* Lu Hsün, pseud.

Chow Tse-tsung. *The May Fourth Movement: Intellectual Revolution in Modern China.* (Harvard East Asian Studies, no. 6) Cambridge, Mass.: Harvard Univ. Pr., 1960.

*Christie, Anthony. *Chinese Mythology.* New York: Tudor Publishing Co., 1969.

Ch'u Hai Tsung Mu T'i Yao (Annotated Bibliography of Plays in Verse). Ed. by Huang Wen-yang. 1736. (reprinted) Peking: People's Literature Press, 1959.

Chu-ko's Lute Repulses the Enemy. See Shih Chieh-t'ing.

Ch'u Tz'u: The Songs of the South. An Ancient Chinese Anthology. See Hawkes, trans.

Ch'ü Yüan. *Li Sao and Other Poems.* Trans. by Yang Hsien-yi and Gladys Yang. Peking: Foreign Languages Press, 1953.

Chuang-tzu. *See* Fung.

Chung-kuo Min Chien Ku-shih Hsuan (Selected Chinese Folktales). See Chia Chih.

Chung-kuo Tung-wu Ku-shih Chi (A Collection of Chinese Animal Tales). Shanghai: People's Literature Press, 1966.

Columbia (University) College. Oriental Studies Program. *A Guide to Oriental Classics.* 2d ed. William Theodore de Bary and Ainslie T. Embree, eds. (Companions to Asian Studies) New York: Columbia Univ. Pr. 1975.

Comenius. *Orbis Pictus: A Facsimile of the First English Edition of 1659.* Intro. by John E. Sadler. London, Eng.: Oxford Univ. Pr., 1968.

Confucius (K'ung Fu Tzu). *Analects. See* Waley, trans., *Analects of Confucius.*

Constant, Samuel Victor. *Calls, Sounds and Merchandise of the Peking Street Peddlers.* Peking: The Camel Bell, 1937.

The Courtesan's Jewel Box: Chinese Stories of the Xth–XVIIth Centuries. See Yang Hsien-yi, trans.

Davidson, Martha. *A List of Published Translations from Chinese into English, French and German.* Washington, D.C.: American Council of Learned Societies, 1952, 1957.

De Bary, William Theodore, ed. *See* Columbia (University) College. Oriental Studies Program.

Dear Monkey. Abr. [from *Monkey*] trans. by Arthur Waley. *See* Waley, Alison.

Dee Goong An. Celebrated Cases of Judge Dee. See Van Gulik, trans.

*Diény, Jean-Pierre. *Le Monde Est à Vous: La Chine et les Livres pour Enfants.* Paris: Gallimard, 1971.

Doré, Henri. *Recherches sur les superstitions en Chine,* no. 4. Shanghai: Le Mission Catholique, 1911–1938.

Dorson, R. M. *See* Eberhard, ed. *Folktales of China.*

The Dragon King's Daughter: Ten T'ang Dynasty Stories. See Yang Hsien-yi, trans.

The Dream of the Red Chamber. See Hung Lou Meng.

Dubs, H. Homer, trans. *Ch'ien Han Shu: The History of the Former Han Dynasty* by Pan Ku. A critical translation, with annotations. Baltimore: Waverly Pr., 1938.

*Eberhard, Wolfram. *Chinese Fairy Tales and Folk Tales.* Trans. from the German by Desmond Parsons. London, Eng.: Kegan Paul, Trench and Trubner, 1937.

_____ *Chinese Festivals.* London, Eng. and New York: Abelard-Schuman, 1958.

* _____, ed. *Folktales of China.* rev. ed. Foreword by Richard M. Dorson. (Folktales of the World) Univ. of Chicago Pr., 1965.

Edwards, E. D. *Chinese Prose Literature of the T'ang Period, A.D. 618–906.* London: Probsthain, 1937. 2 vols.

Embree, Ainslie T., ed. *See* Columbia (University) College. Oriental Studies Program.

Evans, George Ewart, and David Thomson. *The Leaping Hare.* London, Eng.: Faber and Faber, 1972.

*Fawdry, Marguerite. *Chinese Childhood (A Miscellany of Mythology, Folklore, Fact and Fable).* New York: Barron's, 1977.

Feng Meng-lung, comp. *Ku Chin Hsiao Shuo (Stories Old and New).* See *Ku Chin Hsiao Shuo.*

Feng Tzu-k'ai. *Tzu-k'ai Man-hua-lien (Sketches by Feng Tzu-k'ai).* Ed. by Wan Ch'ao-wen. Peking: People's Publishing Co., 1955.

Flowers in the Mirror (Ching Hua Yüan). See Li Ju-chen.

Folk Tales from China. (English language ed.) Peking: Foreign Languages Press, 1962. 5 vols.

Folktales of China. See Eberhard.

The Foolish Old Man Who Moved Mountains: Stories, Songs and Sayings from China. See Gebhardt.

Fu Hsi-hua, ed. *Pai She Chuan Chi (A Collection of Versions of the Legend of the White Snake).* Shanghai: Chung Hua Book Co., 1958.

Fung Yu-lan. *Chuang Tzu: A New Selected Translation with an Exposition of the Philosophy of Kuo Hsiang.* Shanghai: Commercial Pr., 1931.

Gebhardt, Marie-Louise. *The Foolish Old Man Who Moved Mountains: Stories, Songs and Sayings from China.* Illus. by Edith Aberle and Karen Tureck. New York: Friendship Pr., 1969.

Gernet, Jacques. *Daily Life in China on the Eve of the Mongol Invasion, 1250–1276.* Trans. by H. M. Wright. (Daily Life Series, no. 7) New York: Macmillan, 1962; Stanford: Stanford Univ. Pr., 1962 (paper).

Giles, Herbert Allen. *A Chinese Biographical Dictionary.* Shanghai: Kelly and Walsh, 1898; reprinted, Taipei, 1962.

_____ *Glossary of Reference on Subjects Connected with the Far East.* 3d ed. Hong Kong: Kelly and Walsh, 1900. Reprinted 1974.

Giles, Herbert Allen, trans. and annot. *Strange Stories from a Chinese Studio* (*Liao Chai Chih I* by P'u Sung-ling). London, Eng.: Thomas de la Rue, 1880; reprinted New York: Dover, 1970.

*Goodrich, L. Carrington. *A Short History of the Chinese People*. 2d ed. London, Eng.: Allen and Unwin, 1957.

————, trans. *Hsin Pien Tui Hsiang Szu Yen* (*Fifteenth Century Illustrated Chinese Primer*). Facsimile reproduction with introduction, translation, and notes. Hong Kong: Hong Kong Univ. Pr., 1967.

Graham, Angus Charles. *The Book of Lieh-tzu*. (The Wisdom of the East series) London, Eng.: John Murray, 1961. Reprinted, New York: Paragon Book Corp., 1961.

A Guide to Oriental Classics. See Columbia (University) College. Oriental Studies Program.

Han Shih Wai Chuan: Han Ying's Illustrations of the Didactic Applications of the Classic of Songs. An annotated translation. See Hightower, trans.

Han Ying. *Han Shih Wai Chuan: Han Ying's Illustrations of the Didactic Applications of the* Classic of Songs. An annotated translation. See Hightower, trans.

Havoc in Heaven [scenes from the cartoon film of the same title about Monkey]. See Tang.

Hawkes, David, trans. *Ch'u Tz'u: The Songs of the South. An Ancient Chinese Anthology.* Oxford, Eng.: Clarendon Pr., 1959.

———— *The Story of the Stone* (*Hung Lou Meng*): *A Chinese Novel by Cao Xueqin in Five Volumes.* Harmondsworth, Middlesex, Eng.: Penguin Books, 1973–74.

Headland, Isaac Taylor, trans. *Chinese Mother Goose Rhymes.* Illus. with photographs. New York: Fleming H. Revell, 1900.

*Hensman, Bertha. *More Hong Kong Tale-spinners: Twenty-five Traditional Chinese Tales.* Collected by tape-recorder and translated into English. Illus. by Hsieh Chung-wu. Hong Kong: Chinese Univ. of Hong Kong, 1971.

*Hensman, Bertha, and Mark Kwok-ping. *Hong Kong Tale-spinners: A Collection of Tales and Ballads.* Transcribed and translated from storytellers in Hong Kong. Illus. by Hsieh Chung-wu. Hong Kong: Chinese Univ. of Hong Kong, 1968.

Hightower, James Robert, trans. *Han Shih Wai Chuan: Han Ying's Illustrations of the Didactic Applications of the* Classic of Songs. An annotated translation. (Harvard-Yenching Institute Monograph Series, no. 11) Cambridge, Mass.: Harvard Univ. Pr., 1952.

———— *Topics in Chinese Literature, Outlines and Bibligraphies.* (Harvard-Yenching Institute Studies, no. 3) Cambridge, Mass.: Harvard Univ. Pr., 1965.

History of the Former Han Dynasty (*Ch'ien Han Shu*) by Pan Ku. See Dubs, trans.

*Hong Kong Tale-spinners. See Hensman.

Howard, R. C., ed. See Boorman.

Hsi Hsiang Chi. The Romance of the Western Chamber: A Chinese Play Written in the Thirteenth Century. See Hsiung Shih-i, trans.

Hsi Hsiang Chi. The Western Chamber. See Hung Tseng-ling, adapt.

Hsi Yu Chi (*The Pilgrimage to the West* or *The Journey to the West*) by Wu Ch'eng-en. See Waley, trans., *Monkey* by Wu Ch'eng-en; Yu, Anthony C., trans. and ed., *The Journey to the West.*

Hsia, C. T. A History of Modern Chinese Fiction, 1917–1957. With an appendix on Taiwan by Tsai-an Hsia. New Haven: Yale Univ. Pr., 1961.

Hsia Tsai-an. See Hsia, C. T.

Hsiao P'o-ti Sheng-jih (Hsiao P'o's Birthday). See Lao She.

Hsieh Wan-ying. See Ping Hsin, pseud.

Hsin Pien Tui Hsiang Szu Yen (Fifteenth Century Illustrated Chinese Primer). See Goodrich, trans.

Hsiung, Shih-i, trans. Hsi Hsiang Chi. The Romance of the Western Chamber: A Chinese Play Written in the Thirteenth Century. London, Eng.: Methuen, 1935.

_____ Lady Precious Stream (Wang Pao Ch'uan). An old Chinese play done into English according to its traditional style. London, Eng.: Methuen, 1934.

Hsü Lee-hsia. See Ting Nai-tung.

Hsü, Ruth. Chinese Children's Rhymes. With illus. by Teng Kuei. Shanghai: Commercial Pr., 1935.

Hu Shih. Collected Works. Shanghai: Commercial Pr., 1940. Reprinted, Taiwan, 1953. The nine essays on Hung Lou Meng by Hu Shih are contained in vol. 8, sec. 5.

Huang Sung-k'ang. Lu Hsün and the New Culture Movement. Amsterdam: Djambatan, 1957.

Hung, Tseng-ling, adapt. The Western Chamber (Hsi Hsiang Chi). Drawings by Wang Shu-hui. Peking: Foreign Languages Press, 1958. (A serial picture book.)

Hung Lou Meng (The Dream of the Red Chamber). See Hawkes, trans., The Story of the Stone: A Chinese Novel by Cao Xueqin in Five Volumes; McHugh, trans., The Dream of the Red Chamber (Hung Lou Meng); Wang Chi-chen, trans. The Dream of the Red Chamber (Hung Lou Meng) by Tsao Hsüeh-ch'in and Kao Ngoh.

Irwin, Richard Gregg. The Evolution of a Chinese Novel: Shui-hu-chuan. (Harvard-Yenching Institute Series, no. 10) Cambridge, Mass.: Harvard Univ. Pr., 1953.

Jackson, J. H., trans. The Water Margin (Shui Hu Chuan). Shanghai: Commercial Pr., 1937; reprinted, Hong Kong: Commercial Pr., 1963; G & T Co., P. O. Box 328, Cambridge, Mass., 1976.

Jenyns, Soame, trans. A Further Selection from the Three Hundred Poems of the T'ang Dynasty. London, Eng.: John Murray, 1945.

_____ Selections from the Three Hundred Poems of the T'ang Dynasty. London, Eng.: John Murray, 1940.

Johnson, Kinchen, trans. Folksongs and Children-songs from Peiping (Chinese text with English prose translations). Taipei, Taiwan: Orient Cultural Service, 1971. 2 vols. Reprinted from Asian Folklore and Social Life, Monograph vols. 16 and 17, edited by T. K. Lou in collaboration with W. Eberhard. Peiping: Orient Cultural Service, 1932.

Journey to the West, by Wu Ch'eng-en. See Hsi Yu Chi.

Kao Ngoh. See Tsao Hsüeh-ch'in.

Karlgren, Bernhard, trans. The Book of Odes (Shih Ching). Chinese text, transcription, and translation. Stockholm: The Museum of Far Eastern Antiquities, 1950.

Kessen, William, ed. Childhood in China. New Haven: Yale Univ. Pr., 1975. (The report of the American Delegation on Early Childhood Development in the People's Republic of China.)

King, Evan, trans. *See* Lau Shaw.

Ku Chin Hsiao Shuo (Stories Old and New) (San Yen). Feng Meng-lung, comp. For partial translations, *see* Acton, *Four Cautionary Tales;* Birch, *Stories from a Ming Collection;* Chang, H.C., *Chinese Literature: Popular Fiction and Drama;* Yang Hsien-yi and Gladys Yang, *The Courtesan's Jewel Box: Chinese Stories of the Xth–XVIIth Centuries.*

Ku-tai Ying-hsiung ti Shih Hsiang (The Statue of an Ancient Hero). *See* Yeh Shao-chun.

Kuan Han-ching. *Selected Plays*. Trans. by Yang Hsien-yi and Gladys Yang. Shanghai: New Art and Literature Publishing House, 1958.

Lady Precious Stream (Wang Pao Ch'uan). *See* Hsiung Shih-i, trans.

Lai, T. C., trans. and annot. *Selected Chinese Sayings*. Hong Kong: Univ. of Hong Kong Bookstore, 1960.

Lao She, pseud. *Hsiao P'o-ti Sheng-jih (Hsiao P'o's Birthday)*. Hong Kong: Ta Fang Publishing Co., 1966.

Lao She, pseud. *See also* Lau Shaw.

Lau Shaw, pseud. *Rickshaw Boy (Lo-t'o Hsiang-tzu)*. Trans. from the Chinese by Evan King. New York: Reynal and Hitchcock, 1945.

———— *The Yellow Storm*. Trans. from the Chinese by Ida Pruitt. New York: Harcourt, 1951.

The Legendary Creatures of the Shan Hai Ching (The Book of Mountains and Seas [Shan Hai Ching]). *See* Schiffeler.

Legge, James, trans. *(Shih Ching) The Book of Poetry*. Chinese text with English translation. Shanghai: Chinese Book Co., 1931.

———— *The Chinese Classics*. With a translation, critical and exegetical notes, prolegomena, and copious indexes. Biographical note by Lindsay Ride. Concordance tables. Notes on *Memoires* by Arthur Waley. Hong Kong: Hong Kong Univ. Pr., 1960; New York: Oxford Univ. Pr., 1960. (Reprinted from the original edition, Hong Kong: Mission Press, 1861–1872.)

Letters to Young Readers (Chi Hsiao Tu Che). *See* Ping Hsin.

Lewis, Richard, ed. *The Moment of Wonder: A Collection of Chinese and Japanese Poetry*. Illus. with paintings by Chinese and Japanese masters. New York: Dial, 1964.

Li Chi. *Anyang*. Seattle: Univ. of Washington Pr., 1977.

Li Ju-chen. *Flowers in the Mirror (Ching Hua Yuan)*. Trans. and ed. by Lin Tai-yi. Berkeley: Univ. of California Pr., 1965.

Li Po. *The Works of Li Po, the Chinese Poet*, done into English verse by Shigeyoshi Obata, with an introduction and biographical and critical matter translated from the Chinese. New York: Dutton, 1928.

Li Sao and Other Poems by Ch'ü Yüan. *See* Ch'ü Yüan.

Liao Chai Chih I (Strange Stories from a Chinese Studio) by P'u Sung-ling. *See* Giles, trans. and annot.; Van Over, *A Treasury of Chinese Literature.*

Library of Congress. Asiatic Division. *Eminent Chinese of the Ching Period (1644–1912)*. Ed. by Arthur W. Hummel. Washington, DC: U.S. Govt. Print. Off., 1943. 2 vols.

Lieh Nü Chuan (Biographies of Chinese Women). *See* O'Hara.

Lieh-tzu. *See* Graham.

Lin Lan. *Tung-fang Ku-shih (Tales from the Orient)*. Taipei, Taiwan: CAF, 1950.

Lin Shu. *Lin I Hsiao-shuo Ts'ung-shu (Lin's Collected Translations of Novels)*. Shanghai: Commercial Pr., 1914. 97 vols.

Lin Tai-yi, trans. *See* Li Ju-chen.

Lin Yü-t'ang. *Moment in Peking: A Novel of Contemporary Chinese Life.* New York: John Day, 1939.

The Lion Tavern (Shih-tzu Lou). See *Shih-tzu Lou.*

*Liu, Alan P. L. *Book Publishing in Communist China.* Cambridge, Mass.: MIT Center for International Studies Research Program on Problems of International Communication and Security, 1965.

*Liu, James J. Y. *The Chinese Knight-errant.* London, Eng.: Routledge and Kegan Paul, 1967; Chicago: Univ. of Chicago Pr., 1967.

_____ *The Art of Chinese Poetry.* Chicago: Univ. of Chicago Pr., 1966.

Liu Wu-chi. *An Introduction to Chinese Literature.* Bloomington, Ind.: Indiana Univ. Pr., 1966.

Lo Kuan-chung. *San Kuo Chih Yen I (The Romance of the Three Kingdoms).* See Roberts, trans.

Lo Wen-ying ti Ku-shih (The Story of Lo Wen-ying). See Chang T'ien-i.

The Loss of Chieh-t'ing. See *Shih Chieh-t'ing.*

*Lu Hsün, pseud. *A Brief History of Chinese Fiction.* Trans. by Yang Hsien-yi and Gladys Yang. Peking: Foreign Languages Press, 1959.

_____ *Old Tales Retold.* Trans. by Yang Hsien-yi and Gladys Yang. Peking: Foreign Languages Press, 1961. Reprinted 1972.

_____ *Selected Stories.* (With "Lu Hsün's Life and His Short Stories" by Yeh Yi-chen.) Peking: Foreign Languages Press, 1963.

_____ *Selected Works.* Trans. by Yang Hsien-yi and Gladys Yang. Peking: Foreign Languages Press, 1956, 1959. vols. 1 and 3.

Lu Kung, ed. *Meng Chiang Nü Wan Li Hsun Fu Chi (A Collection of Versions of Meng Chiang Nü Travelling Ten Thousand Miles Searching for her Husband).* Shanghai: Shanghai Publishing Co., 1955.

Lu Mar. *Chinese Tales of Folklore.* Illus. by Howard Simon. New York: Criterion Books, 1964.

McHugh, Florence and Isabel, trans. *The Dream of the Red Chamber, Hung Lou Meng: A Chinese Novel of the Early Ching Period.* The English translation is based on the German version . . . trans. and adapt. by Franz Kuhn. The woodcuts . . . reproduced . . . from *Hung Lou Meng T'u Yung,* illustrations and poems to accompany *The Dream of the Red Chamber* produced in 1884 after older models. London, Eng.: Routledge and Kegan Paul, 1958; New York: Pantheon Books, 1958.

Madam White Forever Confined under Thunder Peak Pagoda ("Pai Niang-tzu Yung Chen Lei-fang-t'a"), *see* Chang, H. C.

Mao Tse-tung. *Talks at the Yenan Forum on Literature and Art* (1942). Peking: Foreign Languages Press, 1967.

Meng Chiang Nü Wan Li Hsun Fu Chi (A Collection of Versions of Meng Chiang Nü Travelling Ten Thousand Miles Searching for her Husband). See Lu Kung.

Moment in Peking: A Novel of Contemporary Chinese Life. See Lin Yu-t'ang.

Monkey (Hsi Yu Chi) by Wu Ch'eng-en. *See* Waley, trans.

The Monkey King, Sun Wu-k'ung. A picture story from the cartoon film, *Uproar in Heaven.* Peking: Supplement to *China Reconstructs,* October, 1962. (A serial picture book in English.)

Monkey Subdues the White-bone Demon. 2d ed. Wang Hsing-pei, adapt. Drawings by Chao Hung-pen and Chien Hsiao-tai. Peking: Foreign Languages Press, 1975. (A serial picture book.)

**More Hong Kong Tale-spinners.* See Hensman.

Myrdal, Jan. *Report from a Chinese Village.* New York: Pantheon, 1965.

"The National Central Library, a record," *Philobiblon, A Quarterly Review of Chinese Publications* [whole] no. 4. Nanking: National Central Library, 1947.

The National Library, Peking (Kuo Li Chung Yang T'u Shu Kuan) (A brochure published by the National Library, Peking, 1955).

National Palace Museum, Taipei. *Select Chinese Rare Books and Historical Documents in the National Palace Museum.* Taipei, Taiwan: The Museum, 1971.

*Nebiolo, Gino, ed. *The People's Comic Book: Red Women's Detachment, Hot on the Trail and Other Chinese Comics.* Trans. . . . by Endymion Wilkinson. Introduction by Gino Nebiolo. Garden City, NY: Doubleday, 1973.

*Nunn, G. Raymond. *Publishing in Mainland China.* (MIT Report no. 4) Cambridge, Mass.: MIT Pr., 1966.

Obata, Shigeyoshi, trans. *The Works of Li Po, the Chinese Poet.* Done into English verse by Shigeyoshi Obata, with an introduction and biographical and critical matter translated from the Chinese. New York: Dutton, 1928.

Obraztsov, Serge. *The Chinese Puppet Theatre.* Trans. from the Russian by J. T. MacDermott. Boston: Plays, Inc., 1975 (reprint of 1961 ed.).

O'Hara, Albert Richard, S. J., *The Position of Woman in Early China According to the Lieh Nü Chuan, "The Biographies of Chinese Women."* Hong Kong: The Author, 1955 (printed by Orient Publishing Co.).

"Pai Niang-tzu Yung Chen Lei-fang-t'a" ("Madam White Forever Confined under Thunder Peak Pagoda"). *See* Chang, H. C.

Pai She Chuan Chi (A Collection of Versions of the Legend of the White Snake). See Fu Hsi-hua, ed.

Pan Ku. *Ch'ien Han Shu: The History of the Former Han Dynasty. See* Dubs, trans.

The People's Comic Book: Red Woman's Detachment, Hot on the Trail and Other Chinese Comics. See Nebiolo.

Pilgrimage to the West by Wu Ch'eng-en. *See Hsi Yu Chi.*

Ping Hsin, pseud. *Chi Hsiao Tu Che (Letters to Young Readers).* Shanghai: K'ai-ming Book Co., 1949.

―――― *T'ao Ch'i-ti Shu-ch'i Jih-ch'i (T'ao Ch'i's Summer Diary).* Shanghai: Juvenile Book Pr., 1956.

Polo, Marco. *The Travels of Marco Polo.* Trans. and with an introduction by Ronald Latham. (Penguin Classics) Harmondsworth, Middlesex, Eng.: Penguin Books, 1958.

Price, R. F. *Education in Communist China.* (World Education Series) London, Eng.: Routledge and Kegan Paul, 1970.

Pruitt, Ida. trans. *The Yellow Storm. See* Lau Shau.

P'u Sung-ling. *Liao Chai Chih I. See* Giles, trans. and annot.; *and* Van Over, ed.

The Real Tripitaka and Other Pieces. See Waley.

Records of the Grand Historian of China. See Watson, trans.

Rickshaw Boy (Lo-t'o Hsiang-tzu). See Lau Shaw.

"Riddle Me This" in *China Reconstructs* (June 1957), p. 52.

Roberts, Moss, trans. and ed. *Three Kingdoms: China's Epic Drama (San Kuo Chih Yen I)* by Lo Kuan-chung. New York: Pantheon Books, 1976.

Romance of the Three Kingdoms (San Kuo Chih Yen I). See Roberts. trans.

The Romance of the Western Chamber (Hsi Hsiang Chi). See Hsiung Shih-i, trans.

San Kuo Chih Yen I (Romance of the Three Kingdoms). See Roberts, trans.

San Mao Liu-lang-chi (San Mao Strip Cartoons). See Chang Lo-p'ing.

San Yen. Ku Chin Hsiao Shuo (Stories Old and New). See *Ku Chin Hsiao Shuo*.

The Scarecrow (Tao Ts'ao Jen). See Yeh Shao-chun.

Schiffeler, John Wm. *The Legendary Creatures of the Shan Hai Ching (The Book of Mountains and Seas)*. San Francisco: The Author (511 El Camino del Mar, San Francisco, CA 94121), 1978.

Scott, A. C. *The Classical Theatre of China*. London, Eng.: Allen and Unwin, 1957; reprinted, Westport, Conn.: Greenwood Pr., 1978.

_____ *An Introduction to Chinese Theatre*. With drawings by the author. New York: Theatre Arts Books, 1959.

_____ *Literature and the Arts in Twentieth Century China*. New York: Doubleday, 1963.

_____ *Traditional Chinese Plays*, vol. 2. *Longing for Worldly Pleasures (Ssu Fan), Fifteen Strings of Cash (Shih-wu Kuan)*. Trans., descr., annot., and illus. by A. C. Scott. Madison and London: Univ. of Wisconsin Pr., 1969.

Seven Sisters: Selected Chinese Folk Stories. Peking: Foreign Languages Press, 1965.

Shan Hai Ching. See Schiffeler.

Shen Ts'ung-wen. *A-li-ssu Chung-kuo Yu-chi (Alice's Adventures in China)*. 1928. 2 vols. (Copy not available for full bibliographic details.)

Shih Chi by Ssu-ma Ch'ien. See Watson, trans.

Shih Chieh-t'ing (The Loss of Chieh-t'ing: The Strategy of the Unguarded City or Chu-ko's Lute Repulses the Enemy). Arr. by Liang-shih and others. Shanghai: Hsin Mei-shu Ch'u-pan-she (New Art Book Publishing Co.), 1954. (A serial picture book.)

Shih Ching. See Karlgren, trans., *Book of Odes*; Legge, trans., *Book of Poetry*; Waley, trans., *Book of Songs*.

Shih-tzu Lou (The Lion Tavern: A Story from Shui Hu Chuan, the Tale of the Marshes). Hong Kong: Mei-li Mei-shu-she (Fine Art Book Co.), 1959. (A serial picture book.)

Shu Ch'ing-ch'un. See Lao She, pseud.

Shui Hu Chuan (The Tale of the Marshes). Excerpts translated by Liu Wu-chi are found in his *Introduction to Chinese Literature*. Other partial translations are Buck, *All Men Are Brothers;* Irwin, *The Evolution of a Chinese Novel;* and Jackson, *The Water Margin*.

The Silent Traveller in London. See Chiang Yee.

Ssu-ma Ch'ien. *Shih Chi*. See Watson, trans.

The Statue of an Ancient Hero (Ku-tai Ying-hsiung ti Shih Hsiang). See Yeh Shao-chun.

Stories Old and New (Ku Chin Hsiao Shuo. San Yen). See *Ku Chin Hsiao Shuo*.

The Story of Lo Wen-ying (Lo Wen-ying ti Ku-shih). See Chang T'ien-i.

The Story of the Stone (Hung Lou Meng): A Chinese Novel by Cao Xueqin in Five Volumes. See Hawkes, trans.

The Story on the Willow Pattern Plate. See Thomas.

A Strange Place (Ch'i-kuai ti Ti-fang). See Chang T'ien-i.

Strange Stories from a Chinese Studio (Liao Chai Chih I by P'u Sung-ling). See Giles, trans.

The Strategy of the Unguarded City. See *Shih Chieh-t'ing*.

The Tale of the Marshes (Shui Hu Chuan). See Shui Hu Chuan.

Tales from the Orient (Tung-fang Ku-shih). See Lin Lan.

Tales the People Tell in China. See Wyndham.

T'an Cho-yuan. *The Development of Chinese Libraries under the Ch'ing Dynasty, 1644–1911.* Shanghai: Commercial Pr., 1935.

Tang, Cheng, adapt. *Havoc in Heaven: From the Cartoon Film of the Same Title.* Scenes from the film by Yan Dingxian et al. Illus. in color. Beijing: Foreign Languages Press, 1979.

T'ang Shih San Pai Shou (Three Hundred Poems of the T'ang Dynasty). For translated selections *see* Jenyns, *Selections from the Three Hundred Poems of the T'ang Dynasty;* Obata, *The Works of Li Po . . . ;* and the Waley translations listed below.

T'ao Ch'i-ti Shu-ch'i Jih-ch'i (T'ao Ch'i's Summer Diary). See Ping Hsin.

Tao Te Ching. See Waley, *The Way and Its Power.*

Tao Ts'ao Jen (The Scarecrow). See Yeh Shao-chun.

Thomas, Leslie. *The Story on the Willow Plate.* Adapt. from the Chinese Legend . . . with illus. by the author. New York: Schocken, 1969.

Three Hundred Poems of the T'ang Dynasty. See *T'ang Shih San Pai Shou.*

Three Kingdoms: China's Epic Drama (San Kuo Chih Yen I). See Roberts, trans.

T'ien Han. *The White Snake, a Peking Opera.* Trans. by Yang Hsien-yi and Gladys Yang. Peking: Foreign Languages Press, 1957.

*Ting Nai-tung and Ting Hsü Lee-hsia. *Chinese Folk Narratives: A Bibliographic Guide.* (Bibliographic Aids Series, no. 4) San Francisco: Chinese Materials and Research Aids Service Center, 1975.

Topping, Audrey. *Dawn Wakes in the East.* New York: Harper, 1972.

Tsang Chiu-san. *Society, Schools and Progress in China.* New York and London: Pergamon Pr., 1968.

Tsao Hsüeh-ch'in. *Hung Lou Meng (The Dream of the Red Chamber).* For available translations see *Hung Lou Meng.*

Tsien Tsuen-hsuin. *Written on Bamboo and Silk: The Beginnings of Chinese Books and Inscriptions.* Univ. of Chicago Pr., 1962.

*Tun Li-ch'en. *Annual Customs and Festivals in Peking as Recorded in the Yen-ching Sui-shih-chi.* 2d ed. rev. Trans. and annot. by Derk Bodde. Hong Kong: Hong Kong Univ. Pr., 1965.

Tung-fang Ku-shih (Tales from the Orient). See Lin Lan.

Uproar in Heaven, cartoon film. See *The Monkey King, Sun Wu-k'ung.*

Van Gulik, Robert, trans. *Celebrated Cases of Judge Dee (Dee Goong An): An Authentic Eighteenth Century Chinese Detective Novel.* With an introduction and notes. New York: Dover, 1976.

Van Over, Raymond, ed. *A Treasury of Chinese Literature.* Greenwich, Conn.: Fawcett, 1972.

*Vitale, Guido. *Chinese Folklore: Pekinese Rhymes.* First collected and edited with notes and translation. Hong Kong: Vetch and Lee, 1972 (reprinted from the 1896 ed., published in Peking by the French Bookshop.)

_____ *Chinese Merry Tales.* Collected and edited by Guido Vitale. Peking: Pei-t'ang Press, 1901.

*Waley, Alison, abr. and ed. *Dear Monkey.* Trans. from the Chinese by Arthur Waley. Illus. by Georgette Boner. Glasgow and London: Blackie, 1973.

Waley, Arthur. *The Real Tripitaka and Other Pieces.* London, Eng.: Allen and Unwin, 1952.

Waley, Arthur. *The Way and Its Power: A Study of the Tao Te Ching and Its Place in Chinese Thought*. London, Eng.: Allen and Unwin, 1968.

_____ *Yuan Mei, Eighteenth Century Chinese Poet*. London, Eng.: Allen and Unwin, 1956.

*_____ trans. *Ballads and Stories from Tun-huang: An Anthology*. London, Eng.: Allen and Unwin, 1960.

_____ trans. *The Book of Songs (Shih Ching)*. 2d ed. London, Eng.: Allen and Unwin, 1954.

_____ trans. *Chinese Poems: Selected from 170 Chinese Poems, More Translations from the Chinese, The Temple and The Book of Songs*. London, Eng.: Allen and Unwin, 1946.

_____ trans. *Monkey (Hsi Yu Chi)* by Wu Ch'eng-en. London, Eng.: Allen and Unwin, 1942.

_____ trans. *One Hundred and Seventy Chinese Poems*. London, Eng.: Constable, 1918; New York: Knopf, 1919 (reprinted 1945).

_____ trans and annot. *The Analects of Confucius*. London, Eng.: Allen and Unwin, 1956.

Wang Chi-chen, trans. and adapt. *The Dream of the Red Chamber (Hung Lou Meng)* by Tsao Hsueh-chin and Kao Ngoh). With a preface by Arthur Waley. Garden City, N.Y.: Doubleday, 1929; New Doubleday Anchor Book ed., 1958.

_____ *Traditional Chinese Tales*. New York: Columbia Univ. Pr., 1944.

Wang Hsing-pei, adapt. *Monkey Subdues the White-bone Demon*. 2d ed. Drawings by Chao Hung-pen and Chien Hsiao-tai. Peking: Foreign Languages Press, 1975. (A serial picture book.)

Wang Pao Ch'uan. *Lady Precious Stream*. See Hsiung Shih-i, trans.

The Water Margin (Shui Hu Chuan). See Jackson, trans.

Watson, Burton, trans. *Ssu-ma Ch'ien: Records of the Grand Historian of China*. Trans. from the *Shih Chi* of Ssu-ma Ch'ien. New York: Columbia Univ. Pr., 1961. 2 vols.

The Way and Its Power: A Study of the Tao Te Ching. See Waley.

Werner, E. T. C. *Chinese Ditties*. Tientsin: Tientsin Pr., 1922.

*_____ *A Dictionary of Chinese Mythology*. Shanghai: Kelly and Walsh, 1932; reprinted, New York: Julian Pr., 1961.

_____ *Myths and Legends of China*. With illus. by Chinese artists. London, Eng.: Harrap, 1922.

The Western Chamber (Hsi Hsiang Chi). See Hung Tseng-ling.

The White Snake, a Peking Opera. See T'ien Han.

The White Snake (Pai She). See also *Pai Niang-tzu . . .* and *Pai She Chuan Chi*.

*Wilkinson, Endymion. trans. See Nebiolo.

*Williams, C. A. S. *Encyclopedia of Chinese Symbolism and Art Motives: An Alphabetical Compendium of Legends and Beliefs as Reflected in the Manners and Customs of the Chinese throughout History*. New York: Julian Pr., 1961. (A reissue of the work originally titled *Outlines of Chinese Symbolism and Art Motives. . . .* Shanghai: Kelly and Walsh, 1932.)

Wu Ch'eng-en. *Monkey (Hsi Yu Chi)*. See Waley, trans.

Wylie, A. *Notes on Chinese Literature*. With introductory remarks on the progressive advancement of the art; and a list of translations from the Chinese into various European languages. Shanghai: American Presbyterian Mission Pr., 1902.

Wyndham, Robert, sel. and ed. *Chinese Mother Goose Rhymes*. Pictures by Ed Young. Cleveland: World Publishing Co., 1968.

_____ *Tales the People Tell in China*. New York: Julian Messner, 1971.

Yang, Gladys, trans. *See* Yang Hsien-yi and Gladys Yang.

Yang Hsien-yi and Gladys Yang, trans. *A Brief History of Chinese Fiction* by Lu Hsün. *See* Lu Hsün.

_____ *The Courtesan's Jewel Box: Chinese Stories of the Xth–XVIIth Centuries*. Peking: Foreign Languages Press, 1957.

_____ *The Dragon King's Daughter: Ten T'ang Dynasty Stories*. Peking: Foreign Languages Press, 1954.

_____ *Li Sao and Other Poems*. *See* Ch'ü Yüan.

_____ *Selected Plays*. *See* Kuan Han-ching.

*_____ *See* Lu Hsün. *A Brief History of Chinese Fiction*.

_____ *See* Lu Hsün. *Selected Stories*.

_____ *See* Lu Hsün. *Selected Works*.

_____ *See* T'ien Han. *The White Snake: A Peking Opera*.

Yeh Shao-chun. *Ku-tai Ying-hsiung ti Shih Hsiang* (*The Statue of an Ancient Hero*). Shanghai: K'ai-ming Book Co., 1949.

_____ *Tao Ts'ao Jen* (*The Scarecrow*). Shanghai: K'ai-ming Book Co., 1949.

The Yellow Storm. *See* Lau Shau.

Yen-ching Sui-shih-chi (*Annual Customs and Festivals in Peking*). *See* Tun Li-ch'en.

Yu, Anthony C., trans. and ed. *The Journey to the West*. Univ. of Chicago Pr., 1977–   . 4 vols., of which vols. 1 and 2 have been published.

Index

Chinese names are given in their traditional form, with family name first, followed by the given names, hyphenated if there are two.